A SHORT HISTORY OF ENGLAND'S AND AMERICA'S LITERATURE

Geoffrey Chaucer

A SHORT HISTORY OF ENGLAND'S AND AMERICA'S LITERATURE

by

Eva March Tappan

YESTERDAY'S CLASSICS

ITHACA, NEW YORK

This edition, first published in 2021 by Yesterday's Classics, an imprint of Yesterday's Classics, LLC, is an unabridged republication of the text originally published by Houghton, Mifflin, and Co. in 1906. For the complete listing of the books that are published by Yesterday's Classics, please visit www.yesterdaysclassics.com. Yesterday's Classics is the publishing arm of Gateway to the Classics which presents the complete text of hundreds of classic books for children at www.gatewaytotheclassics.com.

ISBN: 978-1-63334-148-7

Yesterday's Classics, LLC
PO Box 339
Ithaca, NY 14851

PREFACE

THIS book is based upon the following convictions:—

1. That the prime object of studying literature is to develop the ability to enjoy it.

2. That in every work of literary merit there is something to enjoy.

3. That it is less important to know the list of an author's works than to feel the impulse to read one of them.

4. That it is better to know a few authors well than to learn the names of many.

To select those few authors with due regard to what is good in itself and what is historically of value, to choose from the hundreds whose writings have made for literary excellence, is under no circumstances an easy task. It is especially difficult—and especially delightful—for one who can echo most honestly the words of the French critic, "En litterature j'aime tout."

EVA MARCH TAPPAN.

WORCESTER, MASSACHUSETTS,

January, 1905.

CONTENTS

ENGLAND'S LITERATURE

CHAPTER I

Centuries V-XI

THE EARLY ENGLISH PERIOD

CHAPTER II

Centuries XII and XIII

THE NORMAN-ENGLISH PERIOD

CHAPTER III

Century XIV

CHAUCER'S CENTURY

CHAPTER IV

Century XV

THE PEOPLE'S CENTURY

CHAPTER V

Century XVI

SHAKESPEARE'S CENTURY

CHAPTER VII

Century XVIII

THE CENTURY OF PROSE

AMERICA'S LITERATURE

CHAPTER I

1607-1765

THE COLONIAL PERIOD

CHAPTER II

1765-1815

THE REVOLUTIONARY PERIOD

CHAPTER III

THE NATIONAL PERIOD — EARLIER YEARS

1815-1865

THE KNICKERBOCKER SCHOOL

CHAPTER IV

THE NATIONAL PERIOD — EARLIER YEARS

1815-1865

THE TRANSCENDENTALISTS

CHAPTER VII

THE NATIONAL PERIOD — EARLIER YEARS

1815-1865

THE HISTORIANS

CHAPTER VIII

THE NATIONAL PERIOD — EARLIER YEARS

1815-1865

THE SOUTHERN WRITERS

CHAPTER IX

THE NATIONAL PERIOD — LATER YEARS

1865-

REFERENCES

SIGNIFICANT DATES IN ENGLISH LITERATURE

680. Death of Cædmon.

735. Death of Bede.

901. Death of Alfred.

1066. Norman Conquest.

1154. *Anglo-Saxon Chronicle* ends; death of Geoffrey of Monmouth.

1205-25. Layamon's *Brut,* the *Ormulum,* the *Ancren Riwle.*

1346. Battle of Crécy.

1362. *Piers Plowman.* English becomes the official language of the courts.

1380. Wyclif's translation of the Bible.

1400. Death of Chaucer.

1453. Capture of Constantinople by the Turks.

1470. Malory's *Morte d'Arthur.*

1476. Printing introduced into England.

1525. Tyndale's translation of the New Testament.

Before 1547. Blank verse introduced by Surrey, the Sonnet and Italian attention to form introduced by Surrey and Wyatt.

1552 or 53(?). *Ralph Roister Doister,* the first English comedy.

1564. Birth of Shakespeare.

1579. *Euphues; The Shepherd's Calendar.*

1587-93. Marlowe shows the power of blank verse.

1590. *Arcadia;* Books I-III of the *Faerie Queene.*

1590-99. Decade of the Sonnet.

1594. Hooker's *Ecclesiastical Polity,* Books I-IV.

1611. "King James version" of the *Bible.*

1616. Death of Shakespeare.

1623. *First Folio.*

1632-38. Milton's *L'Allegro, Il Penseroso, Comus,* and *Lycidas.*

1642. Closing of the theatres.

1660. The Restoration.

1662. *Hudibras.*

1667. *Paradise Lost.*

1678. *The Pilgrim's Progress.*

1700. Death of Dryden.

1709-11. *The Tatler.*

1711-13. *The Spectator.*

1740. *Pamela,* the first English novel.

1751. Gray's Elegy.

1765. Percy's *Reliques.*

1798. *Lyrical Ballads,* by Wordsworth and Coleridge.

1802-17. *Reviews* established.

1811. Jane Austen's *Sense and Sensibility.*

1812. First part of Byron's *Childe Harold.*

1814. Scott's *Waverley.*

1819-21. Best work of Keats and Shelley.

1830. Tennyson's *Poems, Chiefly Lyrical.*

1836-37. Dickens's *Pickwick Papers.*

1843. First volume of Ruskin's *Modern Painters.*

1848. First volume of Macaulay's *History of England.*

1857. "George Eliot's" first fiction.

1868-69. Browning's *The Ring and the Book.*

SIGNIFICANT DATES IN AMERICAN LITERATURE

1640. *The Bay Psalm Book,* the first book printed in America.

1678. *Anne Bradstreet's poems,* the best American verse of the seventeenth century.

1704. *The Boston News-Letter,* the first American newspaper.

1754. Edwards's *Inquiry into the Freedom of the Will,* the first great American metaphysical book.

1786. Freneau's poems, the best American poetry of the eighteenth century.

1788-89. *The Federalist,* the strongest literary influence in favor of adopting the Constitution.

1798. Brown's *Wieland,* the first American romance.

1817. Bryant's *Thanatopsis,* the first great American poem.

1819. Irving's *Sketch Book,* the first American book to win European fame.

1821. Cooper's *Spy,* the first important American novel.

1827. *The Youth's Companion* founded, the pioneer paper for young people.

1834-38. Sparks's *Life and Writings of George Washington,* the first of the American school of history.

1837. Emerson's *American Scholar,* "our intellectual Declaration of Independence."

1840. *The Dial,* the organ of transcendentalism.

1848. *The Biglow Papers,* the first literary use of dialect in American literature.

1849. Ticknor's *History of Spanish Literature,* a strong influence toward the study of European literature.

1849. Thoreau's *Week,* the first American book of "nature literature."

1850. Hawthorne's *Scarlet Letter,* the greatest American novel.

1852. Mrs. Stowe's *Uncle Tom's Cabin,* the first American novel of purpose.

CHAPTER I

Centuries V–XI

THE EARLY ENGLISH PERIOD

1. Poetry

1. Our English Ancestors

About fifteen hundred years ago, our English ancestors were living in Jutland and the northern part of what is now Germany. They were known as Saxons, Angles, and Jutes, all different tribes of Teutons. They were bold and daring, and delighted in dashing through the waves wherever the tempest might carry them, burning and plundering on whatever coast they landed. If a man died fighting bravely in battle, they believed that the Valkyries bore him to the Valhalla of Odin and Thor, where the joys of fighting and feasting would never end. Yet these savage warriors loved music; they were devoted to their homes and their families; and, independent as they were, they would yield to any one whom they believed to be their rightful ruler. They were honest in their religion, and they thought seriously about the puzzling questions of life and death. They were sturdy in body and mind, the best of material to found a nation. About the middle of the fifth century, they began to go in large numbers to Britain, and there they remained, either slaying or driving to the west and north the Celts who had previously occupied the country. The Angles were one of the strongest Teutonic tribes, and gradually the island became known as the land of the Angles, then Angleland, then England.

However rough the Teutons might be, there was one person whom they never forgot to treat with special honor, and that was the "scop," the maker, or former. It was his noble office to chant the achievements of heroes at the feasts of which the Teutons were so fond. Imagine a rude hall with a raised platform at one end. A line of stone hearths with blazing fires runs down the room from door to door. Between the hearths and the side walls are places for the sleeping-benches of the warriors. In the fires great joints of meat are roasting, and on either side of the hearths are long, rude tables. On the walls are shields and breastplates and helmets, and coats of mail made of rings curiously fastened together. Here and there are clusters of spears standing against the wall. The burnished mail flashes back the blazing of the fires, and trembles with the heavy tread of the thegns, with their merriment and their laughter, for the battle or the voyage is over, and the time of feasting has come. On the platform is the table of the chief, and with him sit the women of his family, and any warriors to whom he wishes to show special honor. After the feasting and the drinking of mighty cups of "mead," gifts are presented to those who have been bravest, sometimes by the chief, and sometimes—an even greater honor—by the wife of the chief herself. These gifts are horses, jewelled chains for the neck or golden bracelets for the arms, brightly polished swords, and coats of mail and helmets. The scop sits on the platform by the side of the chief. When the feasting is ended, he strikes a heavy chord on his harp and begins his song with "Hwæt!" that is, "Lo!" or "Listen!"

2. Growth of the Epic—Beowulf

These songs chanted by the scops were composed many years before they were written, and probably no two singers ever sang them exactly alike. One scop would sing some exploit of a hero; another would sing it differently, and perhaps add a second exploit greater than the first. Little by little the poem grew longer. Little by little it became more united. The heroic deeds grew more and more marvellous, they became achievements that affected the welfare of a whole people; the poem had a hero, a beginning, and an end. The simple tale of a single adventure had become an epic. After a while it was written; and the manuscript of one of these epics has come down to us, though after passing through the perils of fire, and is now in the British Museum. It is called *Beowulf* because it is the story of the exploits of a hero by that name. The scene is apparently laid in Denmark and southern Sweden, and it is probable that bits of the poem were chanted at feasts long before the Teutons set sail for the shores of England. The story of the poem is as follows:—

> *Hrothgar, king of the Danes, built a more beautiful hall than men had ever heard of before. There he and his thegns enjoyed music and feasting, and divided the treasures that they had won in many a hard-fought battle. They were very happy together; but down in the marshes by the ocean was a monster named Grendel,*

who envied them and hated them. One night, when the thegns were sleeping, he came up stealthily through the mists and the darkness and dragged away thirty of the men and devoured them.

Night after night the slaughter went on, for Hrothgar was feeble with age and none of his thegns were strong enough to take vengeance. At length the young hero, Beowulf, heard of the monster, and offered to attack it. When night came, Grendel stalked up through the darkness, seized a warrior, and devoured him. He grasped another, but that other was Beowulf; and then came a struggle, for the monster felt such a clutch as he had never known. No sword could harm Grendel. Whoever overcame him must win by the strength of his own right arm. Benches were torn from their places, and the very hall trembled with the contest. At last Grendel tore himself away and fled to the marshes, but he left his arm in the unyielding grasp of the hero.

Then was there great rejoicing with Hrothgar and his thegns. A lordly feast was given to the champion; horses and jewels and armor and weapons were presented to him, while scops sang of his glory. The joy was soon turned into sorrow, however, for on the following night, another monster, as horrible as the first, came into the hall. It was the mother of Grendel come to avenge her son, and she carried away one of Hrothgar's favorite liegemen.

When Beowulf was told of this, he set out to punish the murderer. He followed the footprints of the fiend through the wood-paths, over the swamps, the cliffs, and the fens; and at last he came to a precipice overhanging water that was swarming with dragons and sea serpents. Deep down among them was the den of Grendel and his mother. Beowulf put on his best armor and dived down among the horrible creatures, while his men kept an almost hopeless watch on the cliff above him. All day long he sank, down, down, until he came to the bottom of the sea. There was Grendel's mother, and she dragged him into her den. Then there was another terrible struggle, and as the blood burst up through the water, the companions of Beowulf were sad indeed, for they felt sure that they should never again see the face of their beloved leader. While they were gazing sorrowfully at the water, the hero appeared, bearing through the waves the head of Grendel. He had killed the mother and cut off the head from Grendel's body, which lay in the cavern.

Beowulf's third exploit took place many years later, after he had ruled his people for fifty years. He heard of a vast treasure of gold and jewels hidden away in the earth, and although it was guarded by a fire-breathing dragon, he determined to win it for his followers. There was a fearful encounter, and his thegns, all save one, proved to be cowards and deserted him. He won the victory, but the dragon had wounded him, and the poison of the wound soon ended his life. Then the thegns built up a pyre, hung with helmets and coats of mail; and on it they burned the body of their dead leader. After this, they raised a mighty mound in his honor, and placed in it a store of rings and of jewels. Slowly the greatest among them rode around it, mourning for their leader and speaking words of love and praise,—

Said he was mightiest of all the great world-kings,
Mildest of rulers, most gentle in manner,
Most kind to his liegemen, most eager for honor.

This is the story of Beowulf as it has come down to us in a single ragged and smoke-stained manuscript. This manuscript was probably written in the eighth or ninth century, and the poem must differ greatly from

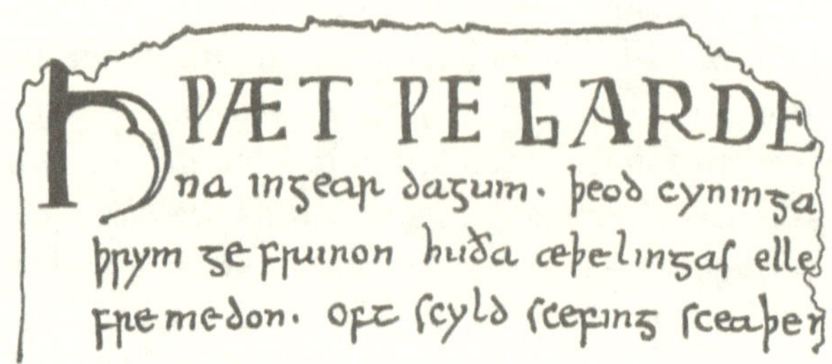

HƿÆT ƿE GARDE
na ingear dagum. þeod cyninga
þrym ge frunon huða æþelingas elle
fremedon. oft scyld scefing sceaþe

A Portion of the First Page of the Beowulf Manuscript

the original version, especially in its religious allusions. In earlier times, the Celts had learned the Christian faith from the Irish; but it was not preached to the Teutons in southern England until 597, when missionaries from Rome made their way to Kent. At first they were allowed to preach on the little island of Thanet only and in the open air; for the wary Teutons had no idea of hearing strange teachings under roofs where magic might easily overpower them. Soon, however, large numbers became earnest converts. Bits of the teachings of the missionaries were dropped into *Beowulf.* Instead of "Fate," the poets said "God;" Grendel is declared to be a descendant of Cain; and the scop interrupts his story of Grendel's envious hatred by singing of the days when God made the heavens and the earth; the ceremonies at the burning of Beowulf are heathen, but the poem says that it was God, the true King of Victory, who led him to the fire-dragon's treasures.

3. Form of Early English Poetry

Many words in Old English are like words in present use, but Old English poetry was different in several respects from the poetry of to-day. The following lines from Beowulf are a good illustration:—

Tha com of more under mist-hleothum
Then came from the moor under the misty-hillside

Grendel gongan, Godes yrre bær;
Grendel going, God's wrath he bore;

mynte se man-scatha manna cynnes
intended the deadly foe of men to the race

sumne besyrwan in sele tham hean.
some one to ensnare in hall that lofty.

To-day we like to hear rhyme at the end of our lines; our ancestors enjoyed not rhyme, but alliteration. In every line there were four accented syllables. The third, the "rime-giver," gave the keynote, for with whatever letter that began, one of the preceding accented syllables must begin and both might begin. The fourth never alliterated with the other three. In the first line quoted, the accented syllables are *com, mor, mist,* and *hle. Mist* is the rime-giver. In the second line, *God* is the rime-giver, while *Gren, gon,* and *bær* are the other accented syllables. The Teutons were very fond of compound words. Some of these words are simple and childlike, such as ban-hus (bone-house), body; ban-loca (bonelocker), flesh. Some, especially those pertaining to the ocean, are poetical, such as mere-stræt (sea-street), way over the sea; yth-lida (wave-sailer) and famig-heals (foamy-necked), vessel.

4. Other Old English Poems

A number of shorter poems have come down to us from the Old English. Among them are two that are of special interest. One of these is *Widsith* (the far-wanderer), and this is probably our earliest English poem. It pictures the life of the scop, who roams about from one great chief to another, everywhere made welcome, everywhere rewarded for his song by kindness and presents. The poem ends:—

Wandering thus, there roam over many a country
The gleemen of heroes, mindful of songs for the chanting,
Telling their needs, their heartfelt thankfulness speaking.
Southward or northward, wherever they go, there is some one
Who values their song and is liberal to them in his presents,
One who before his retainers would gladly exalt
His achievements, would show forth his honors. Till all this is vanished,
Till life and light disappear, who of praise is deserving
Has ever throughout the wide earth a glory unchanging.

The second of these songs is *Deor's Lament.* Deor is in sorrow, for another scop has become his lord's favorite. The neglected singer comforts himself by recalling the troubles that others have met. Each stanza ends with the refrain,—

That he endured; this, too, can I.

Widsith and *Deor's Lament* were found in a manuscript volume of poems collected and copied more than eight hundred years ago. It is known as the Exeter Book because it belongs to the cathedral at Exeter. Another volume, containing both poetry and prose was discovered at the Monastery of Vercelli in Italy. These two volumes and the manuscript of *Beowulf* contain almost all that is left to us of Anglo-Saxon poetry.

5. Cædmon [d. 680]

The happy scop and the unhappy scop are both forgotten. No one knows who wrote either the rejoicing or the lament. The first English poet that we know by name is the monk Cædmon, who died in 680. The introduction of Christianity made great changes in the country, for though the sturdy Englishmen could not lay aside in one century, or two, or three, all their confidence in charms and magic verses, and in runic letters cut into the posts of their doors and engraved on their swords and their battle-axes, yet they were honest believers in the God of whom they had learned. Churches and convents rose throughout the land, and one of these convents was the home of Cædmon. It was founded by Irish missionaries, and was built at what is now called Whitby, on a lofty cliff overlooking the German Ocean. There men and women prayed and worked and sought to live lives of holiness. At one

The Ruins of Whitby Abbey

of their feasts the harp passed from one to another, that each might sing in turn. Cædmon had not been educated as a monk, and therefore he had never learned to make songs. As the harp came near him, he was glad to slip out of the room with the excuse that he must care for the cattle. In the stable he fell asleep; and as he slept a vision appeared to him and said, "Cædmon, sing some song to me." "I cannot sing," he replied, "and that is why I left the feasting." "But you shall sing," declared the vision. "Sing the beginning of created beings." Then Cædmon sang. He sang of the power of the Creator, of his glory, and of how He made the heavens and the earth. In the morning he told the steward of the mysterious gift that had come to him while he slept, and the steward led him joyfully to Hilda, the royal maiden who was their abbess. Many learned men came together, and Cædmon told them his dream and repeated his verses. Another subject was given him, and he made verses on that also. "It is the grace of God," said the council reverently. The habit of a monk was put upon him, he was carefully taught the word of God, and as he learned, he composed poem after poem, following the Bible story from the creation to the coming of Christ, his resurrection and his ascension.

6. Cynewulf, born about 750

The name of one more poet, Cynewulf, is that of the greatest of the authors whose words have come down to us from the early days of England. He, too, was probably of Northumbria, and he must have written about a century after the time of Cædmon. Hardly anything is known of him except his name; but he interwove that in some of his poems in such a way that it could never be forgotten. For this purpose he made use of runes, the earliest of the northern alphabets. Each rune represented not only a letter, but also the word of which it was the initial; for instance:—

C = Cene, the courageful warrior.
Y = Yfel, wretched.
N = Nyd, necessity.
W = Wyn, joy.
U = Ur, our.
L = Lagu, water.
F = Feoh, wealth.

With these runes Cynewulf spelled out his name:—

Then the Courage-*hearted cowers when the King he hears*
Speak the words of wrath—Him the wielder of the heavens
Speak to those who once on earth but obeyed him weakly,
While as yet their Yearning *pain, and their* Need, *most easily*
Comfort might discover.

. . . .

Gone is then the Winsomeness
Of the earth's adornments! What to Us *as men belonged*
Of the joys of life was locked, long ago in Lake-*floods,*
All the Fee *on earth.**

Cynewulf has many beautiful descriptions of nature, sometimes of nature calm and quiet and peaceful; for instance:—

When the winds are lulled and the weather is fair,
When the sun shines bright, holy jewel of heaven,
When the clouds are scattered, the waters subdued,
When no stormwind is heard, and the candle of nature
Shines warm from the south, giving light to the many.

*Stopford Brooke's translation, in *English Literature from the Beginning to the Norman Conquest.*

Cynewulf loved tranquil days and peaceful scenes; but if he wrote the riddles which are often thought to be his, he had not lost sympathy with the wild life of his ancestors on the stormy ocean. The English liked riddles, and this one must have been repeated over and over again at convent feasts and in halls at times of rejoicing:—

Sometimes I come down from above and stir up the storm-waves;
The surges, gray as the flint-stone, I hurl on the sea-banks,
The foaming waters I dash on the rock-wall. Gloomily
Moves from the deep a mountain billow; darkening,
Onward it sweeps o'er the turbulent wild of the ocean.
Another comes forth and, commingling, they meet at the mainland
In high, towering ridges. Loud is the call from the vessel,
Loud is the sailors' appeal; but the rock-masses lofty
Stand unmoved by the seafarers' cries or the waters.

The answer to this is "The hurricane."

An especially beautiful poem of Cynewulf's is called the *Dream of the Rood.* The cross appeared to the poet in a dream,—"the choicest dream," he calls it. It was "circled with light," it was glittering with gems and with gold, and around it stood the angels of God. From it there flowed forth a stream of blood; and while the dreamer gazed in wonder, the cross spoke to him. It told him of the tree being cut from the edge of the forest and made into the cross. Then followed the story of the crucifixion, of the three crosses that stood long on Calvary sorrowing, of the burial of the cross of Christ deep down in the earth, of its being found by servants of God, who adorned it with silver and with gold that it might bring healing to all who should pay it their reverence.

7. Early English Poetry as a Whole

Such was the Early English poetry, beginning with wild exploits of half-fabulous heroes and gradually changing under the touch of Christianity into paraphrases of the Bible story, into legends of saints, and accounts of heavenly visions. It contains bold descriptions of sea and tempest, intermingling, as the years passed, with pictures of more quiet and peaceful scenes. The names of but two poets, Cædmon and Cynewulf, are known to us; but throughout all these early poems there is an earnestness, an appealing sincerity, and an honest, childlike love of nature, that bring the writers very near to us, and make them no unworthy predecessors of the poets that have followed them.

2. Prose

8. Bede, 673–735

About the time of the death of Cædmon, a boy was born in Northumbria who was to write one of the most famous pieces of Early English prose. His name was Bede, or Bæda, and he is often called the Venerable Bede, venerable being the title next below that of saint. When he was a little child, he was taken to the convent of Jarrow, and there he remained all his life. A busy life it was. The many hours of prayer must be observed; the land must be cultivated; guests must be entertained, no small interruption as the fame of the convent and of Bede himself increased. Moreover, this convent was a great school, to which some six hundred pupils, not only from England but from various parts of Europe, came for instruction.

Bede enjoyed it all. He was happy in his religious duties. He "always took delight," as he says, "in learning, teaching, and writing." He found real pleasure in the outdoor work; and, little as he tells us of his own life, he does not forget to say that he especially liked winnowing and threshing the grain and giving milk to the young lambs and calves. He was keenly alive to the affairs of the world, and though libraries were his special delight, he was as ready to talk with his stranger guests of distant kingdoms as of books. In the different monasteries of England there were collections of valuable manuscripts, and Jarrow had one of the most famous of these collections. The abbot loved books, and from each one of his numerous journeys to Rome he returned with a rich store of volumes.

Monk at Work on Book of Kildare

Much of Bede's time must have been given to teaching, and yet, in the midst of all his varied occupations, this first English scholar found leisure to write an enormous amount. Forty-five different works he produced, and they were really a summary of the knowledge of his day. He wrote of grammar, rhetoric, music, medicine; he wrote lives of saints and commentaries on the Bible,—indeed, there is hardly a subject that he did not touch. He even wrote a volume of poems, including a dainty little pastoral, resembling the Latin pastorals, a contest of song between summer and winter, which closes with a pretty picture of the coming of springtime and the cuckoo. "When the cuckoo comes," he says, "the hills are covered with happy blossoms, the flocks find pasture, the meadows are full of repose, the spreading branches of the trees give shade to the weary, and the many-colored birds sing their joyful greeting to the sunshine."

One day the king of Northumbria asked Bede to write a history of England, and the busy monk began the work as simply as if he were about to prepare a lesson for his pupils. He sent to Rome for copies of letters and reports written in the early days when the Romans ruled the land; he borrowed from various convents their treasures of old manuscripts pertaining to the early times; and he talked with men who had preserved the ancient traditions and legends. So it was that Bede's *Ecclesiastical History,* the first history of England, was written. When it was done, he sent it to the king, together with a sincere and dignified little preface, in which he asked for the prayers of whoever should read the book,—a much larger number than the quiet monk expected.

With the difficulty of collecting information, no one could expect Bede's work to be free from mistakes, although he was careful from whom his information came, and he often gives the name of his authority. Bede knew well how to tell a story, and the *Ecclesiastical History,* sober and grave as its title sounds, is full of tales of visions of angels, lights from heaven, mysterious voices, and tempests that were stilled and fires that were quenched at the prayers of holy men. Here is the legend of Cædmon and his gift of song. Here, too, is the famous statement that there are no snakes in Ireland. "Even if they are carried thither from Britain," says Bede, "as soon as the ship comes near the shore and the scent of the air reaches them, they die."

All these books were written in Latin. That was the tongue of the church and of all scholars of the day. It was a universal language, and an educated man might be set down in any monastery in England or on the Continent, and feel perfectly at home in its book-room or in conversation with the monks. Bede was so thoroughly English, however, in his love of nature, his frankness and earnestness, and his devotion to the people of his own land that, although he wrote in Latin, most of his works have a purely English atmosphere. He did not scorn his native tongue, and even in his writing he may have used it more than once, though we know the name of one work only. This was a translation of the *Gospel of St. John,* and it was his last work. He knew that his life was near its close, but he felt that he must complete this translation for his pupils. Some one of them was always with him to write as the teacher might feel able to dictate. The last

A Mediæval Author at Work

day of his life came, and in the morning the pupil said, "Master, there is still one chapter wanting. Will it trouble you to be asked any more questions?" "It is no trouble," answered Bede. "Take your pen and write quickly." When evening had come, the boy said gently, "Dear Master, there is yet one sentence not written." "Write quickly," said Bede again. "The sentence is written," said the boy a few minutes later. "It is well," murmured Bede, and with new strength he joyfully chanted the *Gloria;* and so, in 735, he passed away, the first English scholar, scientist, and historian.

9. Alcuin, 735?–804

In the very year of Bede's death, if we may trust to tradition, Alcuin was born, the man who was to carry on English scholarship, though not on English soil. He was a monk of the convent of York, and was famous for his knowledge. Perhaps some of the English churchmen thought that he was too famous, when they knew that King Charlemagne had heard of his learning, and had persuaded him to leave his own country and come to France to teach the royal children and take charge of education in the Frankish kingdom. For fourteen years, from 782 to 796, he spent nearly all his time at the court of Charlemagne. Moreover, he persuaded many other men of York training to leave England and assist him in teaching the French. He little knew how grateful the English would be in later years that this had been done.

10. Alfred the Great, 848–901

During those years of Alcuin's absence in France, there was dire trouble in Northumbria. King after king was slain by rebels; and finally the Danes, coming from the shores of the Baltic, made their first attacks on the coasts of Northumbria. This was the beginning. Year after year the savage pirates fell upon the land. For more than three quarters of a century the Northumbrians were either fighting or dreading the coming of their heathen foes. At the end of that time, when peace was made with the terrible invaders, Northumbria was a desert so far as literature was concerned. The Danes had struck especially at the monasteries because of the gold and silver vessels and ornaments that were collected in them; and not one monastery remained standing in all the land from the Tyne to the Humber. Libraries famous over Europe had been burned; smoked and bloodstained ruins were alone left to show where men had been taught who had become the teachers of Europe. South of the Humber matters were little better; for there, too, the heathen Danes had swept through and through the country. Priests pronounced the words in their Latin mass books, but very few could understand the language and put a Latin letter into English. The only hope of England lay in her king. It was happy for her that her king was Alfred the

King Alfred

Great, and that this sovereign who could fight battles of swords and spears was of equal courage and wisdom in the warfare against ignorance. In his childhood he had visited Rome, perhaps spent several years in that city. He had paid a long visit at the Frankish court of Charlemagne's son. He had seen what knowledge could do, and he meant that his own people should have a chance to learn. Then it was that France repaid England for the loan of Alcuin, for priests taught in the schools which he had founded were induced to cross the Channel and become the teachers of the English.

There were few English books, however, and there was no one to make them but this busy king; and just as simply as Bede had taken up his pen to write a history of the land, so Alfred set to work to translate books for his kingdom. Among the books that he translated were two that must have been of special interest to the English, Bede's *Ecclesiastical History* and a combined history and geography of the world, written five hundred years before Alfred's day by a Spanish monk called Orosius. The latter had long been a favorite school-book in the convents; but, naturally, a geography that was five hundred years old was in need of revision, and Alfred became not only a translator but a reviser. He never forgot that he was writing for his people, and whenever he came to an expression that would not be clear to them, he either explained it, or omitted it altogether. Whenever he could correct a mistake of Orosius's, he did so.

11. The Language of Alfred's Time

In one way Alfred had not only his translations to make, but his very language to invent. Latin is a finished, exact, accurate language; the English of the ninth century was rude, childish, and awkward, and it was no easy task to interpret the clean-cut wording of the Latin into the loose, clumsy English phrases. Nevertheless, Alfred had no thought of imitating the Latin construction. The following is a literal translation of part of the preface to one of his books that he sent to Wærferth, bishop of Worcester:—

> *Alfred the King bids to greet Wærferth the bishop with loving words and in friendly wise; and I bid this be known to thee that it very often comes into my mind what wise men there were formerly, both clergy and laymen; and what blessed times there were then throughout England; and how kings who had power over the nation in those days obeyed God and his ministers, and they both preserved peace, order, and authority at home and also increased their territory abroad; and how they throve both in war and in wisdom; and also the holy orders how zealous they were both in teaching and in learning, and in all the services that they ought to give to God; and how people from abroad sought wisdom and teaching in this land; and how we must now get them from without if we are to have them.*

Confused as this is, the king's earnestness shows in every word. He knows just what he means to say, and, language or no language, he contrives to say it. Bede's translation of the *Gospel of Saint John* disappeared centuries ago, and this preface of King Alfred's is the first bit of English prose that we possess. Literature had vanished from the north and was making its home in the south.

12. The Anglo-Saxon Chronicle

Another piece of literary and historical work we owe to Alfred, and that is the *Anglo-Saxon Chronicle.* In almost every convent the monks were accustomed to set down what seemed to them the most important events, such as the death of a king, an attack by the Danes, an unusually high tide, or an eclipse of the sun. One of these lists of events was kept in the convent at Winchester, Alfred's capital city, and the idea occurred to him of revising this table, adding to it from Bede's *Ecclesiastical History* and other sources, and making it the beginning of a progressive history of his kingdom. It is possible that Alfred himself did this revising, and it can hardly be doubted that he wrote at least the accounts of some of his own battles with the Danes.

13. Death of Alfred

In 901, it was written in the Chronicle, "This year died Alfred, the son of Ethelwulf." King Alfred left England apparently on the way to literary progress, if not greatness. The kingdom was at peace; the Danes of the north and the English of the south were under one king, and were, nominally at least, ruled by the same laws; churches had arisen over the kingdom; convents had been built and endowed; schools were increasing in number and in excellence; books of practical worth had been translated, probably more than have come down to us; the people had been encouraged to learn the language of scholars, yet their own native tongue had not been scorned, but rather raised to the rank of a literary language. There seemed every reason to expect national progress in all directions, and especially in matters intellectual.

14. Literature during the 10th and 11th Centuries

The contrary was the fact. For this there were two reasons: 1. Alfred's rule was a one-man power. His subjects studied because the king required study. Learned men came to England because the king invited them and rewarded them. At Alfred's death a natural reaction set in. The strong will and the generous hand were gone, the watchful eye of the king was closed. 2. The Danes renewed their attacks. It almost ceased to be a question of any moment whether England should advance; far more pressing was the question whether England should exist. The church was in a low state. The monks did not obey the rules of their orders, and many of the secular clergy were not only ignorant but openly wicked. About the middle of the tenth century, the monk Dunstan became abbot of Glastonbury, and he preached reforms so earnestly that both priests and people began to mend their ways. Moreover, the year 1000 was approaching, and there was a general feeling that in that year the world would come to an end. A natural result of this feeling was that the church became more active, and that great numbers of lives of saints appeared, and sermons, or homilies, as they were called.

These homilies were not so uninteresting as their name sounds. To hold the attention of the people, the preachers were forced to be picturesque, and they gave in minute detail most vivid descriptions of places, saints, and demons about which they knew absolutely nothing. The saints were pictured as of fair complexion, with light hair and blue eyes. Satan was described as having dark, shaggy hair hanging down to his ankles. Sparks flew from his eyes and sulphurous flames from his mouth. The most famous writer of these homilies was Ælfric, abbot of Ensham.

Dedication of a Saxon Church
From an old manuscript

In the first two centuries after Alfred, the old poems composed in the north were rewritten in the form in which they have come down to us, that is, in the language of the south, of the West Saxons; but little was produced that could be called poetry. The *Chronicle* was continued, and one or two bold battle-songs were inserted. A few rude ballads were composed, with little of the old alliteration, and with only a beginning of appreciation of rhyme. One of these was the work of a king, Canute the Dane, who became ruler of England in 1017:—

Merie sungen the munaches binnan Ely
Tha Cnut ching reuther by:
"Rotheth cnites noer the land
And here ye thes Munaches sæng."

Joyously sang the monks in Ely
When Canute the king rowed by.
"Row, knights, nearer the land,
And hear ye the song of the monks."

Glancing back over the literature of England, we can see that it had been much affected by the influence of the Celts. From the sixth century to the ninth the Christian schools of Ireland were famous throughout Europe, and the Irish missionaries taught the religion of Christ to the Northumbrians. The Teutons and the Celts were not at all alike. The Teutons thought somewhat slowly. They were given to pondering on difficult subjects and trying to explain puzzling questions. The Celts thought and felt swiftly; a word would make them smile, and a word would arouse their sympathy. The Teutons liked stories of brave chiefs who led their thegns in battle and shared with them the treasures that were won, of thegns who were faithful to their lord, and who at his death heaped up a great mound of earth to keep his name in lasting remembrance. The Celts, too, were fond of stories, but stories that were full of bright and beautiful descriptions, of birds of brilliant coloring, of marvellous secrets, and of mysterious voices. They liked battle scenes wherein strange mists floated about the warriors and weird phantoms were dimly seen in the gathering darkness.

To say just when and where the Celtic influence touched English literature is not easy; but, comparing the grave, stern resolution of *Beowulf*, with the imaginative beauty, the graceful fancy, and the tender sentiment of the *Dream of the Rood*, and the picturesque and witty descriptions of the homilies, one can but feel that there is something in the literature of the English Teutons which did not come from themselves, and which can be accounted for in no other way than by their contact with the Celts.

15. William the Norman Conquers England

The beginnings of a noble literature had been made in England, but the inspiration had become scanty. The English writer needed not only to read something better than he had yet produced, but even more he needed to know a race to whom that "something better" was familiar. In 1066, an event occurred that brought him both men and models: William the Norman conquered England and became its king.

SUMMARY

Centuries V–XI

THE EARLY ENGLISH PERIOD

1. Poetry	2. Prose
Beowulf.	Bede.
Widsith.	Alfred.
Deor's Lament.	*Anglo-Saxon Chronicle.*
Cædmon.	Lives of saints and homilies.
Cynewulf.	

1. Poetry

Our English ancestors lived in Jutland and the northern part of what is now Germany. They were savage warriors, but loved song and poetry. After their feasts the scop, or poet, sang of the adventures of some hero. Little by little these songs were welded together and became an epic. One epic, *Beowulf,* has been preserved, though much changed by the teachings of the missionaries who came to England in 597. Anglo-Saxon verse was marked by alliteration instead of rhyme.

Besides *Beowulf,* little remains of the Anglo-Saxon poetry except what is contained in the *Exeter Book* and the *Vercelli Book.*

The first poet whom we know by name was the monk Cædmon (seventh century), whose chief work was a paraphrase of the Scriptures. The greatest of the early poets was Cynewulf (eighth century).

2. Prose

One of the most famous pieces of English prose, a translation of the *Gospel according to St. John,* was written by the monk Bede (seventh and eighth centuries). He wrote on many subjects, but his most valuable work is his *Ecclesiastical History.*

Alcuin (eighth century) carried on English scholarship in France. England was harassed by the Danes, but after King Alfred (ninth century) had brought about peace, Alcuin's pupils became teachers of the English.

King Alfred made several valuable translations. The preface of one of them is the earliest piece of English prose that we still possess. *The Anglo-Saxon Chronicle* was formally begun in his reign.

The death of Alfred and the renewed attacks of the Danes retarded the literary progress of England. The preaching of Dunstan and the near approach of the year 1000 called out lives of saints, and homilies written by Ælfric and others. Old poems were rewritten, and rude ballads were composed. The influence of the Celts for beauty, fancy, and wit may be seen in both poetry and prose. English literature had made a good beginning, but needed better models.

CHAPTER II

Centuries XII and XIII

THE NORMAN-ENGLISH PERIOD

16. Advantages of the Conquest

Nothing better could have happened to England than this Norman conquest. The Englishmen of the eleventh century were courageous and persistent, but the spark of inspiration that gives a people the mastery of itself and the leadership of other nations was wanting. England was like a great vessel rolling in the trough of the sea, turning broadside to every wave. The country must fall into the hands of either the barbaric north or the civilized south. Happily for England, the victor was of the south.

The Normans were Teutons, who had fallen upon France as their kinsmen had fallen upon England; but the invaders of France had been thrown among a race superior to them in manners, language, and literature. These northern pirates gave a look about them, and straightway they began to follow the customs of the people whom they had conquered. They embraced the Christian religion and built churches and monasteries as if they had been to the manner born. They forgot their own language and adopted that of France. They intermarried with the French; and in a century and a half a new race had arisen with the bravery and energy of the Northmen and an aptitude for even more courtly manners and even wider literary culture than the French themselves.

17. The Struggle between the French and English Languages

Such were the Norman conquerors of England. How would their coming affect the language and the literature of the subject country? It was three hundred years before the question was fully answered. At first the Norman spoke French, the Englishman spoke English, and both nations used Latin in the church service. Little by little, the Norman found it convenient to know something of the language spoken by the masses of the people around him. Little by little, the Englishman acquired some knowledge of the language of his rulers. Words that were nearly alike in both tongues were confused in pronunciation, and as for spelling,—a man's mode of spelling was his private property, and he did with his own as he would. It is hard to trace the history of the two languages in England until we reach the fourteenth century, and then there are some few landmarks. In 1300, Oxford allowed people who had suits at law to plead in "any language generally understood." Fifty years later, English was taught to some extent in the schools. In 1362, it became the official language of the courts. In 1385, John of Trevisa wrote, "In all the grammar schools of England children give up French and construe and learn in English, and have thereby advantage on one side and disadvantage on another. Their advantage is that they learn their grammar in less time than children were wont to do; the disadvantage is that now grammar-school children know no more French than their left heel knows." In 1400, the Earl of March offered his aid to the king and wrote his letter in English, making no further apology for using his native tongue than the somewhat independent one, "It is more clear to my understanding than Latin or French."

In this contest, three centuries long, English had come off victor, but it was a different English from that of earlier times. Hundreds of new nouns, verbs, and adjectives had entered it, but they had been forced to wear the English garb. To speak broadly, verbs had adopted English endings; adjectives had adopted English comparisons; nouns had given up their case-endings and also their gender in great degree, for the simplest remedy for the frequent conflict between the English and French gender was to drop all distinctions of gender so far as inanimate objects were concerned.

How did the coming of the Norman affect the literature of England? As soon as the shock of conquest was somewhat past, the English unconsciously began, in the old Teutonic fashion, to look about them and see what ways worthier than their own they could adopt. They had refused to become a French-speaking people, but was there any thing in Norman literature and literary methods worthy of their imitation, or rather assimilation?

18. Opening of the Universities and the Crusades

The Normans had a taste for history, they were a religious people, and they thoroughly enjoyed story-telling. Two other influences were brought to bear upon the English: the opening of the universities and the crusades. The first made it possible for a man to obtain an education even if he had no desire to become a priest. The second threw open the treasures of the world. Thousands set out on these expeditions to rescue the tomb of Christ from the power of the unbelievers. Those who returned brought with them a wealth of new ideas. They had seen new countries and new manners. They had learned to think new thoughts.

The opening of the universities made it possible for chronicles to be written, not only by monks in the monasteries, but by men who lived in the midst of the events that they described. Chronicles were no longer mere annals; they became full of detail, vivid, interesting.

19. Devotional Books

The religious energy of the Normans and the untiring zeal of the preachers strengthened the English interest in religious matters. The sacred motive of the crusades intensified it, and books of devotion appeared, not in Latin, like the chronicles, but in simple, everyday English. One of the best known of these was the *Ormulum,* a book which gives a metrical paraphrase of the Gospels as used in the church service, each portion followed by a metrical sermon. Its author kept a sturdy hold upon his future fame in his couplet,—

Thiss boc iss nemmnedd Orrmulum
Forrthi thatt Orm itt worhhte.

He was equally determined that his lines should be

pronounced properly, and so after every short vowel he doubled the consonant. He even gave advance orders to whoever should copy his work:—

> *And whoso shall will to write this book again another time, I bid him that he write it correctly, so as this book teacheth him, entirely as it is upon this first pattern, with all such rhymes as here are set with just as many words, and that he look well that he write a letter twice where it upon this book is written in that wise.*[*]

Another of these books of devotion was the *Ancren Riwle,* a little prose work whose author is unknown. Its object was to guide three sisters who wished to withdraw from the world, though without taking the vows of the convent. It is almost sternly strict, but so pure and natural and earnest that it was deeply loved and appreciated.

20. Romances

The Norman delight in stories and the new ideas given by the crusades aroused in the English a keen love of romance. The conquest itself was romantic. The chivalry introduced by the Normans was picturesque. It adorned the stern Saxon idea of duty with richness and grace. Simple old legends took form and beauty. Four great cycles of romance were produced; that is, four groups of stories told in metre, each centred about some one hero. One was about Charlemagne, one about Alexander the Great, one told the tale of the fall of Troy, and one pictured King Arthur and his knights. This last cycle had a curious history. Before the middle of the

[*] Translated in Morley's *English Writers,* iii.

Sir Launcelot and a Hermit
From an illuminated MS. of 1316

twelfth century, one Geoffrey of Monmouth, a Welsh bishop, wrote in Latin an exceedingly fanciful *History of the Kings of Britain.* It was translated into French by a clerk named Wace; was carried to France; wandered over the Continent, where it was smoothed and beautified, and gained the stories of Launcelot and the Holy Grail; then returned to England, and was put into English verse by the English priest Layamon. He called it the *Brut,* or story of Brutus, a fabled descendant of Æneas, who was claimed to have landed on the shores of England in prehistoric times. This cycle was the special favorite of the English. The marvellous adventures of King Arthur's knights interested those who had been thrilled by the stories of returning crusaders; and the quest of the knights for but one glance of that Holy Thing, the Grail, was in full accord with the spirit of the crusades, an earthly journey with a spiritual gain as its object and reward.

The *Chronicle* came to an end in 1154. The *Ormulum,*

the *Ancren Riwle*, and the *Brut* all belong to the early part of the thirteenth century. They are English in their feeling; but as the years passed, French romances were sung throughout the land,—in French where French was understood, in English translation elsewhere. One of the best liked of these was *King Horn.* Its story is:—

The kingdom of Horn's father is invaded by the Saracens, who kill the father and put Horn and his companions to sea. King Aylmar receives them, and orders them to be taught various duties. Of Horn he says:—

And tech him to harpe
With his nayles scharpe,
Bivore me to serve
And of the cupe lerve,—

the usual accomplishments of the page. The king's daughter, Rymenhild, falls in love with Horn; and no wonder, if the description of him is correct.

He was bright fo the glas,
He was whit fo the flur,
Rofe red was his colur,
In none kinge-riche
Nas non his iliche.

He goes in quest of adventures, to prove himself worthy of Rymenhild. The course of their love does not run smooth. King Aylmar presents a most eligible king as his daughter's suitor; Horn's false friend tries to win her; she is shut up in an island castle; but Horn, in the disguise of a gleeman, makes his way into the castle and wins his Rymenhild. He kills his false friend; he finds that his mother still lives; he regains his father's kingdom; and so the tale ends. This story is thoroughly French in its treatment of woman. In *Beowulf,* the wife of the lord is respected and honored, she is her lord's friend and helpmeet; but there is no romance about the matter. To picture the smile of woman as the reward of valor, and her hand as the prize of victory, was left to the verses of those poets who were familiar with the glamour of knighthood.

21. The Norman-English Love of Nature

This new race, the Norman-English, enjoyed romance, they liked the new and the unwonted, but there was ever a warm corner in their hearts for nature. The dash of the waves, the keen breath of the northern wind, the coming of spring, the song of the cuckoo, the gleam of the daisy,—they loved them all; and in the midst of the romances of knights and Saracens and foreign countries, they felt a tenderness toward what was their very own, the world of nature. Simple, tender, graceful little lyric poems slipped in shyly among the more pretentious histories, religious handbooks, and paraphrases. Here are bits from them:—

Sumer is icumen in,
Lludc sing cuccu!
Groweth sed, and bloweth med,
And springth the wude nu,
Sing, cuccu!

or this:—

Dayes-eyes in the dales,
Notes sweete of nightingales,
Each fowl song singeth,

or this, which has a touch of the French love romance:—

Blow, northern wind,
Send thou me my suetyng.
Blow, northern wind,
Blow, blow, blow!

22. The Robin Hood Ballads

Not only love of nature but love of freedom and love of justice inspired the ballads of Robin Hood, many of which must have originated during this period, though probably they did not take their present form till much later. They are crude, simple stories in rhyme of the exploits of Robin Hood and his men, and they come straight from the heart of the Englishman, that bold, defiant heart which always beat more fiercely at the thought of injustice. Robin and his friends are exiles because they have dared to shoot the king's deer, and they have taken up their abode in "merry Sherwood." There they waylay the sheriff and the "proud bishop," and force them to open their well-filled purses and

A Band of Minstrels
From a fourteenth-century MS.

count out the gold pieces that are to make life easier for many a poor man. These ballads were not for palaces or for monasteries, they were for the English people; and the ballad-singers went about from village to village, singing to one group after another, adding a rhyme, or a stanza, or an adventure at every repetition. Gradually the tales of the "courteous outlaw" were forming themselves into a cycle of romance, but the days of the printing-press came too soon for its completion. Whether Robin was ever a "real, live hero" is not of the least consequence. The point of interest is that the ballads which picture his adventures are the free, bold expression of the sincere feelings of the Englishman in the early years of his forced submission to Norman rule.

23. Value of the Norman-English Writings

The writings of the first two centuries after the Norman conquest are, as a whole, of small worth. With the increasing number of translations, such a world of literature was thrown open to the English that they were dazzled with excess of light. Daringly, but half timidly, they ventured to step forward, to try one thing after another. No one could expect finish and completeness; the most that could be looked for was some beginning of poetry that should show imagination, of prose that should show power. So ended the thirteenth century, in a kind of morning twilight of literature. The fourteenth was the time of the dawning, the century of Chaucer.

SUMMARY

Centuries XII and XIII

THE NORMAN-ENGLISH PERIOD

"Ormulum".
"Ancren Riwle".
Cycles of romance.
Charlemagne.
Alexander.
Fall of Troy.
King Arthur.
Layamon's "Brut".
French romances.
"King Horn".
Nature lyrics.
Robin Hood ballads.

The Norman Conquest affected both language and literature. English, French, and Latin were used in England; but English gradually prevailed, until in 1362 it became the official language of the courts. Many new words had been added and its grammar simplified.

The literary influence of the Normans was for history, religious writings, and story-telling. Two other influences helped to arouse the English to mental activity,—the opening of the universities and the crusades.

The chief immediate literary results of this intellectual stimulus were the chronicles, now written by men who were not monks, and books of devotion. Among the latter was the *Ormulum* and the *Ancren Riwle.*

Love of story-telling manifested itself in four cycles of romance, centring about Charlemagne, Alexander the Great, the fall of Troy, and King Arthur. This last cycle went through the hands of Geoffrey of Monmouth, Wace, Layamon, and others. French romances were popular, especially *King Horn.*

Love of nature inspired simple, sincere lyrics; love of freedom and justice inspired the Robin Hood ballads.

The writings of the twelfth and thirteenth centuries are of little intrinsic value, but foreshadow better work to come.

CHAPTER III

Century XIV

CHAUCER'S CENTURY

24. England in the Fourteenth Century

The fourteenth century was not only the dawning of modern English literature, but it was the dawning of English thought. Before this time kings had thought how to keep their thrones; barons had thought how to prevent kings from becoming too powerful; priests and monks had thought, sometimes how to teach the people, sometimes how to get the most possible from them; but the masses of the English people never seemed to think of anything that was of interest to them all until about the middle of the fourteenth century.

One special reason for this beginning of English thought was that many thousands of Englishmen had become more free than ever before. England had long been controlled by what is known as the feudal system; that is, a tenure of land on condition of service. The cultivated portions of England were divided into great manors, or farms, and each was held by some rich man on condition of giving his service to the king. On these manors lived the masses of the people, the villeins, or peasants. They were obliged as part of their duty to work for their lord a certain number of days every year, and they were forbidden to leave the manor. During the crusades, the lords who went to the Holy Land needed a great deal of money, and they often allowed their tenants to give them money instead of service. Sometimes they sold them land. These crusades came to an end in the thirteenth century, and even during the early years of the fourteenth the peasants were beginning to feel somewhat independent.

In 1338, the Hundred Years' War broke out between England and France. In 1346, an important battle was won at Crécy, not by English knights on horse back with swords and lances, but by English peasants on foot with no weapons except bows and arrows. Then the peasants began to say to one another, "We can protect ourselves. Why should we remain on manors and depend upon knights in armor to fight for us?" Following close upon this battle was a terrible disease, called the Black Death, which swept over England. When it had gone, half of the people of the land were dead. Many of those peasants who survived ran away from the manors, for now that there were so few workmen, they could earn high wages anywhere. Moreover, weaving had been introduced, and if they did not wish to do farm-work, they could support themselves in any city. The king and his counsellors made severe laws against this running away; but they could not well be enforced, and they only made the peasants angry with all who were richer or more powerful than themselves. They began to question, "How are these lords any greater folk than we? How do they deserve wealth any more than we? They came from Adam and Eve just as we did."

The masses of the people, then, were angry with the nobles and the other wealthy men. They were also discontented with the church. After the Black Death there was hardly a person in England who was not mourning the loss of dear friends. Especially the poor longed for the comfort that the church should have given them; but the church paid little attention to their needs. Many of the clergy who received the income from English benefices lived in Italy, and had no further interest in England than to get as much from the land as possible. While the peasants were in such poverty, vast sums of money were being sent to these Italian priests, for fully half the land was in the hands of the church. The church did less and less for men, while the vision of what it might do was growing clearer. Thousands of these unhappy, discontented peasants marched up to London to demand of the king their freedom and other rights and privileges. This was the Peasants' Revolt of 1381. Their demands were not granted, and the revolters were severely punished.

In this century of unrest and change there were four authors whose writings are characteristic of the manner in which four classes of people regarded the state of matters. They were: 1. "Sir John Mandeville," who simply accepted things as they were; 2. William Langland, or Langley, who criticised and wished to reform; 3. Wyclif, who criticised and wished to overthrow; and 4. Chaucer, the good-humored aristocrat, who saw the faults of his times, but gently ridiculed them rather than preached against them.

25. The Voyages and Travels of Sir John Mandeville, Kt.

This account of distant countries and strange peoples purports to have been written by Sir John himself. He claims to be an English knight who has often journeyed to Jerusalem, and who puts forth this volume to serve as a guide-book to those wishing to make the pilgrimage. The introduction seems so "real" that it is a pity to be obliged to admit that the work is probably a combination of a few travellers' stories and a vast amount of imagination, and that, worse than all, there never was any "Sir John." It was first written in French, and then translated into English either in the fourteenth century or the early part of the fifteenth. The traveller has most marvellous experiences. He finds that in the Dead Sea iron will float, while a feather will

Sir John Mandeville on his Voyage to Palestine
From an old MS. in the British Museum

drop to the bottom. "And these be things against kind [nature]," says Sir John. He sees in Africa people who have but one foot. "They go so fast that it is marvel," he declares, "and the foot is so large that it shadoweth all the body against the sun when they will lie and rest themselves." Sometimes he brings in a bit of science. From his observations of the North Star he reasons that "Men may go all round the world and return to their country; and always they would find men, lands, and isles, as well as in our part of the world." When he touches on religious customs, he becomes especially interesting, for in the midst of the unrest and discontent of his age he has no fault to find with the laws or the church; and with all his devotion to the church, he has no blame for those whose belief differs from his own. "They fail in some articles of our faith," is his only criticism of the Moslems.

26. William Langland, 1332–1400

William Langland wrote the *Vision of Piers Plowman.* Very little is known of Langland save that he was probably a clerk of the church. He knew the lives of the poor so well that it is possible he was the son of a peasant living on a manor, and became free on declaring his intention to enter the service of the church. His *Vision* comes to him one May morning when, as he says—in the alliterative verse of *Beowulf* but in words much more like modern English:—

I was wery forwandred and went me to reste*
Under a brode banke bi a bornes† side,

*weary with wandering.
†brook's.

And as I lay and lened and loked in the wateres,
I slombred in a slepyng; it sweyned so merye.*

In his dream he sees "a faire felde full of folke." There are plowmen, hermits, men who buy and sell, minstrels, jugglers, beggars, pilgrims, lords and ladies, a king, a jester, and many others. They are all absorbed in their own affairs, but Repentance preaches to them so earnestly about their sins that finally they all vow to make a pilgrimage to the shrine of Truth. No one can tell them where to find the shrine. At last they ask Piers the Plowman to go with them and show them the way. "If I had plowed and sowed my half-acre, I would go with you," he replied. The pilgrims agree to help him, and he sets them all to work. While they are working, God sends a pardon for them; but a priest who sees it declares that it is no pardon, for it says only that if men do well, they shall be saved.

This ends the vision, but Piers dreams again. "Do well, do better, do best," is the keynote of this dream. One does well who is moral and upright; he does better who is filled with love and kindness; he does best who follows most closely the life of the Christ. Finally, Piers is seen in a halo of light, for this leader who works and loves and strives to save others represents the Christ himself.

This work is the last important poem written in the old alliterative metre of *Beowulf.* It is an allegory, and there are in it such characters as Lady Meed (bribery), Holy Church, Conscience, Sir

*sounded.

Work-well-with-thine-hand, Sir Goodfaith Gowell, Guile, and Reason. Reason's two horses are Advise-thee-before and Suffer-till-I-see-my-time. The liking for allegories came from the French, but the puzzling over hard questions of life and destiny was one of the characteristics of the early Teutons. Langland saw the trouble and wrong around him; he saw the hard lives of the poor and the laws, that oppressed them; he saw just where the church failed to teach and to comfort them; yet this fourteenth-century Puritan never thought of revolt. Some few changes in the laws, more earnestness and sincerity in the church, and above all, an effort on the part of each to "do best,"—and the eager reformer believed that happiness would smile upon the world of England. In 1361, only one year before this poem was written, the Black Death had for the second time swept over the land. For the second time a great wave of hopeless sorrow and helplessness had overwhelmed the hearts of the people. Langland had put into words what was in every one's thoughts. It is no wonder that his poem was read by thousands; that men saw more clearly than ever the evils of the times; that they began to look about them for strength to bear their lives, for help to make them better.

27. John Wyclif, 1324–1384

The strength and help were already on the way, for while Langland was planning some additions to his poem, a learned clergyman named John Wyclif was translating the Bible into the language of the people. Wyclif was a very interesting man. Until he was about forty, he was a quiet student and preacher. Suddenly

John Wyclif

he appeared in public as the opponent of the pope himself. The pope claimed that England had not paid him his proper tax for many years. "We need the money," declared Wyclif, "and surely a people has a right to self-preservation." The king and the clergy supported the bold patriot, and they were not at all annoyed while he preached against the sins of the monks; but when he was not satisfied with calling for the purification of the church, and for better lives on the part of the clergy and the monks, but began to preach and write against transubstantiation and other doctrines, they were indignant. The authorities in England tried to arrest him, and the pope commanded that he be brought to Rome; but still he sent his tracts over the length and breadth of the country. He wrote no more in Latin, but in simple, straightforward English that the plain people could understand. Such is the English of his translation of the Scriptures. The following is a specimen of its language:—

> *Blessid be pore men in spirit: for the kyngdom of hevenes is herum. Blessid ben mylde men: for thei schulen weelde the erthe. Blessid ben thei that mournen: for thei schal be coumfortid. Blessid be thei that hungren and thirsten after rigtwisnesse: for thei schal be fulfillid. Blessid ben merciful men: for thei schal gete mercy. Blessid ben thei that ben of clene herte: for thei schulen se god: Blessid ben pesible men: for thei schulen be clepid goddis children. Blessid ben thei that suffren persecucioun for rightwisnesse: for the kyngdom of heavens is hern.*

Many churchmen honestly believed that it was wrong to give the Bible to those who were not scholars, lest they should not understand it aright; and even more were either shocked or angry at Wyclif's daring to criticise the teachings of the church and the lives of the clergy. Persecution arose against the preacher and his followers. He was protected by powerful friends; but, forty years after his death, his grave was opened, his bones burned, and the ashes tossed scornfully into the river Swift. It was easier, however, for his opponents to fling away his ashes than to destroy his influence upon the people and upon the language. His Bible was in manuscript, of course, because printing had not yet been invented; but it was read and reread by thousands, and the plain, strong words used by himself and his assistants became a part of the every-day language. Moreover, this translation showed that an English sentence need not be loose and rambling, but might be as clear and definite as a Latin sentence; that English as well as Latin could express close reasoning and keen argument.

28. Geoffrey Chaucer, 1340?–1400

While Wyclif was preaching at Oxford and Langland had not yet begun to work on his *Vision,* a young page was growing up in the house of the Duke of Clarence who was destined to become the prince of story-tellers in verse. This young Geoffrey Chaucer was the son of a wine merchant of London. He lived like other courtiers; he went to France to help fight his king's battles, was taken prisoner, was ransomed and set free. He wrote some love verses in the French fashion and translated some French poems, but he would have been somewhat amazed if any one had told him that he would be known five hundred years later as the "Father of English Poetry."

By 1372, the young courtier had become a man "of some respect," and the king sent him on diplomatic missions to various countries, twice at least to Italy. The literature of Italy was far in advance of that of England, and now the works of Dante, Petrarch, and Boccaccio were open to the poet diplomat. Finally, Chaucer was again in England; and when he wrote, he wrote like an Englishman, but like an Englishman who was familiar with the best that France and Italy had to give.

29. The Canterbury Tales

A collection of stories written by Boccaccio was probably what suggested to Chaucer the writing of a similar collection. Boccaccio's stories are told by a company of friends who have fled from the plague-stricken city of Florence to a villa in the country. Chaucer made a plan that allowed even more variety, for his stories are told by a company who were going on a pilgrimage to the shrine of Thomas à Becket at Canterbury. Boccaccio's people were of nearly the same rank; but on a pilgrimage all sorts of folk were sure to meet, and therefore Chaucer was perfectly free to introduce any kind of person that he chose.

The Prioress
From the Ellesmere MS., which is the best as well as the oldest of the Chaucer MSS.

Making a pilgrimage was a common thing in those days, and people went for various reasons: some to pray and make offerings to the saint that they believed had helped them in sickness or trouble, some to petition for a favor, some for the pleasure of making a journey, and some simply because others were going. Travelling alone was not agreeable and not always safe, therefore these pilgrims often set out in companies, and a merry time they made of it. Some even took minstrels and bagpipes to amuse them on the road.

The *Canterbury Tales* is Chaucer's best work. It begins on a bright spring morning, when he had gone to the Tabard Inn in Southwark for the first stage in his pilgrimage to Canterbury. Just at night a party of twenty-nine rode up to the door of the inn, and the solitary traveller was delighted to find that they, too, had set out on the same errand. There was nothing shy or unsocial about this pilgrim, and before bedtime came, he had made friends with them all, and had agreed to join their party. A very cheerful party it was, and these good-natured travellers were pleased with the rooms, the stables, the supper, the wine, and especially with the landlord, Harry Bailey, whom the poet calls "a merry man." After supper the host tells them that he never before saw so cheerful a company together at his inn. Then he talks about their journey. He says he knows well that they are not planning to make a gloomy time of it.

For trewely confort ne myrthe is noon
To ride by the weye doumb as a stoon,

he declares; and he proposes that each one of them shall tell two stories going and two more returning, and that when they have come back, a supper shall be given to the one who has told the best story. This pleases the pilgrims, and they are even more pleased when the cheery landlord offers to go with them, to be their guide and to judge the merit of the tales.

The Wife of Bath
From the Harleian MS.

Then come the stories themselves. There are only twenty-five of them, and three of those are incomplete, for Chaucer never carried out his full plan. They are of all kinds. There are stories of knights and monks; of giants, fairies, miracles; of the crafty fox who ran away with Chanticleer in his bag, but was persuaded by the no less crafty rooster to drop the bag and make a speech of defiance to his pursuers. There are stories of magic swords that would cut through any kind of armor, and there is a tale of "faire Emelye," the beloved of two young knights, one of whom was in prison and could gaze upon her only from afar, while the other was forbidden on pain of death to enter the city wherein she dwelt.

The Squire
From the Ellesmere MS.

After the fashion of his day, Chaucer took the plots of his tales from wherever he might find them, but it is his way of telling the stories that is so fascinating. We cannot help fancying that he is talking directly to us, for he drops in so many little confidential "asides." "I have told you about the company of pilgrims," he says, "and now it is time to tell you what we did that night, and after that I will talk about our journey." At the end of a subject he is fond of saying, "That is all. There is no more to say." He is equally confidential when he describes his various characters, as he does in the *Prologue* before he begins his story-telling. It was no easy task to describe each one of a large company so accurately that we can almost see them, and so interestingly that we are in no haste to come to the stories; but Chaucer was successful. He describes the knight, who had just returned from a journey, and was so eager to make his grateful pilgrimage that he had set out with his short cassock still stained from his coat of mail; the dainty young prioress, who had such perfect table-manners that she never dipped her fingers deep in the gravy—an important matter to table-mates before forks were in use—or let a drop fall on her breast; the sailor, whose beard had been shaken by many a tempest; the physician, who had not his equal in the whole world; the woman of Bathe, with her "scarlet red" stockings, her soft new shoes, and her hat as broad as a buckler; and the gay young squire, whose gown "with sleves longe and wyde" was so richly embroidered that it looked like a meadow "al ful of fresshe floures whyte and reede." Chaucer gives us a picture of the merry company, but more than that, he shows us what kind of people they were. He tells us their faults in satire as keen as it is good-natured. The monk likes hunting better than obeying strict convent rules, and Chaucer says of him slyly that when he rode, men could hear the little bells on his bridle jingle quite as loud as the bell of the chapel. The learned physician was somewhat of a miser, and Chaucer whispers cannily,—

The Parson
From the Ellesmere MS.

For gold in phisik is a cordial,
Therefore he lovede gold in special.

The two characters for whom the poet has most sympathy are the thin and threadbare Oxford student, who would rather have books than gorgeous robes or musical instruments; and the earnest, faithful parish priest, who "Christes Gospel trewely wolde preche," and who never hired some one to take charge of his parish while he slipped away to live an easy life in a brotherhood.

Chaucer
From the Ellesmere MS.

This keen-eyed poet, with his warm sympathy, could hardly have helped loving nature, and he can picture a bright, dewy May morning so clearly that we can almost see "the silver dropes hangyng on the leves." He liked May and sunshine and birds and lilies and roses. He liked the daisy, and when he caught sight of the first one, he wrote:—

And down on knees anon right I me set,
And as I could this freshe flower I grette,
Kneeling always till it inclosed was
Upon the small and soft and sweete grass.

30. Death of Chaucer, 1400

Chaucer's life was not all sunshine, but he was always sunny and bright. He writes as if he knew so many pleasant things that he could not help taking up his pen to tell us of them. His death occurred in 1400, and that date is counted as the end of the old literature and the beginning of the new. Chaucer well deserves the title, "Father of English Poetry;" but when we read his poems, we forget his titles and his learning, and think of him only as the best of story-tellers.

We owe gratitude to Chaucer not only because he left us some delightful poems, but because he broke away from the old Anglo-Saxon metre and because he wrote in English. The *Canterbury Tales* begins:—

Whan that Aprille with hise shoures soote
The droghte of March hath perced to the roote,
And bathed every veyne in swich licour
Of which vertu engendred is the flour;
Whan Zephirus eek with his swete breeth
Inspired hath in every holt and heeth
The tendre croppes, and the yonge sonne
Hath in the Ram his halfe cours y-ronne,
And smale foweles maken melodye
That slepen al the nyght with open eye,
So priketh hem Nature in hir corages,
Thanne longen folk to goon on pilgrimages.

This is written in the 5-beat line, which gives more freedom than the 4-beat line of *Beowulf.* Alliteration is not employed to mark the accented syllables, but only to ornament the verse. Chaucer used many French words and often retained the French endings; but he used them so easily and so appropriately that they seemed to become a part of the language. Another service and an even greater one he rendered to the English tongue. People in different parts of England spoke in English, to be sure, but in widely differing dialects. Chaucer wrote in what was known as the Midland dialect, and his work was so good and so well liked that it had a powerful influence to *fix* the language; that is, to make his writings and his vocabulary models for the authors who succeeded him.

SUMMARY

Century XIV

CHAUCER'S CENTURY

"Sir John Mandeville."	*John Wyclif.*
William Langland.	*Geoffrey Chaucer.*

The weakening of the feudal system brought about the dawning of English thought. The causes of this weakening were:—

1. The lords, wishing to become crusaders, often accepted money instead of work.

2. In the Hundred Years' War the peasants discovered their power.

3. The Black Death lessened the number of workers, and enabled men to find farm-work where they chose and to demand what wages they liked.

4. The introduction of weaving made it possible for peasants to support themselves without working on the land.

Harsh laws aroused discontent with the government; the negligence of the clergy aroused discontent with the church. This discontent showed itself finally in the Peasants' Revolt of 1381.

Four writers are typical of the four chief classes of people:—

1. "Sir John Mandeville," who accepted things as they were.

2. William Langland, who in *Piers Plowman* showed his wish to bring about reforms.

3. John Wyclif, who wished to overthrow rather than to reform. He and his assistants translated the Bible into English. Its clear, strong phrasing became a part of the every-day speech, and did much to fix the language by showing its powers.

4. Geoffrey Chaucer, who good-naturedly ridiculed the faults of his times. Chaucer's great work is the *Canterbury Tales,* which was probably suggested by Boccaccio's *Decameron.* Chaucer abandoned the early Anglo-Saxon metre and wrote in rhymed heroic verse. His work was so excellent that it fixed the Midland dialect as the literary language of England.

CHAPTER IV

Century XV

THE PEOPLE'S CENTURY

31. The Imitators of Chaucer

Chaucer's poetry was so much better than any that had preceded it that the poets who lived in the early part of the fifteenth century made many attempts at imitation. They were not very successful. Chaucer wrote, for instance:—

The bisy larke, messager of day,
Salueth in hir song the morwe gray;
And fiery Phœbus riseth up so brighte
That al the orient laugheth of the lighte,
And with his stremes dryeth in the greves
The silver droppes hangyng on the leves.

One of Chaucer's imitators wrote:—

Ther he lay to the larke song
With notes newe, hegh up in the ayr.
The glade morowe, rody and right fayr,
Phebus also casting up his bemes,
The heghe hylles gilt with his stremes,
The syluer dewe upon the herbes rounde,
Ther Tydeus lay upon the grounde.

The best of these imitators was a king, James I of Scotland, who was captured by the English when he was a boy of eleven, and was kept a prisoner in England for nineteen years. During his captivity he fell in love with the king's niece, and to her he wrote the tender verses of *The Kings Quair.** He describes his loneliness as follows:—

Bewailing in my chamber thus allone,
Despeired of all joye and remedye,
For-tiret of my thought and wo-begone,
And to the wyndow gan I walk in hye,
To see the warld and folk that went forbye,
As for the tyme though I of mirthis fude
Mycht have no more, to luke it did me gude.

He catches sight of the princess walking in the garden,

The fairest or the freschest younge floure
That ever I sawe, methought, before that houre.

He gazes at her; then,

And in my hede I drew rycht hastily,
And eft sones I lent it out ageyne,
And saw hir walk that verray womanly,
With no wight mo, bot only women tueyne,
Than gan I studye in myself and seyne,
Ah! suete, are ye a warldly creature,
Or hevinly thing in likeness of nature?

So it is that the captive king wrote his love, with a frank, admiring imitation of Chaucer, but so simply and so naturally that he is more than a name on a printed page; and it is really a pleasure to know that the course of his love ran smooth, and that he was finally allowed to return to his kingdom with the wife whom he had chosen. This seven-line stanza was not original with him by any means, but because a king had used it, it became known as "rhyme royal."

*Book.

32. Sir Thomas Malory

This century began and ended with royalty, for in its early years King James wrote its best poetry, and toward its end Sir Thomas Malory—of whom little is known—wrote its best prose, the *Morte d'Arthur,* the old stories of King Arthur grown more full, more simple, and more beautiful than ever. "Thys noble and Joyous book," Caxton called it when he put it into print. At the close of Arthur's life he bids, according to Malory, "Syr Bedwere" to throw the sword Excalibur into the lake. Syr Bedwere obeys. Then says the author:—

> *He threwe the swerde as farre in to the water as he myght, & there cam an arme and an hande aboue the water and mette it, & caught it and so shake it thryse and braundysshed, and then vanysshed awaye the hande wyth the swerde in the water. . . . Than syr Bedwere toke the Kyng vpon his backe and so wente wyth hym to that water syde, & whan they were at the water syde euen fast by the banke houed a lytyl barge wyth many fayr ladyes in hit, & emange hem al was a quene, and al they had blacke hoodes, and al they wepte and shryked whan they sawe Kyng Arthur. "Now put me in to the barge," sayd the kyng, and so he dyd softelye.*

33. The Age of Arrest

The fifteenth century is sometimes called the "age of arrest" because it is not marked by any great literary work like that of Chaucer. There are good reasons why no such work should have been produced. First, the greater part of the century was full of warfare. The Hundred Years' War did not close until 1453, and there was hardly time to sharpen the battle-axes and put new strings to the bows before another war far more fierce than the first broke out, and did not come to an end until 1485. This was the War of the Roses, which was fought between the supporters of rival claimants to the English throne. Sometimes one side had the advantage and sometimes the other; and whichever party was in power put to death the prominent men of the opposing party. Second, there was not only no rest or quiet in the kingdom for great literary productions, but at least half of the nobles, the people of leisure, were killed in the terrible slaughter. Third, the church, which paid no taxes, owned so much of the land that the whole burden of taxation had to be borne by only a part of the people.

Poor in literature as this century of fighting was, there were two reasons why it was good for the "common folk." In the first place, knighthood was becoming of less and less value, partly because of the increasing use of gunpowder, but even more because the English had at last learned that a man encased in armor so heavy that he could hardly mount his horse without help was not so valuable a soldier as a man on foot with a bow or a battle-axe. In the second place, war could not be carried on without money, and money must come by vote of the House of Commons, which represented, however poorly and unfairly, the masses of the people. If the king and his counsellors wished to obtain money, they were obliged to pay more attention than ever before to the desires of the people.

34. Ballads

It was from the common folk that the most interesting literature of the century came, the ballads. An age of turmoil and unrest was, as has been said, no time for elaborate literary work, but the flashes of excitement, the news of a battle lost or a battle won, the story of some brave fighter returning from the war,—all these inspired short, strong ballads. Of course there had been many ballads before then, especially those of Robin Hood, but the fifteenth was the special century of the ballad, the time when the strong undercurrent of this poetry of the people came most conspicuously to the surface. No one knows who composed these ballads, but the wording shows that many of them came from Scotland, and were inspired by the wild forays that were continually taking place between the Scotch and the English who dwelt near the border line of the two countries. The most famous of all the border ballads is that of *Chevy Chase,* which begins:—

The Persé out of Northomberlonde,
and a vowe to God mayd he
That he wold hunte in the mountayns
off Chyviat within days thre
In the magger of doughté Dogles,
and all that ever with him be.

A ballad is not merely a story told in rhyme; it has several distinctive marks:—

1. It plunges into the tale without a moment's delay. There is not a shade of Chaucer's leisurely description. *Chevy Chase* does not even stop to explain who the two heroes, Percy and Douglas, may be.

2. It does something and says something. Every word counts in the story. We know from their deeds and words what the ballad people think, but "He longed strange countries for to see," or he "fell in love with Barbara Allen," is about as near a description of their thoughts as the ballad ever gives.

3. It is very definite. If people are bad, they are very bad; and if they are good, they are very good. "Alison Gross" is "the ugliest witch in the north countrie." The bonny maiden is the fairest flower of all England. Colors are bright and strong:—

O bonnie, bonnie was her mouth
And cherry were her cheeks;
And clear, clear was her yellow hair,
Whereon the red blude dreeps.

Comparisons are of the simplest; the maiden has a milk-white hand, her cheeks are red as a rose, and her eyes are blue as the sky.

4. The metre is almost always 4, 3, 4, 3; that is, the first and third lines contain four accented syllables, the second and fourth contain three. The second and fourth lines rhyme, sometimes the first and third also. The final syllable often receives an accent even when there would be none in prose.

5. Most of the ballads show the touch of the Celt. There are weird stories of the return of ghostly lovers; there are fascinating little gleams of fairyland, of beauty and of happiness, but often with a shade of sadness or loneliness, the unmistakable mark of the Celtic nature,

that could turn from smiles to tears in the flashing of a moment.

O sweetly sang the blackbird
That sat upon the tree;
But sairer grat Lamkin
When he was condemned to die.

We do not know who composed the older ballads. Indeed, each one seems to have grown up almost like a little epic. The gleeman wandered from village to village, singing to groups of listeners, whose rapt eagerness was his inspiration. He sang his song again and again, each time adding to it or taking from it, according to whether his invention or his memory was the better. Moreover, there was no private ownership in ballad land. Any ballad was welcome to a line or a stanza from any other. Little by little the song grew, until finally its form was fixed by the coming of the printing-press.

35. Mystery Plays

The fifteenth century was the time when the mystery or miracle play was at its best. This kind of play originated in the attempts of the clergy to teach the people, and was common on the Continent long before the coming of the Normans to England. There were few books and few who could read. Therefore the clergy conceived the idea of acting in the church short plays presenting scenes from the Bible. To give room for more people to hear, the play was soon performed on a scaffold in the churchyard. Gradually the acting was given up by the priests and fell into the hands of the parish clerks; then into those of the guilds, or

A Mystery Play at Coventry
From an old print

companies of tradesmen, for long before the fifteenth century the men of each craft had formed themselves into a guild. Slowly the plays became cycles, each cycle following the Bible story from *Genesis* to the end of the *Gospels,* sometimes to the resurrection. Each guild had in charge the presentation of one story or more. The acting was no longer in the churchyards, but at different convenient stations in the town. The stage was a great two-story or three-story wagon called a pageant. An important part of the scenery was "hell mouth," represented by a pair of widely gaping jaws full of smoke and flames, into which unrepentant sinners were summarily hurled and from which Satan issued to take his part in the drama. The plays were always acted in the biblical order. When one play was ended, the pageant moved on, leaving the place free for the next play, so that a person remaining at any one station could see the whole cycle.

To modern ideas there are some things in these plays that seem irreverent; for instance, the representation of God the Father on the stage. In one of the plays of the creation he is made to say familiarly:—

Adam and Eve, this is the place
That I have graunte you of my grace
To have your wonnyng[*] in;
Erbes, spyce, frute on tree,
Beastes, fewles,[†] all that ye see,
Shall bowe to you, more and myn.[‡]
This place hight paradyce,
Here shall your joys begynne,
And yf that ye be wyse,
From thys tharr[§] ye never twynne.[¶]

Again, when the angels appear to the shepherds to sing of peace on earth, one of the shepherds says, "I can sing it as well as he, if you will help;" and he tries to imitate the heavenly song.

The makers of the mystery plays knew as well as the writers of homilies that if the attention of the people was to be retained, there must be amusement as well as instruction, and therefore they did not hesitate to introduce comical scenes. The antics of Satan were made to provide a vast amount of amusement; and even more respectable scriptural characters were impressed

[*] dwelling.
[†] fowls.
[‡] great and small.
[§] need.
[¶] depart.

A Scene from Everyman

This is a photograph of the reproduction of the play given by the Ben Greet Company in 1903. It represents Everyman on his pilgrimage, followed by Beauty, Strength, Discretion, and Five Wits. Good Deeds and Knowledge are in the background.

into the service of making fun to gratify the demands of the spectators. After Noah has built his ark, he requests his wife to come into it, but she objects. Noah ought not to have worked on that ark one hundred years before telling her what he was doing, she says; at any rate, she must go home to pack her belongings; she does not believe it will rain long, and if it does, she will not be saved without her cousins and her friends. She is finally persuaded to enter the ark. At last the door is closed, and Noah might well offer up a prayer of gratitude or sing a hymn of praise for the safety of himself and his family; but, instead, he proceeds to give most prosaic directions to his sons to take good care of the cattle, and to his daughters-in-law to be sure to feed the fowls.

With all their crudeness, these plays are often gentle and sympathetic. Joseph watches over Mary most lovingly. "My daughter," he tenderly calls her. At the crucifixion John's words of comfort to the sorrowing mother are very touching. "My heart is gladder than gladness itself," says Mary Magdalene at the resurrection. Such were the plays that pleased the people; for they were simple, childlike, warm-hearted, ready to be amused, satisfied with the rudest jesting, and accustomed to treat sacred things with familiarity, but with no conscious irreverence. Going to a mystery play, like going on a pilgrimage, was a religious duty; but the mediæval mind saw no reason why duty and amusement should not be agreeably united.

36. Miracle Plays and Moralities

In England these plays were more frequently called miracle plays, though this name was applied elsewhere only to dramas based not upon biblical scenes, but upon legends of saints or martyrs. Often one kind of play blended with another; for instance, *Mary Magdalene* introduces scenes from the life of Christ, like a mystery; it follows out the legends of the heroine, like a miracle; it also leads to a third variety of play, the morality, in that it introduces abstract characters, such as Sloth, Gluttony, Wrath, and Envy, for in the morality the characters were the virtues and vices. What amusement was in them was made by the Devil and a new character, the Vice, who played tricks on Satan in much the fashion of the clown or fool of later days. At first sight, the morality seems dreary reading, especially when compared with the liveliness and rapid action of the mystery. There is no dreariness, however, to one who reads between the lines and is mindful of how intensely real the story was to those who listened to it in the earlier ages. One of the best of the moralities is *Everyman*, which was taken from the Dutch. In this play, Death, God's messenger, is sent to bid the merry young Everyman to make the long journey. Everyman pleads for a respite, he offers a bribe, he begs that some one may go with him. "Ye, yf ony be so hardy," Death replies. Then Everyman in sore distress appeals to Fellowship to keep him company.

For no man that is lyvynge to daye
I will not go that lothe journaye,

replies Fellowship. Kindred refuse the petition. Good Deeds would go with him, but Everyman's sins have so weighed her down that she is too weak to stand. At last Knowledge leads him to confession. He does penance and starts on his lonely pilgrimage. One by one, Beauty, Strength, Honor, Discretion, and his Five Wits forsake him. Good Deeds alone stands as his friend, and says sturdily with renewed strength, "Fere not, I wyll speke for the." Everyman descends fearfully but trustfully into the grave. Knowledge cries, "Nowe hath he suffred that we all shall endure;" and the play ends with a solemn prayer,—

And he that hath his accounte hole and sounde,
Hye in heven he shall be crounde,
Unto whiche place God brynge us all thyder
That we may lyve body and soule togyder.

This is not entertaining, but it is far from being dull. With the simple stage setting of four centuries ago, the realistic grave, and the ghastly, ashen gray figure of Death, it must have thrilled and solemnized the hushed listeners as neither play nor sermon could do in later generations.

37. Introduction of Printing into England, 1476

In the last quarter of the century there were two notable events that were destined to do more for the masses of the people than anything that had preceded. The first of these events was the introduction of printing into England. Through these centuries of the beginning of literature, plays, homilies, poems, and lengthy books of prose had all been copied by the pen on parchment or vellum. Cheap picture books were printed on a coarse, heavy paper from wooden blocks, and some of these "block books" contained text also; but to print with movable types was a German invention of the middle of the century. Fortunately for English book lovers, an Englishman named William Caxton, who was then living in Germany, was interested in the wonderful new art, and paid well for lessons in typesetting and all the other details of the trade. He was not only a keen business man, who thought money could be made by printing, but he was also a man of literary taste and ability, and the first English book that he printed was a translation printed of his own, called *The Recuyell of the Historyes of Troye.* He wrote triumphantly to a friend that his book was "not written with pen and ink as other books be." This was in 1474. Two years later, he and his press came to England, and there he printed volume after volume. The *Canterbury Tales,* Malory's *Morte d' Arthur,* Æsop's *Fables,* and nearly one hundred other volumes came from his press.

In the simple, primitive fashion of the fifteenth century, which ascribed to Satanic agency whatever was new or mysterious, there were many people in England who looked upon Caxton's magical output of books as unquestionably the work of the devil; but the press was still kept busy, and the price of books became rapidly less. Before Caxton began to print, they were enormously expensive. A library of twenty or thirty volumes was looked upon as a rare collection; and it was no wonder, for the usual rate for copying was a sum equal to-day to nearly fifty cents a page. Caxton's most expensive book could be purchased for about $30. How

Caxton Presented to Edward IV
Earl Rivers giving the book to the king, while Caxton kneels beside him

amazed he would have been if he could have looked forward to 1885 and seen one of his earlier and less perfect volumes sold for nearly $10,000!

38. Signs of Progress

England was not so wildly enthusiastic over literature that every tradesman or even every noble who could command a few pounds hastened to purchase a book; but the mere fact that there were books for sale at a price lower than had been dreamed of before was a hope and an inspiration. It was easier to see books, to borrow them, to know about them; and little by little the knowledge filtered down through the various classes of people, until that one printing-press at Westminster had given new thoughts and new hopes to thousands.

Earliest Known Representation of a Printing-Press

New thoughts were coming from yet another source. Columbus had discovered what was supposed to be a shorter way to India; Vasco da Gama had rounded Africa; hundreds had gazed with wide-open eyes upon the ship of the Cabots as it sailed from the English wharfs, and had followed the "Grand Admiral" as he walked about the streets on his return, with all the glory of his discoveries about him. No one yet suspected that he had landed on the shores of a continent, but it was enough to hear the sailors' stories of strange plants and animals and people. Who could say what other marvels might be discovered?

Then came the end of the century. The homes of the masses of the people had made small addition of comfort; the noble treated the peasants who still lived on his land with perhaps small increase of respect; but for all that, the fifteenth century was marked by the increasing importance of the common people. They had shown their prowess in fighting; they held more firmly the money-bags of the kingdom; the ballads were theirs; the mystery plays were theirs; the new art of printing would benefit them rather than the wealthy nobles; the discovery of America would be to their gain, and it was already a stimulus to their intellect and their imagination. The sixteenth century was at hand, and men had a right to expect from it such a display of universal intellectual ability as England had never known.

SUMMARY

Century XV

THE PEOPLE'S CENTURY

James I. of Scotland.
Sir Thomas Malory.
Ballads.
Mystery plays.
Moralities.

The poets of the early part of the century tried to imitate Chaucer. Of these imitators, King James I of Scotland was the best. Toward the end of the century, Sir Thomas Malory wrote the best prose, the *Morte d'Arthur.*

Only a small amount of good literature was produced because:—

1. The Hundred Years' War and the Wars of the Roses filled the age with fighting.

2. A large number of the nobles were slain.

3. The people were heavily taxed.

The common people gained in power because, first, the use of gunpowder made knighthood of decreasing value; and, secondly, the money needed for this warfare could be obtained only by vote of the House of Commons.

From the common folk came the most interesting literature of the time, the ballads. They have no introduction; they are definite; their metre is usually 4, 3, 4, 3; they generally show a Celtic touch. A ballad is often the work of many hands.

The miracle plays were at their best. They were acted first by the clergy; then by members of guilds. They were followed by the moralities, of which *Everyman* is the best example.

Toward the end of the century, there were two notable events which aroused and stimulated the people. They were:—

1. The introduction of printing into England by William Caxton, followed by a decrease in the price of books and a much more general circulation of them.

2. Foreign discoveries by Columbus, Da Gama, the Cabots, and others.

The distinguishing mark of the age was the increasing importance of the common people.

CHAPTER V

Century XVI

SHAKESPEARE'S CENTURY

39. Revival of Learning in Europe

For three hundred years after the Norman Conquest, English writers were inclined to follow French models. Then came Chaucer, who, thoroughly English as he was, retold Italian stories, and was for some years greatly influenced by Italian literature. Italy was looked upon as the land of knowledge and light, and it was the custom for Englishmen who wished for better educational advantages than Oxford or Cambridge could afford, to go to that country to study in some one of the great universities.

Italian scholars were deeply interested in the writings of the Greeks and Romans. For many years they had been collecting ancient manuscripts, and in 1453 an event occurred which brought more of them to Italy than ever before. This event was the capture of Constantinople by the Turks. Constantinople had been the home of many Greek scholars, who now fled to Italy and brought the priceless manuscripts with them. Then there was study of the classics indeed. More and more students went from other countries to Italy. More and more copies of those manuscripts were carried to different parts of Europe. Among the ancient writings was clear, concise prose, so carefully finished that every word seemed to be in its own proper niche; there were beautiful epics and much other poetry; there were essays, histories, biographies, and orations. Printing had come at just the right time to spread this new ancient knowledge over the Continent and England. All western Europe was aroused. People felt a new sense of boldness and freedom. They felt as if in the years gone by they had been slow and stupid. Now they became daring and fearless in their thought. They were eager to learn, to do, to understand. This movement was so marked that a name was given to it, the Renaissance, or new birth, for people felt as if a new life had come to them. The Renaissance did not affect all countries alike. In Italy, the minds of men turned toward sculpture and painting; in Germany, to a bold investigation of religious teachings; in England, toward religion and literature.

A second influence that helped to arouse and inspire was the increased knowledge of the western world. Columbus died in 1506, but now that the way had been pointed out, one explorer after another crossed the western seas. South America was rounded and found to be a vast continent. North America was a group of islands, people thought; and men set out boldly to find a channel through them, to discover a "Northwest Passage." Finally, Magellan's ship went around the world; and, behold, the world was much larger than had been supposed. Before the wonder of this had faded from the minds of men, there came another amazing discovery, for Copernicus declared, "The earth is not the centre of the universe; it is only a satellite of the sun." This was not accepted at once as truth, but the mere suggestion of it broadened men's thoughts. There was good reason why the world should begin to awake.

40. Henry VIII and the Men about Him

The influence of the Renaissance was not strongly felt in England before the time of Henry VIII, who came to the throne in 1509. Around him centred the literature of the early part of the century. Indeed, he himself attempted verse more than once. *Pastime with Good Company* is ascribed to him.

Pastime with good company
I love, and shall until I die,
Gruche so will, but none deny,*
So God be pleased, so live will I.
For my pastance,†
Hunt, sing, and dance,
My heart is sett;
All goodly sport
To my comfort,
Who shall me let?‡

Henry VIII was no great poet, but he liked literature, and he liked to appear as its patron. His early tutor was one of the most prominent literary men of the day, the poet John Skelton. Skelton says:—

The honor of Englond I lernyd to spelle
In dygnite roialle that doth excelle.

*grudge whoso will.
†pastime.
‡hinder.

Skelton was a fine classical scholar, and was perfectly able to write smooth, easily flowing verses, but he deliberately chose a rough, tumbling, headlong metre. He hated Cardinal Wolsey, and of him he wrote:—

So he dothe vndermynde,
And suche sleyghtes dothe fynde,
That the Kynges mynde
By hym is subuerted,
And so streatly coarted
In credensynge his tales,
That all is but nutshales
That any other sayth:
He hath in him suche fayth.

Little wonder is it that Wolsey cordially returned the poet's dislike.

This harsh, scrambling metre Skelton knew how to adapt to more poetical thoughts. His best known poem is on "Phyllyp Sparowe," the pet bird of a young school-girl. It is of the mistress that he writes:—

Soft and make no din,
For now I will begin
To have in remembrance
Her goodly dalliance
And her goodly pastaunce
So sad and so demure,
Behaving her so sure,
With words of pleasure
She would make to the lure
And any man convert
To give her his whole heart.

Skelton was a witty man, and many of the "good stories" of his day were ascribed to him. It is easy to see how Henry VIII would be influenced even as a child by the careless boldness, poetical ability, and rollicking good nature of this man who was as brilliant as he was learned. No one knows how much of Henry's interest in poetry was due to the guidance of his tutor. Elizabeth closely resembled her father, and must have been influenced by his love of literature. It may be that we owe some generous part of the literary glory of the Elizabethan age to the half-forgotten John Skelton with his "jagged" rhymes.

41. Sir Thomas More, 1480–1535

Another friend of Henry VIII was Sir Thomas More. Sir Thomas was so learned that when he was hardly more than a boy he could step upon the stage in the midst of a Latin play and make up a part for himself; and he was so witty that his improvised jests would set the audience into peals of laughter. The year that Henry came to the throne More wrote the lives of Edward V and of Richard III, and this was the first English historical work that was well arranged and written in a dignified style. The little book by which he is best known was written in Latin and had

Sir Thomas More, 1480–1535
From Holbein's Court of Henry VIII

a Greek title, *Utopia,* or "nowhere." This describes a country as More thought a country ought to be. In that marvellous land everything was valued according to its real worth. Gold was less useful than iron; therefore the chains of criminals were made of gold. Kings ruled, not for their own glory, but for the sake of their people. No one was idle, and no one was overworked. War was undertaken only for self-defence, or to aid other nations against invasion. This book is interesting not only because it pictures what so brilliant a man as Sir Thomas More thought a country should be, but because it proves that people were thinking with a boldness and freedom that would not be suppressed. In many respects More proved to be a true prophet, for some of the laws that he suggested became long ago a part of the British constitution.

42. Religious Questioning

In Utopia every man was allowed to follow whatever religion he thought right. This question of religion, whether to obey the church implicitly or to decide matters of faith for one's self, was dividing Germany into two parties, and was arousing a vast amount of thought and discussion in England. Many held firmly to the old faith; but many others were inclined to investigate the teachings of the church, and to wish to compare them with the words of the Bible. English had changed greatly since Wyclif's day, and an English scholar named William Tyndale was determined that the Bible should be given to the people in the language of their own time. "If God spare my life," he said to a clergyman who opposed him, "ere many years I will cause a boy that driveth the plough shall know more of the Scripture than thou dost." There was "no room" in England to make his translation, as he said, and therefore Tyndale went to Germany, and in 1525 printed with the utmost secrecy an English version of the *New Testament.* Some English merchants paid for the printing, and the books found their way over the country in spite of the king's opposition. The *Old Testament* was afterward translated under his direction and partly by himself.

Not more than two years after Tyndale's *New Testament* was printed, Henry became bent upon securing a divorce from his wife, but the pope refused. Then Henry declared that he himself was the head of the church in England. Parliament was submissive, the English clergy were submissive, and in 1534 the Church of England separated from the Church of Rome. Whoever believed that the authority of the pope was superior to that of the king was declared a traitor. Prominent men were not suffered to hold their own opinions in quiet; and among those who were dragged forward and compelled to say under oath whether they accepted Henry as the head of their church was Sir Thomas More. He was too honorable and truthful to assent to what he did not believe; and King Henry, who had claimed to feel great admiration and affection for him, straightway gave the order that he should be executed. Tyndale, too, Henry had pursued even after his withdrawal to the Continent. Such was the treatment that this patron of literature bestowed upon two of the three or four best writers of English prose that lived during his reign.

43. Sir Thomas Wyatt, 1503–1542, and Henry Howard, Earl of Surrey, about 1517–1547

At King Henry's court there were two men in whom every one who met them was interested. The elder was Sir Thomas Wyatt. He was a learned man, he spoke several languages, he was a skilful diplomatist and statesman. He was also a man of most charming manners, and was exceedingly handsome. The younger was the Earl of Surrey. These two men were warm friends, and they were both interested in poetry. Both knew well the Greek and Latin and Italian literatures; and they appreciated not only the freedom of thought and fancy brought in by the Renaissance, but also the carefulness with which the Italian poetry as well as the classical was written. Why should not that same carefulness, that same love for not only saying a good thing but saying it in the best way, be followed in English, they questioned. They were especially pleased with the Italian sonnet, a form of verse that needs the greatest care and accuracy of arrangement in its rhymes, the number of lines and of accents, the ending of the octave, the first eight lines, its connection with the sestet, the last six, and the summing up of the thought at the end.* They brought to England, not the glow and brilliancy of the Renaissance, but the realization that literary composition had definite requirements, that the thought was not enough, but that the form in which the thought was presented was also of importance.

*For a sonnet of Sir Philip Sidney's, see page 104. For one of Milton's, see page 157.

Surrey introduced another form of verse to the English, blank verse, or, as the Italians called it, "free verse." It was in this style that he translated two books of the *Æneid,* smoothly and easily, and with a sincere appreciation not only of the classical beauty of form, but of the beauty of thought and description.

These two men could not be long among Henry's courtiers without feeling both his favor and his disfavor. Wyatt was imprisoned on some trivial charge more than once, and Surrey was beheaded on a groundless accusation of treason. For years their writings were passed from one to another in manuscript, for it would have been thought great lack of taste and delicacy to allow one's poems to be printed; and not until ten years after Surrey's death did they come out in print. The book in which they appeared is known as *Tottel's Miscellany,* a collection of short poems which was published in 1557. This book is interesting, but it is rarely pleasant reading. It has not a touch of humor. The poets wrote of the wretchedness and mutability of the world. The love-poems were especially doleful. The lover complains—"complains" is the favorite word—of his lady's absence; he laments "how impossible it is to find quiet" in his love. Yet even on so lugubrious a subject as "The lover complains of the unkindness of his love," Wyatt is beautiful and graceful. He writes:—

My lute, awake! perform the last
Labour that thou and I shall waste;
And end that I have now begun:
And when this song is sung and past,
My lute, be still, for I have done.

44. Masques and Interludes

While Skelton was preparing the way for satire, while Tyndale and Sir Thomas More were writing excellent prose, while Wyatt and Surrey were teaching English poets not only how to write sonnets and blank verse, but also that the form of a poem should be as carefully watched as the outline and coloring of a picture, the drama was not forgotten. Mysteries and moralities still flourished, but these were not sufficiently entertaining for Henry VIII and his merry court. Two kinds of plays came into great favor, the masques and the interludes. Masques were at first only dumb shows, or pantomimes. In one of them a mock castle was seen, from whose windows six ladies in gorgeous raiment looked forth. The king and five knights in even more brilliant attire appeared and besieged the castle. When the ladies could no longer resist, they came down, flung open the gates, and joined their besiegers in a merry dance. At the close of the dance, each maiden led her knight into the castle, which was then drawn swiftly out of sight. There is little to tell about a masque; but with the opportunity to display gracefulness and beauty and magnificence and skill in the use of arms, there must have been enough to see to amuse even the merry young king.

A Masquer

The second kind of entertainment that was enjoyed by king and nobles was the interludes which were acted between the courses of feasts or at festivals. They are a little like real plays because they are in dialogue, and they are a little like moralities because they sometimes introduce the Vice and other abstract characters. Here the resemblance to the morality ends, for they are often full of wild merriment and jest. The one best known is *The Foure P's: a very Mery Enterlude of a Palmer, a Pardoner, a Potecary, and a Pedlar.* Each one tells such big stories of what he has seen and done that finally the pedlar declares that they are all liars, and that he will give the palm to the one who can tell the biggest lie. Probably the audience listened with roars of laughter as one attempt followed another. The dialogue was rough and sometimes coarse, but it was easy and natural, and it was preparing the way for the graceful wit and the flowing speech of the Elizabethan stage. John Heywood was the author of *The Foure P's.* Sir Thomas More had introduced him to the king, and he remained in the royal favor long after More had been put to death, rising from some humble position in which he served his sovereign for eight pence a day to that of special provider of amusements for the court.

45. The First English Comedy, Ralph Roister Doister, probably 1552 or 1553

Henry VIII died in 1547, and during the six years that the boy Edward VI was on the throne, the first English comedy made its appearance. English scholars were still deeply interested in the classics, and the comedies of Plautus had been played at court many years before. This first English comedy was written by an English schoolmaster and clergyman named Nicholas Udall. He was the author of some dignified translations from the Latin, and his play, *Ralph Roister Doister,* is modelled on the plays of Plautus. The hero, Ralph himself, is a conceited simpleton, upon whom Merrygreek, a hanger-on, plays tricks without number. Ralph is bent upon marrying "a widow worth a thousand pound," and here Merrygreek plays his worst prank. A scrivener has written a love-letter for Ralph, part of which reads:—

Yf ye will be my wife,
Ye shall be assured for the time of my life,
I wyll keep you right well: from good raiment and fare
Ye shall not be kept: but in sorrowe and care
Ye shall in no wyse liue: at your owne libertie,
Doe and say what ye lust: ye shall neuer please me
But when ye are merrie: I will bee all sadde
When ye are sorie: I wyll be very gladde
When ye seek your heartes ease: I will be vnkinde
At no time. In me shall ye muche gentlenesse finde.

Merrygreek reads this letter to the widow, and changes the punctuation so as to give it exactly the opposite meaning and arouse the wrath of Dame Custance. It hardly seems possible that instead of such labored jesting as this we shall have in less than fifty years the light, witty merriment of Shakespeare's Portia; but the days of Queen Elizabeth were at hand, and in that marvellous time all things came to pass.

46. The First English Tragedy, Gorboduc, 1562

In 1558, Queen Elizabeth came to the throne. There

was much rejoicing on the part of the nation, and yet not all was happiness and harmony in England. The country was poor; it had few if any friends; Catholics and Protestants quarrelled bitterly; supporters of Elizabeth and supporters of Mary Stuart were sometimes almost at swords' points. It was fitting that the first significant literary work of Elizabeth's reign should owe its origin to a realization of the condition of affairs. This work was a drama, the first English tragedy. Its authors were Thomas Sackville and Thomas Norton, two young men of the Inner Temple. In 1561, the members of the Inner Temple were to have a grand Christmas celebration twelve days long, and these two young men determined to write a play to show what disasters might befall a disunited nation. This play was called at first *Gorboduc*, later *Ferrex and Porrex*. It was modelled upon the work of the Latin author, Seneca, who was much read in England, but the plot was based upon an old British legend of a kingdom's discord.

King Gorboduc divides his kingdom between his two sons, Porrex and Ferrex. Porrex slays his brother. Their mother kills Porrex. The people rise and kill both Gorboduc and the queen, and the story ends with a long speech on the dangers of such a situation. So many horrors are piled upon horrors that the play seems like a burlesque; but it was no burlesque in the days of its first appearance. Learned councillors and other great folk of the kingdom listened with the utmost seriousness, and the queen sent a command that it should be repeated at court.

Gorboduc is in several ways quite different from

Ralph Roister Doister. In the first place, it is connected with the masques in that it has pantomime, for there is a "dumb show" before each act, foreshadowing what is to come; for instance, before division of the kingdom between the two sons, the fable is shown of the bundle of sticks which could not be broken until they were separated. Before the murder of Ferrex, a band of mourners clad in black walk solemnly across the stage three times. At the end of each act a "Chorus," that is, a single actor in a long black robe, appears and moralizes on the events of the act. Again, *Ralph Roister Doister* was written in rhyming couplets, while the new tragedy was written in the blank verse which Surrey had introduced from Italy. It was not very agreeable blank verse, however, as it came from the pens of the two young Templars, for there is a pause at the end of almost every line, and the monotony is somewhat tiresome; for instance:—

Within one land one single rule is best;
Divided reigns do make divided hearts:
But peace preserves the country and the prince.

47. Increasing Strength of England

One reason for the popularity of *Gorboduc* was that Englishmen were beginning to realize more strongly than ever before that the country was theirs. The queen loved her land and her subjects, and the people of England were quick to feel the new sense of harmony between the ruler and the ruled. England became rapidly stronger. Her sea-captains sailed fearlessly into the Arctic and Pacific Oceans. More than this, they sailed straight into Spanish harbors and burned the merchant vessels lying at anchor; and they lay in wait for Spanish ships coming from the New World, captured them, and bore their vast treasure of gold and silver back to England. There was no enemy to guard against except Spain, and even toward Spain England grew more and more fearless.

All this audacious freedom was reflected in the literature of the time, especially in the boldness with which English writers attempted anything and everything. This boldness was something entirely new in religious writings. Every middle-aged man in England could remember three religious revolutions, three times within the space of less than a quarter of a century when men who had not changed their faith to agree with that of their sovereign had been in danger of death at the stake. Religious poems had been careful and timid, but now they became frank and cheerful. Great numbers of ballads were written, but few of them were as good as the old ones; for their chief object now was to tell of some recent event, that is, to be newspapers rather than poems. Of translations there seemed no end, translations not only from the Greek and Latin, but also from the Italian, for Italy was still the land of culture and light. The Celtic love for stories could now be satisfied, for there were tales and romances from Italy, from the wonder-book of early English history, and even from the legends of Spain. The stories told by returning sea-captains were not to be scorned, throbbing with life as they were, glowing with pictures of the strange new world, and thrilling with wild encounters on the sea.

48. The Early Elizabethan Drama

It was not enough to hear stories told. In that age of action, people must see things done; and the drama flourished more and more. Theatres were built, the first in 1576. The queen was very fond of the drama, and this in itself was a great encouragement, for Elizabeth was England, and England was Elizabeth. All kinds of dramas flourished. The mystery plays were not yet given up; moralities, comedies, tragedies, and all sorts of mongrel dramas appeared. The metre employed was in quite as uncertain a state; for these bold writers of plays were ready to try everything. Sometimes they imitated the blank verse of *Gorboduc;* sometimes they followed such metreless metre as these lines from *Ralph Roister Doister:—*

> *Ye may not speake with a faint heart to Custance,*
> *But with a lusty breast and countenance.*

Sometimes lines of seven accents were tried, sometimes lines of five, sometimes of ten, and sometimes there was no attempt at metre, but the play was written in prose.

The years rolled on rapidly. The sixties were past, the seventies were nearly gone. In 1579, the special need of English literature was form. Both prose and poetry needed the finish and carefulness of which Wyatt and Surrey had been the apostles. In 1579 and 1580, three new writers arose, who laid before the lovers of poetry fresh and winning examples of what might be accomplished by poetic thought united with careful form. These three writers were John Lyly, Edmund Spenser, and Sir Philip Sidney.

49. John Lyly, 1554?–1606

Hardly anything is known of John Lyly before 1579 save that he was a university man and attached to the court. His first book, *Euphues*, that is, "the well endowed by nature," was long looked upon as a model for polite conversation, and affected the style of writing of all literary England for many years. It has a slender thread of story whereon are hung various moral and educational ideas. So far there is nothing unusual in it. Its peculiarity lay in its style. Lyly uses the balanced sentence to excess, stiffens it with alliteration, and loads it down with similes, a large proportion of them drawn from a half-fabulous natural history. One of his sentences is:—

> *If Trauailers in this our age were . . . as willing to reap profit by their paines as they are to endure perill for their pleasure, they would either prefer their own soyle before a strange Land or good counsell before their owne conceyte.*

Another sentence declares:—

> *As the Egle at euery flight looseth a fether, which maketh hir bald in hir age: so the trauailer in euery country looseth some fleece, which maketh him a beggar in his youth.*

This affected manner of talking and writing fell in with the whim of the age, and was soon the height of the fashion. Foolish and unnatural as it seems, it brought to English prose precisely what that prose needed, that is, a plan for each sentence. Far too many a writer, not only in King Alfred's time but long afterward, had plunged into his sentences with the utmost audacity, trusting to luck to bring him out; but whoever wrote in euphuistic fashion was obliged to plan his sentences and choose his words.

Euphuism was only one of the little affectations of style that influenced the literature of Elizabethan times. Throughout the rest of the century and far into the next one poetic disguise after another was welcomed.

50. Edmund Spenser, 1552–1599

One of the most popular of these disguises was the pastoral, wherein the characters are spoken of as shepherds and shepherdesses. They have the sheep and the crook, but in their thought they are anything but simple shepherds. The first of these pastorals was written by Edmund Spenser, and is called *The Shepherd's Calendar.* Spenser was a London boy, who began to write poetry in his school-days, but almost nothing else is known of him until he wrote this poem. Before it was quite completed, he met one of the most interesting young men of the age, Sir Philip Sidney, and was invited to his home at Penshurst. From the first the two young men were very congenial. Tradition says they spent day after day under the beech-trees, reading the works of the old Greek philosophers and talking of poetry. When *The Shepherd's Calendar* was published, it was dedicated to Sidney,—

To him that is the president
Of noblesse and of chevalree.

The *Calendar* is a collection of poems, one for each month of the year. They are not at all alike. One, of course, was in praise of the queen; but there were fables, satires, and allegory, besides the five poems that pertain strictly to country life. For February there is a story of a "bragging brere," or briar rose, who takes it upon him to scold a grand old oak for being in his way, and appeals to the husbandmen to cut it down, for he says it is

Hindering with his shade my lovely light,
And robbing me of the swete sonnes sight.

The oak is hewn down; but when winter is come, the brere, too, meets his death, for now he has not the shelter and support of the oak that he scorned. For August there is a merry little roundelay about the meeting of shepherd "Willie" with shepherdess "Perigot." So it is that Spenser describes his heroine:—

Well decked in a frocke of gray,
Hey ho gray is greete,
And in a kirtle of greene say,
The greene is for maidens meete.
A chapelet on her head she wore,
Hey ho chapelet,
Of sweete violets therein was store,
She sweeter than the violet.
My sheep did leave theyr wonted foode,
Hey ho seely sheepe,
*And gazed on her, as they were wood,**
Woode as he, that did them keepe.

These poems of Spenser's were so much better than any others written since Chaucer's day that all the lovers of poetry were interested, and Spenser was often spoken of as the "new poet." He was without means, and by influence of his friends a government position was

*mad.

obtained for him in Ireland. A few months before he went on board the vessel that was to bear him across the Irish Sea, he wrote to an old school friend to return a little package of manuscript which had been lent him to read, and "whyche I pray you heartily send me with al expedition," he said. The little package was to return to England some ten years later, but much was to happen in the literary world before that came to pass.

In the first place, pastorals became so much the fashion that there was even a rewriting of old poems, so that "youths and maidens" might appear as "swains and nymphs" or as "shepherds and shepherdesses." *Euphues* was not a pastoral, but its smoothness and careful attention to sound were in full accord with this mode of writing. Soon after Spenser had gone to Ireland, his friend, Sir Philip Sidney, wrote a book that was almost equally smooth. It was written merely for amusement and to please the Countess of Pembroke, his favorite sister, but for more than three hundred years it has pleased almost every one who has read it.

51. Sir Philip Sidney, 1554–1586

Sir Philip belonged to a noble family; he received every advantage of education and travel; he was of so singularly sweet a nature and so brilliant an intellect that he was loved and admired by every one who knew him. Yet he was not at all spoiled, he felt only the more eager to prove himself worthy of this love and admiration. When only twenty-three, he was sent to Prague as the ambassador of his country. He was even thought to be a fit candidate for the throne of Poland, but here Queen

Elizabeth said no. "I will not brook the loss of the jewel of my dominions," declared this autocratic sovereign.

Sir Philip's book was named *Arcadia,* or as it was usually called, The *Countess of Pembroke's Arcadia.* It is a kind of pastoral romance, wherein young men and maidens wander about in a beautiful forest. They fall in love with one another; they kill lions; they carry on war with the Helots of Greece; they are taken by pirates and have encounters with bears; and all this occurs in a fabulous country, a wilderness of faerie. The very story is a wilderness. There is no especial plot, and the characters are not drawn like real men and women. But why should they be so drawn? They are half-enchanted wanderers roaming on happily through a magical forest. Page after page Sidney wrote, never stopping for revision, rambling on wherever his fancy led; with the loved sister beside him slipping away each leaf, as his pen traced the bottom line, to see what had come next in the fascinating tale of faerie. Even the sound of the words is charming. The sentences are often long, but clear and graceful and musical. There is

Sir Philip Sidney 1554–1586

more than mere pleasantness of sound in the *Arcadia,* however, for it is full of charming bits of description, and of true and noble thoughts. Here is the merry little shepherd boy, "piping as though he should never grow old." Here is "a place made happy by her treading." Here, too, "They laid them down by the murmuring music of certain waters." It is but a picture of himself when Sidney writes, "They are never alone that are accompanied with noble thoughts," and "Keep yourself in heart with joyfulness." One of his friends said long after the author's death that Sidney had intended to rewrite his book and make it into an English romance with King Arthur for its hero; but it is so graceful and charming in its present form that no one could wish to have it made over.

The *Arcadia* was handed about in manuscript from one friend to another. Wherever it was read, it was praised and imitated, but it was not printed till 1590. Printing was for common folk, not for nobles and courtiers; and the lovers of poetry were in the habit of making manuscript books of their favorite poems. Before the end of the century, however, some of these books did come to the printing-press. As if to console them for their humiliation, most high-sounding titles were given them, and we have *The Paradise of Dainty Devices, Britton's Bower of Delights, The Phenix's Nest, England's Helicon,* etc.

52. Later Elizabethan Drama

It was the time of the pastoral, but hundreds of sonnets were being written and passed about in manuscript. Besides this, the drama was almost ready to burst forth with a magnificence of which no one could have dreamed who had seen only the crude attempts of less than half a century earlier. Scores of plays had been written. They were good plays, too, wonderfully far in advance of the previous attempts. Many of them were well worth acting, and are well worth reading to-day; even though the writers had not yet adopted a standard verse, and had not mastered the art of making their characters *live,* that is, of making a character show just such changes at the end of the play as a human being would show if he had been through such experiences as those delineated. This was the greatest lack in these dramas. Their greatest beauty lay in the little songs scattered through the scenes. In the Elizabethan days everybody loved music and everybody sang. Servants were chosen with an ear to their voices, that they might be able to join in a glee or a catch. The words of the songs must be musical; but the Elizabethans demanded even more than this. Poetry was plentiful, and the songs must be real poetry. Therefore it was that such dainty little things appeared as *Apelles' Song:*—

Cupid and my Campaspe played
At cards for kisses,—Cupid paid;
He stakes his quiver, bow and arrows,
His mother's doves and team of sparrows:
Loses them too; then down he throws
The coral of his lip, the rose
Growing on 's cheek (but none knows how);
With these the crystal of his brow,
And then the dimple of his chin:
All these did my Campaspe win.
At last he set her both his eyes;

She won, and Cupid blind did rise.
O Love, has she done this to thee?
What shall, alas! become of me?

This song is in Lyly's play of *Alexander and Campaspe,* for the famous euphuist wrote a handful of plays which were presented before the queen. He wrote in prose, but some makers of plays employed rhyme, some blank verse, and some a mingling of all three. There was great need of a standard verse suited to the requirements of the drama, a line not so short as to suggest doggerel, and not so long as to be cumbersome and unwieldy. Blank verse was perhaps slowly gaining ground, but before it could be generally accepted as the most fitting mode of dramatic expression, some writer must use it so skilfully as to show its power, its music, and its adaptability.

53. Christopher Marlowe, 1564–1593

Such a writer was Christopher, or "Kit," Marlowe, one of the "university wits," as one group of playwrights was called, because nearly all of them had been connected with one or the other of the great universities. He is thought to have lived in somewhat Bohemian fashion, but little is certainly known of his life save that he took his degree at Cambridge. His *Tamburlaine* was acted in 1587 or 1588. Five years later, Marlowe died; but in those five years he wrote at least three plays, the *Jew of Malta,* the *Tragical History of Doctor Faustus,* and *Edward II,* which showed what magnificent use could be made of blank verse.

In his prologue to *Tamburlaine* he promises to lead

his audience "from jigging veins of rhyming mother wits," and he keeps his promise nobly. The Scythian hero, Tamburlaine, is a shepherd who becomes the conqueror of sovereigns. One scene was the laughing-stock of the time, that in which Tamburlaine enters, drawn in his chariot by two captive kings with bits in their mouths. Marlowe had no sense of humor to keep him from such an absurdity; his mission was to give the poets some idea of what might be done with blank verse; and those who laughed loudest listened with admiration to such lines as these:—

Our souls, whose faculties can comprehend
The wondrous architecture of the world,
And measure every wandering planet's course,
Still climbing after knowledge infinite,
And always moving as the restless spheres,
Will us to wear ourselves, and never rest,
Until we reach the ripest fruit of all,
That perfect bliss and sole felicity,
The sweet fruition of an earthly crown.

Remembering that the speaker is Tamburlaine, the heathen shepherd, to whom a throne is the loftiest glory that imagination can reach, there is no bathos in the closing line. The only fault is in the use of the word "earthly."

Marlowe knew well how to use proper names in his verse; and Queen Elizabeth, with her love of music and her equal love of the magnificence of the royal estate, must have enjoyed:—

And ride in triumph through Persepolis?
Is it not brave to be a king, Techelles?

Usumcasene and Theridamas,
Is it not passing brave to be a king,
And ride in triumph through Persepolis?

Marlowe could write lightly and gracefully, as in his "Come live with me and be my love." Then he is charming, but it is his power rather than his grace that lingers in the mind. More than once there are such lines as,—

Weep not for Mortimer,
That scorns the world, and, as a traveller,
Goes to discover countries yet unknown,—

lines that might well have come from the pen of Shakespeare. These are from the closing scene of *Edward II,* Marlowe's last and finest play.

54. Events from 1580 to 1590

So the years passed in England from 1580 to 1590, but one poet, Spenser, was shut away from the literary life of his countrymen, which was becoming every day more glorious. A castle and a vast tract of land in Ireland had been given him, and there he dwelt and wrote; but all the time he felt like a prisoner, and he called his Irish home "that waste where I was quite forgot." When he came from Ireland in 1589 or 1590 to pay a visit to England, he found several changes. Mary Queen of Scots had been beheaded, and the most timid Protestant no longer feared revolution and a Roman Catholic sovereign. The Spanish Armada had been conquered by the bravery of English captains and the tempests of the heavens; England was mistress of the seas, and her bold mariners were free to go where they would. The thoughts of many were turning toward the New World, and Sir Walter Raleigh had even attempted to found a colony across the seas. One note of sadness mingled with the joy of the nation. Sir Philip Sidney was dead, and was mourned by a whole kingdom. The bravery with which he met the enemy in the fatal battle of Zutphen, the self-forgetful courtesy with which he refused, until another should have drunk, the water that would have eased his suffering, the gentle patience with which he bore the long weeks of agony before the coming of the end,—all this touched the English heart as it had never before been touched. So enduring was the love which he inspired that Fulke Greville, one of his boyhood companions, who outlived him by twenty-two years, asked that on his own tomb might be written, "Servant to Queen Elizabeth, Councillor to King James, and Friend to Sir Philip Sidney." Sidney requested that his *Arcadia* should be destroyed, but his sister could not bear to fulfil such a wish, and in 1590, while Spenser was in England, it was printed.

55. The Faerie Queene

Spenser brought with him from Ireland the little package that he had carried away, now grown much larger. Sir Walter Raleigh had visited him, and as they sat under the alders by the river, Spenser had read aloud the first three books of the *Faerie Queene,* for these were in the precious little package. The poem was published in 1590. It begins:—

A gentle Knight was pricking on the plaine,
Ycladd in mightie armes and silver shielde,
Wherein old dints of deepe woundes did remaine,

The cruell markes of many a bloody fielde;
Yet armes till that time did he never wield:
His angry steede did chide his foming bitt,
As much disdayning to the curbe to yield:
Full iolly knight he seemd, and faire did sitt,
As one for knightly giusts and fierce encounters fitt.

This "gentle knight" represented Holiness, who was riding forth into the world to contest with Heresy. Spenser planned to write twelve books, each of which was to celebrate the victory of some virtue over its contrary vice. At the end of the twelfth book the knights were to return to the land of Faerie. King Arthur was then to represent the embodiment of all these virtues, and he was to wed the Queen of Faerie, who was the Glory of God. Together with this was a very material allegory, if it may be so called, in which Elizabeth is the Queen of Faerie, Mary of Scotland is Error, etc. So far even the double allegory is reasonably clear; but as the poem goes on, it wanders away and away, and is so mingled with other allegories and changes of characters that it is impossible to trace a connected story through even the six books that were written of the twelve that Spenser planned.

The Red Cross Knight
From the Faerie Queene

Tracing the story is a small matter, however. One need not read an imaginative poem with a biographical dictionary and a gazetteer. The allegory of the struggle of evil with good is beautiful; but one need not trouble himself about the allegory. Read the poem simply for its exquisite pictures, its wonderfully rich and varied imagery, and the ever-changing music of its verse, and you will share in some degree the pleasure which for three hundred years Spenser has given to all true lovers of poetry.

56. The Decade of the Sonnet, 1590–1600

From 1590 to 1600 the sonnet was the prevailing form of the lyric. Sonnets were written in sequences, as they were called, that is, in groups, each group generally telling the story of the author's love for some lady fair who was either real or imaginary. Spenser wrote beautiful, musical sonnets, but Sidney's *Astrophel and Stella,* a sequence which was not published till 1591, gives one such a feeling that it *must* be sincere that to read it seems almost like stealing glances at his paper as he wrote. One of his best sonnets is:—

With how sad steps, O Moon, thou climb'st the skies!
How silently, and with how wan a face!
What, may it be that even in heavenly place
That busy archer his sharp arrows tries!
Sure, if that long-with-love-acquainted eyes
Can judge of love, thou feel'st a lover's case,
I read it in thy looks; the languisht grace,
To me, that feel the like, thy state descries:
Then, even of fellowship, O Moon, tell me,
Is constant love deem'd there but want of wit?
Are beauties there as proud as here they be?

Do they above love to be lov'd, and yet
Those lovers scorn whom that love doth possess?
Do they call virtue there ungratefulness?

57. Richard Hooker, 1554?–1600

During this decade an important piece of prose was written by a clergyman named Richard Hooker. He was a man of much learning, but so shy that when he was lecturing at Oxford he could hardly look his students in the face. Even his shyness could not hide his merits, and he was appointed to a prominent position in London. It was not long, however, before he wrote an earnest appeal to the archbishop to give him instead some humble village parish. London was full of controversies, sometimes very bitter ones, between the Church of England and the Puritans. Hooker was far too gentle to meet disagreement and discord, but in his later and more quiet home he produced a clear, strong book called the *Ecclesiastical Polity,* which defended the position of the church, giving the reasons why he believed it to have the right to claim men's obedience. Prose in plenty had been written for some special purpose, but this was something more than a mere putting of words together to express a thought; it was not only an argument, it was literature, and even those who were not interested in its subject read it for the grave harmony of its style and the dignity of its phrasing.

58. William Shakespeare, 1564–1616

It was in this same decade that the full glory of the drama was to burst forth. In 1564, the year of Marlowe's birth, a child was born in the village of Stratford on the river Avon who was to become the greatest of poets. His father, John Shakespeare, was a well-to-do man, and held various offices in the village. This boy, William, grew up much as did other boys of the place. He went to school, studied Latin and possibly a little Greek. Coventry was near, and there mystery plays were performed. Kenilworth Castle was only fifteen miles away; and when Shakespeare was eleven years old, Queen Elizabeth was its guest. No bright boy would let such chances go by to see a mystery play or to have a glimpse of his country's queen and the entertainments given in her honor. In 1568, a company of London actors came to Stratford. John Shakespeare as bailiff gave them a formal welcome to the village; and it is probable that among the earliest memories of his son were the sound of their drums and trumpets, the beating of hoofs, and the sight of banners and riders, of gorgeous costumes flashing in the sun and gayly caparisoned horses prancing down the street to the market-place.

More than a score of times the prancing steeds and their riders visited Stratford; and the country boy, living quietly beside the Avon, must have had many thoughts of the great world of London that was the home of those fascinating cavalcades. He would not have been a real boy if he had not determined to see that marvellous city before many years should pass.

Not long after the festivities of Kenilworth, John Shakespeare began to be less successful in his business affairs. Thirteen or fourteen was not an early age for a boy to be taken from school who did not intend to

Shakespeare's Birthplace at Stratford

go to the university; and it is probable that the boy William left school at that age and began to earn his own living. For some years from that time the only thing known of him is that he often crossed the fields by a narrow lane that led to Shottery and the cottage of Anne Hathaway, and that before he was nineteen she became his wife. In 1586, the young man of twenty-two, with no trade, with himself and wife and three children to support, with only dreams and courage and genius for capital, made his way to London, possibly on horseback, but more probably on foot. 1586 was the year of Sidney's death. There could hardly be a greater inspiration toward honor and uprightness for a young man on his first visit to London than to see the whole city grieving for the death of one but ten years older than himself simply because he whom they had lost was pure and true and noble.

Just what Shakespeare did during those first two years in London is not known, but he must have been connected in some way with the theatre and have won the confidence of those in control, for as early as 1588 he was trusted to "retouch" at least one play. This retouching was regarded as perfectly allowable. There was no copyright law, and as soon as a play had been printed, any theatre had a right to use it, and any author had a right to alter it as he chose. Two years later, the unknown young man from the country had made a place for himself, and in 1590, the year in which Spenser brought the first part of the *Faerie Queene* to London, Shakespeare's merry little comedy, *Love's Labour's Lost,* was acted. This play does not reach the heights of tragedy, of course, or even of his later comedies, but it is freely and lightly drawn; it is full of fun and frolic, and fairly sparkles with witty repartee. Shakespeare had caught the fashion of euphuism, and he made fun of it so merrily that its greatest devotees must have been amused.

Play followed play: comedy, tragedy, history. It was no idle life that he led, for the writing of five or six plays is generally ascribed to the years 1590–1592; and it must be remembered, too, that he was actor as well as author. It was in 1592 that the dramatist Chettle wrote of his excellent acting, and said, moreover, that he had heard of his uprightness of dealing and his grace in writing. Shakespeare was no longer an unknown actor. He was recognized as a successful playwright, and also as a poet, for his *Venus and Adonis* and *Lucrece* had won a vast amount of admiration. "The mellifluous and honey-tongued Shakespeare," one of the critics called him, and spoke with praise of his "sugerd sonnets" that were passed about among his friends.

59. Historical Plays

After some merry, sparkling comedies, such as *A Midsummer Night's Dream* and *The Comedy of Errors*, there came a time when the poet seemed fascinated by the history of his own land. In writing historical drama Shakespeare was never a student-author; Elizabethan life moved too rapidly for much searching of old manuscripts and records. Shakespeare's special power as a dramatist of history lay in his sympathetic imagination by which he understood the men of bygone days. He read their motives, he pictured them as he could imagine himself to have been in their circumstances and with their qualities; and more than once his interpretation of some historical character, opposed as it was to the common belief of his time, has been proved by later investigation to be correct.

Then came the *Merchant of Venice* and a group of comedies, some of which have touches of boisterous rant, while some are happy, romantic, and charmingly graceful. In the *Merchant of Venice* perhaps quite as much as in any other play, Shakespeare shows his power to make us hold a character in the balance. Shylock is cruel and miserly, but we cannot help seeing with a touch of sympathy that he is oppressed and lonely; Bassanio is a careless young spendthrift, but so boyish and so frank that we forget to be severe; Portia is perfectly conscious of the value of her wealth and her

William Shakespeare. 1564–1616
The Chandos Portrait

beauty, but at love's command she is ready to drop both lightly into the hands of Bassanio.

Shakespeare's writing extended over a space of about twenty years, half of which time belonged to the sixteenth century and half to the seventeenth. If he had died in 1600, we should think of him as a dramatist of great skill in writing comedy, whether refined and merry or rough and somewhat boisterous, and in writing historical plays presenting the history of his own country; but, save for some hint that *Romeo and Juliet* might give, we should have no idea of his unrivalled power in writing tragedies. Those as well as his deeper comedies belonged to the following century.

SUMMARY

Century XVI

SHAKESPEARE'S CENTURY

John Skelton.
Sir Thomas More.
William Tyndale.
Sir Thomas Wyatt.
Earl of Surrey.
"Tottel's Miscellany".
John Heywood.
Nicholas Udall.
Thomas Sackville.
Thomas Norton.
John Lyly.
Edmund Spenser.
Sir Philip Sidney.
"The Elizabethan Miscellanies".
Christopher Marlowe.
Richard Hooker.
William Shakespeare.

The minds of the English people and also their literature were strongly affected, first, by the Renaissance; second, by increased knowledge of the western world; and, third, by the discovery that the earth is not the centre of the universe.

During the reign of Henry VIII, English literature centred around him. John Skelton was his tutor; Sir Thomas More one of his courtiers.

Religious questions were much discussed. William Tyndale translated the New Testament. Henry's disagreement with the pope led to the separation of the Church of England from the Church of Rome.

About the middle of the century, the courtiers Wyatt and Surrey introduced the Italian sonnet and the carefulness of Italian poetry. Surrey introduced blank verse. Their poems were published in *Tottel's Miscellany.*

The drama progressed step by step. Mysteries and moralities still flourished. Masques and interludes came into favor. John Heywood wrote the most successful interludes. The first English comedy was *Ralph Roister Doister,* written by Nicholas Udall. The first English tragedy was *Gorboduc,* written by Sackville and Norton.

In the reign of Elizabeth the power of England increased; literature manifested greater boldness. Religious writings, translations, and stories appeared in great numbers, but the glory of the latter half of her reign was the drama. All species of drama flourished; all kinds of metre and also prose were employed. The pressing needs were, first, carefulness of form; and, second, an appropriate and generally accepted metre. A strong influence in favor of carefulness of form was exerted by the *Euphues* of Lyly, by *The Shepherd's Calendar* of Spenser, and succeeding pastorals, and by Sidney's *Arcadia* and also his sonnets circulated in manuscript.

The drama now increased rapidly in excellence, but still had no standard metre and did not attain to the highest success in the delineation of character. It contained, however, beautiful little songs. Finally, Marlowe showed the capabilities of blank verse, and this became the accepted metre.

In 1590, the first three books of the *Faerie Queene* were published. During the following decade the sonnet flourished. Hooker wrote his *Ecclesiastical*

Polity, and the glory of the drama burst forth in the works of William Shakespeare, who solved the great dramatic problem, how to make the characters seem like real people.

CHAPTER VI

Century XVII

PURITANS AND ROYALISTS

60. Shakespeare in the Seventeenth Century

In 1603, Queen Elizabeth died and James of Scotland became the sovereign of England. The inspiration of the age of Elizabeth lingered for some years after her death, and the work of Shakespeare, its greatest glory, extended far into the reign of James. His genius broadened and deepened, and he gave to the new century his deeper comedies and a superb group of tragedies, *Hamlet, King Lear,* and others. His plays grow more intense, more powerful. Sometimes he uses bitter irony. Stern retribution is visited upon both weak and wicked. There is a touch of gloom. Magnificent as these dramas are, it is good to come away from them to the ripple of the sea, to the breeze of the meadow land, to his last group of plays, the joyous and beautiful romantic dramas, such as the *Winter's Tale, Cymbeline,* and, last of all, it may be, *The Tempest,* that marvellous production in which a child may find a fairy tale, a philosopher suggestion and mystery and that "solemn vision" of life that comes in the midst of the wonders of the magic island.

When Shakespeare's sonnets were written and to whom they were written is not known. If the whole aim of their author had been to puzzle his readers, he could not have succeeded better. Some seem to have been written to a man, others to a woman. Some are exquisitely beautiful, some are fairly rollicking in boyish mischievousness. Some express sincere love, some are apparently trying to see how far a roguish mock devotion can be concealed by charm of phrase and rhythm. Here are such perfect lines as

Bare, ruin'd choirs, where late the sweet birds sang.

Here is his honest

My mistress' eyes are nothing like the sun,
Coral is far more red than her lips' red,—

wherein he makes fun of the poetic rhapsodies of Elizabethan lovers. Here, too, is his mischievous sonnet, which pictures—though in most musical language—a woman chasing a hen, while her deserted lover begs her to come back and be a mother to him! These sonnets were published without their author's permission, and he took no step to explain them. Every student of the poet's work has his own interpretation. Which is correct, Shakespeare alone could tell us.

Shakespeare is the world's greatest poet. His genius consists, first, in reading men and women better than anyone else has ever read them, knowing what a person of certain traits would do under certain circumstances, and how the scenes through which that person passed would affect his character; second, in his ability to express that knowledge with such perfection of form and such brilliancy of imagination as has never been equalled; third, in the fact that his power both to read and to express was sustained. The dramatists who preceded him and those who worked by his side often had flashes and gleams of insight and momentary powers of expression that were worthy of him; but the power to see clearly throughout the five acts of a play and to express with equal excellence and consistency the character of the clown and of the king was not theirs.

William Shakespeare was no supernatural being; he was a very human man. Certainly he never thought of himself as sitting on a pinnacle manufacturing English classics. He threw himself into his poetry, but he never forgot that he was writing plays for people to act and for people to see. No really good work of literature flows from the pen without thought. Shakespeare worked very rapidly, but the thinking was done at some time, either when he took up his pen or beforehand. He was a straightforward business man, who paid his debts and intended that what was due to him should be paid. He loved his early home and planned, perhaps from the time that he left it, to return to Stratford. Money came to him rapidly, especially after 1599, when the Globe Theatre was built, in which he seems to have owned a generous share. Two years earlier he had been able to buy New Place in Stratford, and about 1611 he returned to his native town. A vast change it must have been to the man whose dramas had won the admiration of the people and of their queen, to come to a quiet village now grown so puritanical that its council had solemnly decreed that the acting of plays within its limits should be regarded as an unlawful deed. He was away from his London friends and their brilliant meetings at the

Mermaid Inn, of which one of them, Francis Beaumont, wrote:—

What things have we seen
Done at the Mermaid! heard words that have been
So nimble and so full of subtle flame,
As if that everyone from whence they came
Had meant to put his whole wit in a jest,
And had resolved to live a fool the rest
Of his dull life.

No word of complaint or of loneliness has come down to us. In Stratford were his wife, his two daughters, and the little granddaughter, Elizabeth. There are traditions of visits from his old friends. He had wealth, fame, the home of his choice. In the village of his birth the poet died in 1616, and was buried in the church that still stands beside the river Avon.

61. Sir Walter Raleigh, 1552–1618

Wonderful people were those Elizabethans; for every one seemed to be able to do everything. Perhaps the best example of the man of universal ability is Sir Walter Raleigh, an explorer, a colonizer, the manager of a vast Irish estate, a vice-admiral, a captain of the guard, and a courtier whose flattery could delight even so well flattered a woman as Queen Elizabeth. Moreover, when King James imprisoned him under a false charge of treason, this soldier and sailor and colonizer became an author and produced among other writings a *History of the World.* He tells the story clearly and pleasantly. Sometimes he is eloquent, sometimes poetical; e.g. he speaks of the Roman Empire as a tree standing in the middle of a field. "But after some continuance," he says, "it shall begin to lose the beauty it had; the storms of ambition shall beat her great boughs and branches one against another; her leaves shall fall off, her limbs wither, and a rabble of barbarous nations enter the field and cut her down."

Several of the literary giants who began their work in the days of Queen Elizabeth are counted as of the times of James. The greatest of these were the philosopher Francis Bacon and the dramatist Ben Jonson.

62. Francis Bacon, 1561–1626

Francis Bacon seems to have been "grown up" from his earliest childhood. He was the son of Elizabeth's Lord Keeper, and it is said that as a boy his dignity and intelligence delighted her Majesty so much that she often questioned him on all sorts of subjects to see what he would answer. One day when she asked how old he was, he replied with all the readiness of an experienced courtier, "I am two years younger than your Majesty's happy reign." When he was little more than a youth, he declared gravely that he had "taken all knowledge" for his province. In most young men this would have been an absurd speech, but in view of what Bacon actually accomplished it seems hardly more than the truth. He was only thirteen when he entered the university, but during his three years of residence, this boy put his finger on the weak spot in the teaching and study of the day. The whole aim seemed to be, he declared, not to discover new truths, but to go over and over the old ones.

Nothing would have pleased him better than to have

means enough to live comfortably while he thought and wrote, but he had no fortune. "I must think how to live," he said, "instead of living only to think." The young man of eighteen looked about him, and concluded to study law and try to win the patronage of the queen. In his legal studies he was so successful that his reasoning and eloquence were equally pleasing; but the queen's patronage was beyond his reach, for she would give him only just enough favor to keep him ever hoping for more.

In the midst of his disappointments he wrote ten essays, which were published in 1597. They were on such subjects as Study, Expense, Followers and Friends, Reputation, etc., and they seemed in many respects more like the reflections of a man of sixty-three than one of thirty-six. They are so full of wisdom, and the wisdom is expressed so clearly and definitely, that some parts of them seem almost like a sequence of proverbs. Among the sentences most quoted are these:—

> *Some books are to be tasted, others to be swallowed, and some few to be chewed and digested; that is, some books are to be read only in parts; others to be read, but not curiously; and some few to be, read wholly and with diligence and attention. . . . Reading maketh a full man, conference a ready man, and writing an exact man.*

After James came to the throne, Bacon was raised from one position to another, until at last he became Lord High Chancellor. He lived with the utmost magnificence; he had fame, wealth, rank, and the favor of his sovereign. He had also enemies, and before three years had passed, a charge of accepting bribes was brought against him. He was declared guilty; but his real guilt was far less than that of such a deed if done two centuries later; for the acceptance of bribes, or gifts, by men in high legal positions was a custom of long standing. No attempt was made to show that these gifts had made him decide even one cause unjustly.

Bacon's public life was ended, but it is quite possible that the few years which remained to him were his happiest, for, living quietly with his family, he had at last the leisure for thought for which he had longed. Some time before this he had published more essays, and he had already begun the great work of his life, the *Instauratio Magna,* that is, the "great institution" of true philosophy. This undertaking was the outgrowth of his boyish criticism of Oxford. He planned that the work should give a summary of human knowledge in all branches and should point out a system by which advancement might be made. The philosophers of the day were satisfied with words rather than things; in seeking for knowledge of nature, for instance, it seemed to them the proper scholastic method, not to study nature herself but to reason out what seemed to be a fitting law. In Bacon's *Novum Organum,* or "new instrument," he taught that in the study of nature, or in the study of the action of the human mind, men ought, first, to notice how nature and the mind worked, and from this knowledge to derive general laws. The former way of reasoning was called deductive, i.e., first make the rule and then explain the facts by it. Bacon's philosophy was inductive, i.e., first collect examples and from them form a rule. Inductive reasoning was not original with Bacon by any means. His glory lies in his eliminating all inaccurate, worthless notions, and in his firm belief that all reasoning should lead to advancement of knowledge and to practical good. He said, "I have held up a light . . . which will be seen centuries after I am dead;" and he was right, for it is according to his system that all progress in laws, in commerce, and in science has been made.

63. The "King James Version" of the Bible, 1611

Bacon wrote in Latin because he believed that, while English might pass away, Latin would live forever; but in 1611, while he was coming to this decision, the Bible was again translated, and the translation was so excellent and later events made its reading so universal, that this one book alone would almost have saved the English language, if there had been any possibility of its being forgotten. This version was the one which is now in general use, the "authorized version," or the "King James version," as it is called. Simply as a piece of literature, it is of priceless value. The sonorous rhythm of the *Psalms,* the dignified simplicity of the *Gospels,* the splendid imagery of the *Revelation,*—all these are expressed in clear, concise, and often beautiful phrase, whose influence on the last three hundred years of English literature cannot be too highly esteemed.

64. Ben Jonson, 1573?–1637

When Shakespeare returned to Stratford he left London full of playwrights. Many of them had great talent in some one line. Ford and Webster had special power in picturing sorrow and suffering; Beaumont and Fletcher, who worked together, constructed their plots with unusual skill and wrote most exquisite little songs; Chapman has many graceful, beautiful passages; Dekker, as Charles Lamb said, had "poetry enough for anything:" but there was no second Shakespeare. He stood alone, better than all others in all respects. The playwright who stood nearest to him in greatness was Ben Jonson. He was nine years younger than Shakespeare. He was a London boy, and knew little of the simple country life with which Shakespeare was so familiar. His stepfather taught him his own trade of bricklaying, much to the boy's disgust, for he was eager to go on in school. This privilege came to him through the kindness of strangers, and, as one of his friends said later, he "barrelled up a great deal of knowledge." For a while he served as a soldier in the Netherlands. All this was before he was twenty, for at that age he had found his way to the theatre and was trying to act. As an actor, he was not a great success, but he soon showed that he could succeed in that "retouching" of old plays which served young writers as a school for the drama. The next thing known of him is that in 1597, when he

Ben Jonson
1573?—1637

was twenty-four years of age, he wrote a play called *Every Man in His Humour*, which was presented at the theatre with which Shakespeare was connected. There is a tradition that Shakespeare was much interested in the young writer, that he persuaded the managers that the play would be a success, and that he himself took part in it.

This maker of plays who had "barrelled up a great deal of knowledge" was most profoundly interested in the classic drama. The ancient dramatists believed that in every play three laws should be carefully observed. The first was that every part of a drama should help to develop one main story; this was the unity of plot, and was obeyed by Shakespeare as well as Jonson. The second was that the time required by the incidents of a drama should never be longer than a single day; this was the unity of time. The third was that the whole action should occur in one place; this was the unity of place. In the romantic drama, like Shakespeare's plays, the characters develop, and the reader sees at the end of a play that they have been changed by the experiences that they have met with. In Jonson's plays, the characters have only one day's life, and they are the same at the end as at the beginning. Shakespeare's characters seem alive, and we discuss them, their deeds, and their motives, as if they were men and women of history. We may talk of Jonson's plots, but no one thinks of his characters as ever having lived. The law of unity of place prevented the writer from moving his scene easily and naturally as in real life, and this adds to their unrealness. Another respect in which the two writers were quite unlike was that Shakespeare seems to mingle with his characters and to sympathize with every one of them, no matter how unlike they are, while Jonson stands a little one side and manufactures them; for instance, both wrote plays whose scenes were laid in Rome. Shakespeare shows us the thoughts and feelings of his Romans, but he is careless in regard to manners and customs; Jonson is exceedingly accurate in all such details, but he forgets to put real people into his Roman dress. The result is that, while Shakespeare's Romans are men and women like ourselves, Jonson's are hardly more than lay figures. Shakespeare treats a Roman "like a vera brither;" Jonson treats even his English characters as persons whose faults he is free to satirize as much as he chooses. In his first comedy he takes the ground that every one has some one special "humour," or whim, which is the governing power of his life. He names his characters according to this theory, and his Kno'well, Cash, Clement, Downright, Wellbred, etc., recall the times of the morality plays.

Why is it, then, that with this unrealness, this lack of human interest, such excellence should have been found in the plays of Jonson? It is because he observed so closely, because he was so learned and strong and manly, and especially because his fancy was so dainty and beautiful that no one could help being charmed by it. He wrote a number of plays. Every one of them is worth reading; but really to enjoy Jonson, one must read what he wrote when he forgot that the faults of his time ought to be reformed, that is, his masques, which he composed to please the king; for somehow James discovered that this pedant could forget his pedantry, that this wilful, satirical, overbearing, social, genial, warm-hearted author of rather chilly plays could write most exquisite masques. In masques Jonson saw no need of observing the unities; it was all in the land of fancy, and here his fancy had free rein. Of course he praised King James with the utmost servility; but to give such praise in a masque to be acted before the king was not only good policy but it was a custom, and almost as much a literary fashion as writing sonnets or pastorals. In the masque most elaborate scenery was employed, and every device of light and dancing and music. In the *Masque of Oberon,* for instance, the satyrs "fell suddenly into an antick dance full of gesture and swift motion." The crowing of the cock was heard, and, as the old stage directions say, "The whole palace opened, and the nation of Faies were discovered, some with instruments, some bearing lights, others singing,"—and Jonson knew well how to write graceful song that was perfectly adapted to these fascinating scenes. He is rarely tender, but in his *Sad Shepherd,* an unfinished play, there are the exquisite lines:—

Here she was wont to go, and here, and here!
Just where those daisies, pinks, and violets grow;
The world may find the spring by following her;
For other print her airy steps ne'er left:
Her treading would not bend a blade of grass,
Or shake the downy blow-ball from his stalk.

Scattered through Jonson's plays are such beautiful bits of poetry as this; and when we read them, we forgive him his Downright and Wellbred and his affection for the unities.

65. The Tribe of Ben

Jonson became Poet Laureate, the first poet regularly appointed to hold that position; but his courtly honors can hardly have given him as much real pleasure as the devotion of the younger literary men, the "Tribe of Ben," as they were called, who gathered around him with frank admiration and liking.

The romantic plays that most resembled the drama of Shakespeare were written in partnership by two men, Francis Beaumont and John Fletcher. Hardly anything is known of their lives except that they were warm friends and kept bachelor's hall together. Beaumont was twenty and Fletcher twenty-seven when their partnership began; and it lasted for ten years, or until the death of Beaumont, after which Fletcher continued alone. Working together was a common practice among the dramatists, and sometimes we can trace almost with certainty the lines of a play written by one man and those written by his fellow-worker; but in the case of Beaumont and Fletcher, the closest study has resulted in little more than elaborate guesswork. These two come nearest to Shakespeare on his own lines, that is, they can read men well, and they can put their thoughts into beautiful verse; but in the third point of Shakespeare's greatness they are lacking; Shakespeare could sustain himself, Beaumont and Fletcher often fail. Their characters are not always what their natural traits and circumstances should have made them.

Beaumont died in 1616, the year of Shakespeare's death. Seven years later, thirty-six of Shakespeare's plays were collected and published in a book which is known as the *First Folio.* Ben Jonson wrote the dedication, "To the memory of my beloved Master William Shakespeare, and what he hath left us." His poem is fairly glowing with love and appreciation and admiration for the man who would not observe the unities. It is full of such enthusiastic lines as,—

Soul of the age!
The applause, delight, the wonder of our stage!

He was not of an age, but for all time.

While I confess thy writings to be such
As neither Man nor Muse can praise too much.

Ben Jonson was not given to singing indiscriminate praises, and these words speak volumes for the sturdy friendship between the two men who differed so honestly about what pertained to their art. Stories were told many years afterwards of the "wit-combats" which had taken place between the two; of Jonson's solid, learned arguments and Shakespeare's inventive, quick-witted retorts. It would be worth a whole library full of ordinary books to have a verbatim report of only one of those merry meetings.

66. Closing of the Theatres, 1642

Ben Jonson died in 1635, and only seven years later the drama came to an abrupt end by the breaking out of the Civil War and the passage of a law closing the theatres. Perhaps the coming of the end should not be called abrupt, for the glory of the Elizabethan drama had been gradually fading away. Looking back upon it from the vantage ground of nearly three centuries, it is easy to see that the beginning of the downfall was in the work of rugged, honest, obstinate, and altogether delightful Ben Jonson; for with him the drama first put an attempt to reform society before an attempt to picture society, an exaggeration of a single trait of a man before a delineation of the whole character of the man. Little by little the first inspiration vanished, and did not leave behind it the ability to distinguish good from evil. Beautiful lyrics and worthless doggerel stood side by side. There was a demand for "something new." Plots were no longer probable or fascinatingly impossible, they were simply improbable. Characters gradually ceased to be interesting. Worse than this, they were often unpleasant. The court of his Majesty James I. was not marked by an exquisite decorum in either speech or manner. Vulgarity and coarseness filtered down from the throne to the theatres; it was time that they were closed.

67. Increasing Power of the Puritans

A second reason for the decadence of the drama is so intertwined with the first that they can hardly be separated, namely, the ever-increasing power of the Puritans. Even before 1611, their influence had become so strong that in numerous places besides Stratford it was forbidden to act plays. Many years earlier, even before Shakespeare first went to London, some of the Puritans wrote most earnestly against play-acting. One spoke of "Poets, Pipers, Plaiers, Jesters, and such-like caterpillars of a Commonwealth;" but he had the grace to except some few plays which he thought of better character than the rest. One strong reason why the

Puritans opposed plays at that time was because they were performed on Sundays as well as week-days, and people were inclined to obey the trumpet of the theatre rather than the bell of the church. Sunday acting was given up, and as the years passed, not only the Puritans, but those among their opponents who looked upon life thoughtfully, began to feel that the theatre, with the immorality and indecency of many of the plays then in vogue, was no place for them. It was abandoned to the thoughtless, to those who cared little for the character of a play so long as it amused them, and to those who had no dislike for looseness of manners and laxness of principles. Such was the audience to whom playwrights had begun to cater. In 1642 came war between the king and the people. In 1649 King Charles was beheaded, and until 1660 the Puritan party was in power.

68. Literature of the Conflict

Aside from the work of the dramatists, whose business it was to gratify the taste of their audiences, what kind of writing would naturally be produced in such a time of conflict, when so many were becoming more and more thoughtful of matters of religious living and when the line between the Puritans and the followers of the court was being drawn more closely every year? We should look first for a meditative, critical spirit in literature; then for earnestly religious writings, both prose and poetry, from both Puritan and Churchman; and along with these a lighter, merrier strain from the courtier writers, not necessarily irreligious, but distinctly non-religious.

69. John Donne, 1573–1631

This is precisely what came to pass; but in this variety of literary productions there was hardly an author who was not influenced by the writings of a much admired preacher and poet named John Donne, the Dean of St. Paul's. His life covered the reign of James and two thirds of that of Elizabeth, but just when his poems were written is not known. They are noted for two qualities. One of these was so purely his own that no one could imitate it, the power to illuminate his subject with a sudden and flashing thought. That is why stray lines of Donne's linger in the memory, such as—

I long to talk with some old lover's ghost,
Who died before the god of love was born.

Unfortunately, it was the second quality which was so generally imitated. This was, not the flashing out of a thought, but the wrapping it up and concealing it so that it requires a distinct intellectual effort to find out what is meant; for instance, in the very poem just quoted are the lines:—

But when an even flame two hearts did touch,
His [Love's] office was indulgently to fit
Actives to passives; correspondency
Only his subject was; it cannot be
Love, if I love who loves not me.

Of course one finally reasons it out that Donne means to say love should inspire love, that "I love" and "I am loved" should "fit;" but by that time the reader is inclined to agree with honest Ben Jonson, who declared that Donne "for not being understood would perish."

Sometimes, again, Donne conceals his thought in so complicated, far-fetched a simile that one has to stop and reason out its significance. He writes of two souls, his own and that of his beloved:—

If they be two, they are two so
As stiff twin compasses are two;
Thy soul, the fixed foot, makes no show
To move, but doth if th' other do.

And though it in the centre sit,
Yet when the other far doth roam,
It leans and hearkens after it,
And grows erect as that comes home.

These "conceits," as they were called, greatly influenced the poets of the age. There were also two other influences, that of Ben Jonson for carefulness of form and expression, and that of Spenser, still remembered, for beauty and sweetness and richness of imagery; but of these three influences, that of Donne was by far the strongest.

70. John Milton, 1608–1674

Of the poets who wrote between 1625 and 1660, John Milton stands for the poetry of meditation. He was born in 1608, the son of a wealthy Londoner. The father was anxious that his son should devote himself to literature; and when he saw how perfectly the boy's wishes harmonized with his own, he left him absolutely free to follow his own will. Less freedom in some respects might have been better; for this boy of twelve with weak eyes and frequent headaches went to school daily, had also tutors at home, and made it his regular practice to study until midnight. He entered Cambridge at sixteen, not the ideal bookworm by any means, for he was so beautiful that he was nicknamed the "Lady of Christ's College."

While Milton was still a student, he wrote his *Hymn on the Morning of Christ's Nativity,* a most exquisite Christmas poem. The stanzas are perfect wherein his learning serves only for adornment and his mind is full of the thought of the Christ Child; but some of those toward the end of the poem, which are a little weighed down by his learning, have less charm. This poem, one of Milton's earliest as it was, has a kind of unearthly sweetness of melody and clearness of vision. It seems to have come from another world; to have been written in a finer, rarer atmosphere. The feeling deepens on reading *L'Allegro, Il Penseroso,* the masque *Comus,* and *Lycidas,* all composed within six years after Milton left the university and while he was devoting himself to music and study at his father's country home. He was only twenty-nine when the last of these poems was written. The first two, whose titles may be translated "The Cheerful Man" and "The Thoughtful Man," are descriptions, not of nature, but of the way nature affects the poet when he is in different moods. It is interesting to compare Milton's work with that of earlier times. In *L'Allegro* he writes:—

John Milton
1608–1674

Mountains on whose barren breast
The labouring clouds do often rest:
Meadows trim with daisies pied;
Shallow brooks and rivers wide:
Towers and battlements it sees
Bosomed high in tufted trees.

Surrey loved nature, but this is the way he describes a similar scene:—

The mountains high and how they stand!
The valleys and the great main land!
The trees, the herbs, the towers strong,
The castles and the rivers long!

Poetry made noble progress in the century that lay between the two writers.

L'Allegro and *Il Penseroso* reveal Milton himself. *L'Allegro* speaks of jest and laughter and dancing and mirth; but Milton is not made mirthful, he is only an onlooker, he is never one of those who have—

Come forth to play
On a sunshine holyday.

Shakespeare we admire and love; Milton we admire. Of the other poems, *Comus* is a masque which was presented at Ludlow Castle. *Lycidas* is an elegy in memory of a college friend. It follows the pastoral fashion, and the best way to enjoy it is to read it over and over until the "flock" and "shepherd" and "swain" no longer seem artificial and annoying; and then come appreciation and pleasure. Milton had ever the courage of his convictions. Even in *Comus* and *Lycidas,* a masque and an elegy, there are stern lines rebuking the evils of the times and the scandals of the church. It was easy to see on which side Milton would stand when the struggle broke out between the king and the Puritans.

71. Milton as a Pamphleteer

When it was plain that war must come, Milton was travelling on the Continent, honored and admired wherever he went by the men of greatest distinction. He had planned a much longer stay; but "I thought it base to be travelling for amusement abroad while my fellow-citizens were striking a blow for freedom," he said, and forthwith he set off for England. War had not yet broken out, but this earnest Puritan began to write pamphlets against the Church of England and against the king. In his pamphlets of controversy he seizes any weapon that comes to hand; dignified rebuke, a whirlwind of denunciation, bitter sarcasm, or sheer insolence and railing, but never humor. In his prose he has small regard for form or even for the convenience of his readers; in his *Areopagitica,* a plea for freedom of the press, his sentences are overpowering in their length; three hundred words is by no means an unusual number: and yet, whether his sentences are long or short, simple or involved, there is seldom wanting that same magnificent flow of harmony that is the glory of his poetry. Milton is always Milton.

Among his pamphlets are some that he wrote on divorce. In the midst of the war, he, the stern Puritan, married young Mary Powell, the daughter of an ardent Royalist. After one gloomy month she returned to her own more cheerful home, and in the two years that passed before she would come back to him, he comforted himself by arguing in favor of divorce.

Charles was executed in 1649, and when Cromwell became Lord Protector, Milton was made his Latin secretary. Milton seems cold and unapproachable, but in one weighty act during the years of his secretaryship he comes nearer to us than at any other time. The son of the dead King Charles was in France, and in his behalf a Latin pamphlet had been written by one of the most profound scholars of the time, upholding the course of Charles and declaring those who brought him to his death to be murderers. The Royalists were jubilant, for they thought no adequate reply could be given. The Puritans who knew John Milton best were confident, for they believed that he could confute the reasoning. It was a work requiring study and research as well as skill in argument. Milton began but very soon the question came to him, whether to complete the paper or to save himself from blindness, for he found that his sight was rapidly failing. He made his choice and wrote his *Defence of the English People.* Three years later, sitting in total darkness, he wrote,—

> *What supports me, dost thou ask?*
> *The conscience, Friend, t' have lost them overplied*
> *In liberty's defence, my noble task.*

72. Milton's Sonnets

From 1637 to 1660 Milton wrote nothing but these stern, earnest pamphlets and a few sonnets, one in honor of Cromwell, and one, *On the Late Massacre in Piemont,* that sounds like the fiercest denunciations of a Hebrew prophet. One sonnet is on his own blindness;

and here every one must bow in reverence, for, shut up in hopeless darkness, he grieves only lest his "one talent" is lodged with him useless, and the last line fairly glows with a transfigured courage,—

They also serve who only stand and wait.

Milton had need of courage, for in 1660 the power of the Puritans was gone. The country was tired of their strict laws, and Charles II, son of the beheaded Charles, was brought back in triumph to the throne of his fathers. Milton might well have been pardoned for feeling that his sacrifices were wasted. He was not without consolation, however, for in his mind there was an ever brightening vision of a glorious work that he hoped to accomplish even in his darkness.

Printing-Office of 1619

73. The Religious Poets, Herbert, Crashaw, Vaughan

Leaving for a while Milton, the poet of meditation, we return to the other writers of the time of contest between the king's claim and the people's right; first, to the religious authors, poets, and prose writers. The best known work of most of them was done between 1640 and 1650, save for that of George Herbert, who died in 1633.

74. George Herbert, 1593–1633

Herbert was born of a noble family, and was expected to do honor to it by entering court life. At first all things went smoothly. He had hardly taken his degree before honors were shown him which seemed the first steps to political advancement. In a very short time, however, the friends died upon whom he had depended for influence with King James; and he suddenly concluded to enter the church. His fashion of deciding momentous questions with a startling promptness he carried into other matters; for, three days after meeting the young woman who won his heart, their marriage took place. Again, when a more important position was offered him than the one which he held, he refused to accept it; but having yielded to the archbishop's arguments, he ordered the proper canonical garments to be made ready on the following morning, put them on at once, and was inducted before night.

This man of rapid decisions had a sweet face and a gentle, courteous manner that won him friends wherever he went. He was the most modest of men, and in his

George Herbert
1593–1633

last sickness he directed that his poems should be burned, unless the friend to whom he entrusted them thought they would be of advantage to "any poor, dejected soul."

The writings were printed, and became very popular. The name of the volume was *The Temple.* It contained more than one hundred and fifty short religious poems. They have not the richness of the lyrics of the dramatists, they have not the learning or the imagination of Milton; but they are so sincere, so earnest, and so practical that they were loved from the first. Herbert's is an every-day religion; he is not afraid to speak of simple needs and simple duties. In his *Elixir,* which begins with the childlike petition,—

Teach me, my God and King,
In all things Thee to see,
And what I do in anything,
To do it as for Thee,—

he inserts the homely, helpful stanza,—

A servant with this clause
Makes drudgery divine:
Who sweeps a room as for Thy laws,
Makes that and th' action fine.

Herbert is full of conceits. After writing a beautiful little poem about the blessing of rest being withheld from man that for want of it he may be drawn to God, he named his poem *The Pulley!* He wrote verses in the shape of an altar and in the shape of wings; he wrote verses like these:—

I bless Thee, Lord, because I GROW
Among the trees, which in a ROW
To Thee both fruit and order OW.

But one willingly pardons such whims to the man who could write the christianized common sense of *The Church Porch* and the tender, sunlit verses of—

Sweet day, so cool, so calm, so bright.

75. Richard Crashaw, 1615–1650

The names of two other religious poets of the time are familiar, Richard Crashaw and Henry Vaughan. Crashaw, as well as Herbert and Vaughan, was of the Church of England, but he afterwards became a Roman Catholic and spent his last years in Italy. In 1646 he published *Steps to the Altar* and also *Delights of the Muses;* the first a book of religious verse, the second of secular.

Crashaw is best remembered by a single line of religious verse, the translation of his Latin line in reference to Christ's changing of water into wine,—

The conscious water saw its Lord and blushed,—
Vidit et erubuit nympha pudice Deum;

and also by his lightly written but half-earnest verses, *Wishes to His (Supposed) Mistress:—*

Whoe'er she be,
That not impossible she,
That shall command my heart and me.

He goes on endowing her with every beauty and every virtue. He writes:—

Her that dares be
What these lines wish to see:
I seek no further; it is she.

He ought to end here, but he continues for several stanzas more. He is somewhat like the writers of seven or eight centuries earlier in his way of beginning a poem and writing on and on without any very definite plan. If some kind critic had only looked over the shoulder of this man who was capable of composing such charming bits of verse, we might have had from him some rarely beautiful poems.

76. Henry Vaughan, 1621–1695

Crashaw died in 1650, the year in which Henry Vaughan, the Silurist, or Welshman, wrote his *Silex Scintillans,* or "sparks from the flintstone." He explains the title in one of his poems:—

Lord! thou didst put a soul here. If I must
Be broken again, for flints will give no fire
Without a steel, O let thy power cleer
The gift once more, and grind this flint to dust!

The allusion to his being "broken" is explained, by the fact that a long illness had turned his mind upon heaven rather than upon earth. Eternity was his one thought. His poem, *The World*, begins superbly:—

I saw eternity the other night,
Like a great ring of pure and endless light
All calm as it was bright.

This is a conceit, to be sure, but it is a glorious one.

Vaughan loves nature, and his *Bird* is as tender as it is strong. One might fancy that it was Robert Burns himself who speaks:—

Hither thou com'st. The busie wind all night
Blew through thy lodging, where thy own warm wing
Thy pillow was. Many a sullen storm,
For which coarse man seems much the fitter born,
Rain'd on thy bed
And harmless head.
And now, as fresh and cheerful as the light,
Thy little heart in early hymns doth sing
Unto that Providence whose unseen arm
Curb'd them, and cloath'd thee well and warm.

Vaughan sees what is beautiful in the world and loves it; but all the while he looks through it and beyond it. Herbert, whose life and poems were his model, wrote:—

A man that looks on glass,
On it may stay his eye;
Or if he pleaseth, through it pass,
And then the heavens espy.

So it is that Vaughan looks upon nature. Even in his lines to a little bird, he says that though the birds of light make a land glad, yet there are night birds with mournful note, and ends,—

Brightness and mirth, and love and faith, all flye,
Till the day-spring breaks forth again from on high.

All that he writes comes from his own experience. There is not a hint of glancing at his audience; every poem sounds as if it had been written for his own eyes and for those of no one else. There is somewhat of the charm of "Jerusalem the golden" in his—

My soul, there is a countrie,
Afar beyond the stars;

but the poem which has been the most general favorite is:—

They all are gone into the world of light,
And I alone sit ling'ring here!
Their very memory is fair and bright,
And my sad thoughts doth clear.

77. Writers of Religious Prose

These three men, Herbert, Crashaw, and Vaughan, the Church of England clergyman, the Roman Catholic priest, and the Welsh physician, produced the best religious poetry of England during the Commonwealth and the troublous times preceding the same period. There were also three prominent writers of religious prose, Thomas Fuller, Jeremy Taylor, and Richard Baxter.

78. Thomas Fuller, 1608–1661

Fuller was a clergyman of the Church of England. He was so eloquent that his sermons were said to have been preached to two audiences, those within the room and those who filled the windows and the doors. "Not only full but Fuller," the jesters used to say. Fuller published in 1640 his *Holy and Profane State,* which was sparkling with bits of wisdom. "She commandeth her husband by constantly obeying him," is one of his epigrams. His sermons were always interesting, for he was not only earnest and able, but he was quaintness itself. His subjects are a study. One series of sermons was on "Joseph's Party-colored Coat." One was on "An ill match wel broken off;" and had for its text, "Love not the world."

Fuller's best known book is not religious but historical, and is the outgrowth of his experience as an army chaplain; for while he was with the king's soldiers, he spent his spare time collecting bits of local information about prominent persons. He wandered about among the people, listening for hours at a time to the garrulous village gossips for the sake of obtaining some one good story, some bit of reminiscence, or an ancient doggerel rhyme, as the case might be; and he put them all into his book, *The Worthies of England,* or *Fuller's Worthies,* as it is commonly called. He describes one man as a "facetious dissenting divine," another as a "pious divine;" of another he says, "He did first creep, then run, then fly into preferment; or rather preferment did fly upon him without his expectation." He says of another man, "He was a partial writer," but adds consolingly that he is "buried near a good and true historian." He is full of quaint antitheses and conceits; for example, he says that gardening is "a tapestry in earth," and that tapestry is a "gardening in cloth." Of the sister of Lady Jane Grey he writes that she wept so much that "though the roses in her cheeks looked very wan and pale, it was not for want of watering."

79. Jeremy Taylor, 1613–1667

The second of the religious writers, Jeremy Taylor, was the author of *Holy Living* and *Holy Dying.* He was one of the chaplains of King Charles, though there was some hesitation about appointing him because of his youth. The young man was equal to the occasion, however, for he begged the archbishop to pardon that fault and promised to mend it if he lived. He certainly deserved anything that England could offer if the account of his early sermons is at all accurate, which says his audience was forced to take him for "some young angel, newly descended from the visions of glory."

Jeremy Taylor is always fresh and bright and interesting. In whatever he says, there is some turn of thought, some bit of sweetness or gentleness that is unlike the work of others. His similes especially are so simple and natural that once heard, they cannot be forgotten. He says:—

> *I have seen young and unskilful persons sitting in a little boat, when every little wave sporting about the sides of the vessel, and every motion and dancing of the barge seemed a danger, and made them cling fast upon their fellows: and yet all the while they were as safe as if they sat under a tree, while a gentle wind shaked the leaves into a refreshing and cooling shade. And the unskilful, inexperienced Christian shrieks out whenever his vessel shakes . . . and yet, all his danger is in himself, none at all from without.*

He loves nature, and he notices all the little things as well as the great. In likening the comforting words of a true friend to the coming of spring, he says:—

> *But so have I seen the sun kiss the frozen earth, which was bound up with the images of death and the colder breath of the north; and then the waters break from their enclosures, and melt with joy and run in useful channels; and the flies do rise again from their little graves in walls, and dance awhile in the air to tell that there is joy within.*

80. Richard Baxter, 1615–1691

The third of these writers of religious prose was Richard Baxter. In his youth he spent one month at court, but found a courtier's life unendurable. He became a clergyman of the Church of England and finally a thoroughgoing Puritan. He wrote *The Saint's Everlasting Rest;* and he might well turn his mind toward rest, for he lived in the midst of danger and persecution. "Methinks," he wrote, "among my books I could employ myself in sweet content, and bid the world farewell, and pity the rich and great that know not this happiness; what then will my happiness in heaven be, where my knowledge will be perfect?" Aside from Baxter's earnestness, his great charm lies in his simplicity and directness. Whoever reads the book feels as if the author were talking rather than writing, and talking directly to him and to no one else. He is sincere and powerful, but entirely without embellishments. He said he never had "leisure for polishing or exactness or any ornament." He thought of nothing but the good that he might do. When some one praised his books, he replied, "I was but a pen, and what praise is due to a pen?"

81. The "Cavalier Poets"

Entirely different from these earnest, serious preachers was a merry little group of "Cavalier Poets," as they have been called, all, save one, closely connected with the court of Charles I. In this group were four who were superior to the others of their class. They were Thomas Carew, Sir John Suckling, Richard Lovelace, and Robert Herrick.

82. Thomas Carew, 1589–1639

Carew was sewer, or cup-bearer to King Charles, and was a favorite at the court. He would probably have won just as much praise from the gay company around him if he had written as carelessly as some of them, but that was not Carew's way. His poems are not deep and powerful, but they are never careless. He begins with a thought, perhaps a very simple one, but he is as careful to express it smoothly and gracefully as if it were a whole epic. His lyrics are his best known work, especially the song, *Ask Me no More.* Quite different are they in tone from those of the "complaining" lovers of *Tottel's Miscellany.* Carew ventures to write *The Lady to Her Inconstant Servant;* but in Surrey's poems the "servant" never dreamed of being inconstant. Carew knows how to appreciate beauty, but again and again he turns from a pretty face to the qualities of heart and mind. Perhaps as well known as *Ask Me no More* are the first two stanzas of *Disdain Returned:—*

He that loves a rosy cheek,
Or a coral lip admires,
Or from star-like eyes doth seek
Fuel to maintain his fires,
As old Time makes these decay,
So his flames must waste away.

But a smooth and steadfast mind,
Gentle thoughts and calm desires,
Hearts, with equal love combined,
Kindle never-dying fires;
Where these are not, I despise
Lovely cheeks or lips or eyes.

83. Sir John Suckling, 1608–1642

Sir John Suckling used to laugh at Carew for being so careful to make his poems smooth and finished; for he himself tossed off a rhyme as lightly as one blows away a bit of thistledown. Somehow in reading the best of Suckling's poems, we can never get away from the feeling that Sir John himself is reciting them to us, and we fancy the mischievous sparkle of his eyes as he queries,—

Why so pale and wan, fond lover?
Prithee, why so pale?
Will, when looking well can't move her,
Looking ill prevail?
Prithee, why so pale?

Suckling wrote a gay little letter in rhyme to "Dick," who may have been Richard Lovelace, telling him about a wedding that he had attended. It is all merry and bright, but when he comes to talk about the bride, he is fairly bubbling over with fun.

Her feet beneath her petticoat,
Like little mice stole in and out,
As if they fear'd the light:

But O she dances such a way!
No sun upon an Easter-day
Is half so fine a sight.

This gay young courtier, rich, handsome, and talented, met with a sad fate. He spent four years wandering over the Continent, fought for the king of Sweden, returned to London, left the court for a time, but hastened back to aid the Royalist party. After the final victory of the Puritans, he fled from England.

In Spain he endured the most fearful tortures of the Inquisition, but finally escaped. All this was before he was thirty-four, for in that year of his age he died.

84. Richard Lovelace, 1618–1658

Richard Lovelace had a life equally full of changes. He, like Suckling, was a court favorite. He too was rich, handsome, and talented; and he too stood firmly by the man whom he believed to be his rightful sovereign. For the king's sake he bore imprisonment, and it was in prison that he wrote *To Althea,* with its famous lines,—

Stone walls do not a prison make,
Nor iron bars a cage!

There are two more lines of Lovelace's that are as familiar as any proverb,—

I could not love thee, dear, so much,
Loved I not honour more.

The woman whom he loved believed him to be dead, and married another man. He was in despair, and he cared little what became of him. He threw away his fortune, and finally died in the depths of poverty.

85. Robert Herrick, 1594–1674

The fourth of these Cavalier poets, and by far the greatest, was Robert Herrick. His life was quite different from that of the others in that he knew nothing of days at court. He had some fourteen years of quiet at Cambridge, and then twenty years of greater quiet as minister of a little country parish. He wrote more lyrics than any of his fellow poets, and a large number of them have that unexplainable quality which makes us say, "That is just the thought for the place."

"Robin" was one of the few men who are every inch alive. He loved the old Greek dances, but he could find amusement in watching his parishioners circle around an English Maypole. He wrote a *Thanksgiving* for his little house, his watercress, his fire, his bread, and his "belovéd beet" as simply and as sincerely as a child. Herrick enjoyed everything.

Where care
None is, slight things do lightly please,

he says gayly. He calls upon music,—

Fall on me like a silent dew,
Or like those maiden showers,
Which, by the peep of day, do strew
A baptism o'er the flowers;

but he is equally ready to chat in rhyme about his maid "Prewdence," his hen, his cat, his goose, or his dog Tracy.

Herrick wrote two collections of poems, *The Hesperides* and *Noble Numbers. The Hesperides* is all aglow with sunshine; it is full of "brooks, of blossoms, birds, and bowers," as he says in his argument. Chaucer writes of the springtime and of the longing that it gives folk to go on pilgrimage, but there is even more of the springtime eagerness to go somewhere under the open sky in Herrick's *Corinna's Going a-Maying.*

Get up, get up for shame! the blooming morn
Upon her wings presents the god unshorn.
See how Aurora throws her fair
Fresh-quilted colours through the air:
Get up, sweet slug-a-bed, and see
The dew bespangling herb and tree.

To "Julia" he writes a crisp little Night Piece,—

Her eyes the glow-worm lend thee,
The shooting stars attend thee;
And the elves also,
Whose little eyes glow
Like the sparks of fire, befriend thee.

He writes to "Corinna" or "Perilla" or "Anthea," but not with the agonies of Elizabethan lovers; for he seems to have no more choice among them than that one name will suit his line and another will not.

His religious poems, *Noble Numbers,* are somewhat different from those of the other writers of religious verse. He is no hermit, no recluse. "God is over the world, then let us enjoy it," is the spirit of his verse. He does not long for the mystic joys of martyrdom; he does not often beg for more blessings either spiritual or temporal; but he is grateful for what he has, and does not doubt that goodness and mercy will follow him all the days of his life. Even in his *Litany* there are no agonies of doubt and uncertainty. He prays for comfort, and he expects to receive it.

In the hour of my distress,
When temptations me oppress,
And when I my sins confess,
Sweet Spirit, comfort me.

. . . . . .

When the Judgment is reveal'd,
And that open'd which was seal'd;
When to Thee I have appeal'd,
Sweet Spirit, comfort me.

There is an unmistakable tone of sincerity in the following lines, one of the first poems in *Noble Numbers:—*

> *Forgive me, God, and blot each line*
> *Out of my book that is not Thine.*
> *But if, 'mongst all, thou find'st here one*
> *Worthy thy benediction;*
> *That one of all the rest shall be*
> *The glory of my work and me.*

One little corner of his writings is so unlike the rest of his poems that it might pass for the work of another author; but, save for that, Herrick is the most delightful, frank, refreshing man that one can imagine, fairly running over with the joy of living and with the cheerfulness that comes from finding great pleasure in small pleasures.

86. Izaak Walton, 1593–1683

One author who will not fall into line with the others of his day is Izaak Walton. The confusion and troubles of the Civil War did not suit him, and he slipped away to the country to find peace and quiet. He lived to be ninety years old, but not in loneliness, for his friends were always ready to go to see this man with his brightness, intelligence, and gentle, whimsical humor. He was not without occupation in his country home, for there he wrote the lives of several famous men of his time, Donne and Herbert among them. These *Lives* are so tender and sincere that they seem to be simple talks about friends who were dear to him, an ideal mode of writing biographies. Best of his works, however, is *The Compleat Angler.* In one way it is a wise little treatise on the different kinds of fish and the best modes of catching them; but its charm lies not in information about hooks and bait but in Walton's genuine love of the country and in the quaintness of his thoughts. He treats fishing with gravity, whether mock or real it is sometimes hard to tell. "Angling is somewhat like poetry," he declares learnedly, "men are to be born so;" and he gives as the epitaph of a friend, "An excellent angler, and now with God." "Look about you," he says, "and see how pleasantly that meadow looks; nay, and the earth smells so sweetly too: Come let me tell you what holy Mr. Herbert says of such days and flowers as these, and then we will thank God that we enjoy them,"—and he recites,—

Sweet day, so cool, so calm, so bright.

It is no marvel that his old friends never forsook the man who could chat so simply and delightfully. He is especially charming when he talks of music, whether it be the "smooth song which was made by Kit Marlow" or the inimitable melody of the nightingale. Of the latter he writes:—

> *But the nightingale, another of my airy creatures, breathes such sweet loud music out of her little instrumental throat, that it might make mankind to think miracles were not ceased. He that at midnight, when the very labourer sleeps securely, should hear, as I have very often, the clear airs, the sweet descants, the natural rising and falling, the doubling and redoubling of her voice, might well be lifted above earth, and say, "Lord, what musick hast thou provided for the Saints in Heaven, when thou affordest bad men such musick on Earth!"*

87. The Restoration, 1660

The year 1660 found England tired of Puritan control. Across the Channel was the son of Charles I., and he was invited to return and rule the land, as has been said. Unfortunately, he could not even rule himself, and his idea of being king was simply to have plenty of money and amusement. At first the nation could hardly help sympathizing with him and his merry Cavalier friends; for the last years had been dull and gloomy. After the supreme power fell into the hands of the Puritans, they suppressed as far as possible all public amusements, and they made no distinction between the brutalities of bull-baiting and the simple dancing around a Maypole which had so entertained Herrick. Much of this unreasonable strictness was due to men who were not really Puritans at heart, but who had joined the ruling party for the sake of power; and these men went beyond the others in severity in order to make themselves appear zealous converts.

88. Samuel Butler, 1612–1680

It is possible that some of these turncoats had a sly relish of a book which came out in 1662 and which threw the merry monarch and his court into gales of laughter. Its name was *Hudibras,* and it was written by one Samuel Butler. Among the few facts known of his life is that he was for some time a member of the household of a Puritan colonel. The gentleman never guessed that a caricature of himself was to be the laughing-stock of the son of the king whom his party had beheaded. This Puritan becomes in Butler's hands a knight who sets out with his squire, quite in the mediæval fashion, to range the country through and correct abuses. Thus is Sir Hudibras described:—

For he was of that stubborn crew
Of errant saints, whom all men grant
To be the true Church Militant:
Such as do build their faith upon
The holy text of pike and gun;
Decide all controversies by
Infallible artillery,
And prove their doctrine orthodox,
By Apostolic blows and knocks.

There was much comfort in this satire for the men who had been beaten by the "infallible artillery."

Nobody cares much to-day which side Butler made fun of. We value *Hudibras* for its amusing similes, its real wisdom, and its witty couplets, such as:—

The sun had long since in the lap
Of Thetis taken out his nap,
And, like a lobster boiled, the morn
From black to red began to turn.

Great conquerors greater glory gain
By foes in triumph led than slain.

He that complies against his will
Is of his own opinion still.

Butler is said to have expected a reward from the king and to have been disappointed. This was quite in the style of Charles II, whose gratitude was reserved for the favors which he hoped to receive.

89. Milton's Later Years

The only gratitude that can be felt toward Charles himself is for his negative goodness in not persecuting to the death John Milton, a man who had been so prominent during the Commonwealth and who had written the *Defence of the English People.* The poet was left to spend his later years in peace; and then it was that his mind turned toward a plan of his youth that had long been laid aside for the time of quiet that he hoped would come. He wished to write some long poem on a subject that was worthy of his ability. Just what that subject should be was not easy to decide. He thought of taking King Arthur for a hero and writing a British epic; but his plan broadened until he determined to write—

Of man's first disobedience, and the fruit
Of that forbidden tree, whose mortal taste
Brought death into the world, and all our woe,
With loss of Eden, till one greater Man
Restore us, and regain the blissful seat.

These are the first lines of *Paradise Lost.* The poem is based upon Revelation xii. 7-9, the third chapter of Genesis, and other passages in the Bible. Satan rebels against God and with his angels is cast out of heaven into the flames of hell. While they lie in chains, the world is created, and man is given the Garden of Eden for his home. Satan rouses his angels to revenge themselves by tempting man. He himself makes his way to Eden and persuades Eve to disobey the command of God. Adam joins her in the sin, and both are driven from Eden; but a vision is granted to show that man shall one day find redemption.

To treat so lofty a theme in such manner that the treatment shall not by contrast appear trivial and unworthy is a rare triumph. Milton has succeeded so far as success is possible. His imagination does not fail; his poetic expression is ever suited to his thought; the mere sound of his phrases is a wonderful organ music, for Milton is master of all the beauties and intricacies of poetic harmony. Short extracts give no idea of the majesty of the poem, though there are scores of lines that have become familiar in every-day speech.

The mind is its own place, and in itself
Can make a heaven of hell, a hell of heaven.

Not to know me argues yourselves unknown.

The world was all before them, where to choose.

Milton ever suits the word to the thought. To express harshness of sound he says:—

On a sudden open fly,
With impetuous recoil and jarring sound,
Th' infernal doors, and on their hinges grate
Harsh thunder.

There is the very hush of evening in the lines,—

Then silent night
With this her solemn bird and this fair moon.

Here is gliding smoothness:—

Liquid lapse of murmuring streams.

Milton had thought that the vision shown to Adam of the final redemption of man was all-sufficient; but a Quaker friend who had read the manuscript said to him, "Thou hast said much of Paradise lost, but what hast thou to say to Paradise found?" This simple question inspired Milton's second long poem, *Paradise Regained,* which he—and he only—preferred to the first. After this he wrote *Samson Agonistes,* a tragedy which conforms in every way to the rules of the Greek drama. These poems were dictated in his blindness. One sonnet, written during those years of darkness, explains the power by which he endured so crushing a misfortune:—

When I consider how my light is spent
Ere half my days, in this dark world and wide,
And that one talent which is death to hide,
Lodg'd with me useless, though my soul more bent
To serve therewith my Maker, and present
My true account, lest he returning chide;
"Doth God exact day-labour, light denied?"
I fondly ask: but Patience, to prevent
That murmur, soon replies, "God doth not need
Either man's work, or his own gifts; who best
Bear his mild yoke, they serve him best: his state
Is kingly; thousands at his bidding speed,
And post o'er land and ocean without rest;
They also serve who only stand and wait."

A child may find pleasure in the musical sound of *Paradise Lost,* but the fullest enjoyment and appreciation of the poem require familiarity not only with the Bible, but with classical literature. Four years after Milton's death a book came out which to children is a fascinating story and to the learned a marvellously perfect allegory, while to thousands of humble seekers after the way in which they should walk it has been a guide and an inspiration. This book is *The Pilgrim's Progress.*

90. John Bunyan, 1628–1688

It was written by John Bunyan, a man whose life was in many ways the opposite of Milton's, for he was poor and almost without even the simplest beginnings of education. There is small reason for thinking that Milton ever looked upon himself as in any respect a wrongdoer; but the rude village lad suffered for two years agonies of remorse for what he feared was the unpardonable wickedness of his boyhood. At last the light burst upon him. He believed that the sins of his youth had found forgiveness, and he had but one desire, to preach forgiveness to every one whom he could reach. His trade was that of a tinker, and as he went from place to place, he preached wherever any one would listen. There was little trouble in gathering audiences together; for the untaught villager began to show a vividness of speech, a rude eloquence, which held his hearers as if they were spellbound.

John Bunyan
1628–1688

Those were not days when a man might preach what he would. Charles II looked upon all dissenters as opposed to him. Bunyan had become a dissenter, and it did not occur to him to conceal his faith or even to preach with less boldness. He was promptly arrested and thrown into jail. "Will you promise to do no more preaching if you are set free?" the king's officers asked. Outside the jail were his wife and two little daughters, one of them especially dear to him because of her blindness; but Bunyan refused to make the promise. For twelve years he was a prisoner in Bedford Jail, doing whatever work he could get to support his family. At the end of that time he was free for a while, then came a second imprisonment. It was within the walls of the jail that he wrote *The Pilgrim's Progress,* the most perfect allegory ever produced. In this story, or "dream," Christian—no glittering knight, but a plain, every-day citizen—flees from the City of Destruction in quest of the Celestial City. He has many troubles; he falls into the Slough of Despond; he has to go by roaring lions; he encounters Apollyon; he passes through the Valley of Humiliation; he is beaten and persecuted at Vanity Fair; he wanders out of the way and falls into the hands of Giant Despair of Doubting Castle; and he goes tremblingly through the Valley of the Shadow of Death. But his way is not all gloom. He finds friendly entertainment and counsel at the House of the Interpreter; at the house built by the Lord of the Hill he rests "in a large upper chamber, whose window opened toward the sunrising, the name of the chamber was Peace;" he is shown far away the beauties of the Delectable Mountains, which are in Emmanuel's Land; the key of promise opens the way out of Doubting Castle. At last he and his friends stand beside the River of Death, which alone lies between them and the Celestial City; and when they have passed through the flood, behold two Shining Ones are beside them to help them up the hill to the City whose foundation is higher than the clouds. A heavenly host comes out to meet them and gives them ten thousand welcomes.

"Call at the gate," bid the Shining Ones, and the King commands that it shall be opened unto them. They go in, and all the bells of the City ring for joy. The dreamer looked in after them and he says, "The City shone like the sun; the streets also were paved with gold, and in them walked many men with crowns on their heads, palms in their hands, and golden harps to sing praises withal. . . . And after that they shut up the gates; which, when I had seen, I wished myself among them."

The Pilgrim's Progress is a wonderful book. It is the result of a thorough knowledge of the Bible, sincere religious feeling, and a glowing imagination that made real and tangible whatever thought it touched. No other writer could safely venture to name his characters Faithful or Pliable or Ignorance; but Bunyan makes these abstractions real. Faithful has other qualities than faithfulness, and he talks with Christian not like a shadow, but like a real human being. When Christian fights with Apollyon, there is no strife of phantoms, but a veritable contest, wherein Apollyon gave him a fall and would have pressed him to death had not Christian by good fortune succeeded in catching his sword and giving him a deadly thrust. The English of the book is pure and strong; but its great power lies neither in its English nor in the perfection of the allegory, but in the fact that in picturing his own religious struggles, Bunyan pictured those of many another man. "Look in thy heart and write," said Philip Sidney. One hundred years later, the unlettered tinker in Bedford Jail obeyed unconsciously the behest of the heir of the richest culture that England could give, and sent forth a masterpiece.

Bunyan wrote several other books, all of value, but none equal to *The Pilgrim's Progress.* After his release from prison and to the end of his life he devoted himself to the preaching that he loved.

91. John Dryden, 1631–1700

Neither Bunyan nor Milton wrote with any thought of pleasing the age in which he lived. Bunyan says explicitly,—

Nor did I undertake
Thereby to please my neighbor; no, not I.
I did it mine own self to gratify.

Milton surely had no preference of his own age in mind when he spent his last years on a work which he had little reason to think would find many readers among his contemporaries. The most important writer of the closing years of the century was their opposite in this respect. His name was John Dryden. He was born in 1631, of a Puritan family. Up to 1660, he wrote nothing that attracted any attention except a eulogy of Cromwell, but in that year he produced a glowing welcome to Charles II, wherein he declared that—

For his long absence Church and State did groan.

We owe much to Dryden, but his name would be even greater if he had not deliberately made up his mind to please the age in which he lived, and which, unfortunately, was an age of neither good morals nor good manners. The theatres, closed in 1642, were now flung open, and there was a call for plays. Many were written, but they were of quite different character from the plays of the sixteenth century. The Shakespearian inspiration had vanished, and the French desire for polish and carefulness of form now held sway. If the hero of a play was in circumstances that would naturally arouse deep feeling, the writer was expected to polish every phrase, but whether the speech sounded sincere was a matter of small moment. Indeed, it was regarded as in much better taste to repress all genuine emotion. This was enough to make a play cold and unreal; but another popular demand was still more destructive of a really great dramatic period, namely, that the plays should imitate the indecent manners of the court. A successful play, then, was required to be polished in form, gay and witty, but cold, and often vulgar and profane. Dryden yielded to this demand, especially in his comedies, but he was otherwise honest in his work, for he wrote carefully and thoughtfully. No other dramatic poet of the age was his equal; and, indeed, about whatever he wrote there was a certain strength and power that won attention and respect.

John Dryden
1631–1700

Dryden was careful to choose popular themes. He wrote a poem on the events of the year 1667, namely, the Great Fire of London, the Plague, and the War with the Dutch; not poetical subjects by any means, but subjects in which every one was interested and which afforded good opportunity for lines that would win applause, such as the following, which says that the English seaman—

Adds his heart to every gun he fires.

Life began to move easily and pleasantly with Dryden. He was favored by the king; his company was sought by men of rank, he was comfortable financially. His next step was to write satire. The country was full of plot and intrigue. Whoever wished to stand well with the king and his party must do his best to support them. Then it was that Dryden wrote his most famous satire, *Absalom and Achitophel.* In this there is a kind of character-reading that is quite different from Shakespeare's. Shakespeare was interested in all kinds of people and understood them because he sympathized with them. Dryden's aim in his satire was not to understand and sympathize, but to pick out the weakest points of his victims, to sting and to hurt. One man he described as—

Stiff in opinions, always in the wrong,
Was everything by starts and nothing long,
But in the course of one revolving moon
Was chymist, fiddler, statesman, and buffoon.

Dryden was ready to undertake any kind of literary work that was demanded by the times, and in the midst of his satires he wrote the *Religio Laici,* or "religion of a layman," and here he deserves honest praise. This poem is an argument in favor of the Church of England. To express difficult arguments in verse is not easy, but

Dryden has succeeded. His poem is clear and natural in its wording, smooth, dignified, and easy to read.

Shall I speak plain, and in a nation free
Assume an honest layman's liberty?
I think, according to my little skill,
To my own mother Church submitting still,
That many have been saved, and many may,
Who never heard this question brought in play.
The unlettered Christian, who believes in gross,
Plods on to Heaven and ne'er is at a loss;
For the strait gate would be made straiter yet,
Were none admitted there but men of wit.

Only a few years later Dryden became a member of the Roman Catholic Church and wrote *The Hind and the Panther,* wherein the milk-white hind represents the Church of Rome; the panther, beautiful but spotted, the church he had abandoned. Dryden could write witty lines, but his sense of humor was not strong enough to save him from the absurdity of setting two of the beasts of the field into theological argument. Still, here were the same excellencies as in the *Religio Laici,* the same grace and vigor. The poem deserved applause and won it.

Dryden translated the Æneid and other works. He wrote two beautiful odes for St. Cecilia's Day. In the second, known as *Alexander's Feast,* are many lines of the sort that stay in the memory, such as:—

None but the brave deserves the fair.

Sweet is pleasure after pain.

War, he sung, is toil and trouble;
Honour but an empty bubble.

Dryden's prose is of great value because of its clear, bracing style and general excellence. He wrote much criticism, not only in his *Essay of Dramatic Poesy,* but in the prefaces to his various plays; and criticism, aside from stray paragraphs, was something new in English literature. His sentences have not the majestic sonorousness of Milton's, but every phrase has its work to do and is placed where it can do that work best. In the hands of Dryden prose became a keen-edged instrument.

The year 1700 is marked by the death of this poet, critic, dramatist, and satirist. The seventeenth century had seen the noblest imaginative work of Shakespeare; the thoughtfulness for form of Ben Jonson; the accurate reasoning of Bacon; the gay trivialities, sometimes touched with seriousness, of the Cavalier poets; the tender grace of Walton; the earnestness, aspiration, and devotion of the writers of religious prose and poetry; the majesty of *Paradise Lost;* the spiritual symbolism of *The Pilgrim's Progress;* and now, last of all, had come John Dryden, who stood in the story of the century for the development of critical judgment. The glow of the Elizabethan inspiration had long since passed away. Looking forward to the eighteenth century, one could not hope to find a great imaginative poetry or a marked originality, but one could justly expect an unusual development of literary moderation and correctness.

SUMMARY

Century XVII

PURITANS AND ROYALISTS

First Quarter of the Century.

Francis Bacon.
Shakespeare's later work.
Ben Jonson.
Beaumont and Fletcher.
John Donne.

Literature of the Conflict and the Commonwealth.

John Milton, earlier poems and pamphlets.
Izaak Walton.

Religious poets:
George Herbert.
Richard Crashaw.
Henry Vaughan.

Religious Prose Writers:
Thomas Fuller.
Jeremy Taylor.
Richard Baxter.

Cavalier Poets:
Thomas Carew.
Sir John Suckling.
Richard Lovelace.
Robert Herrick.

Literature of the Restoration.

Samuel Butler.
Milton, later poems.
John Dryden.
John Bunyan.

In the early years of the seventeenth century Shakespeare produced his finest plays, the deeper comedies and the tragedies. His sonnets were published. Raleigh typifies the Elizabethan of universal ability.

Bacon wrote his *Instauratio Magna.* In 1611, the "King James version" of the Bible was produced.

Next to Shakespeare in greatness, but strongly contrasted with him in method of work and cast of mind, was Ben Jonson. His most interesting work is his masques. The romantic plays most like Shakespeare's were those of Beaumont and Fletcher. In 1623, thirty-six of Shakespeare's plays were collected and printed.

The drama gradually became less excellent; partly because it ceased to reflect life, partly because Puritan influence resulted in abandoning the theatre to the careless and immoral. In 1642 the theatres were closed.

The writers of the Commonwealth were all influenced to some extent by the "conceits" of Donne. Their writings were, first, meditative and critical, represented by the earlier work of Milton, many of his shorter poems and his pamphlets; second, earnestly religious, represented by the work of Herbert, Crashaw, and Vaughan in poetry and that of Fuller, Taylor, and Baxter in prose; third, in the lighter, merrier strain of the Cavalier poets, Carew, Suckling, Lovelace, and Herrick who also wrote religious poems. Izaak Walton belongs to none of these classes. *The Compleat Angler* is his best work.

After the Restoration of 1660 Butler caricatured the Puritans in *Hudibras;* Milton produced his greatest work, *Paradise Lost;* and Bunyan wrote the best of allegories, *The Pilgrim's Progress.*

The greatest writer of the last years of the century was Dryden. The drama revived, but valued polish rather than sincerity, and demanded indecency and the repression of emotion. Dryden lowered his work by yielding to the taste of the times. He wrote plays, poems on popular subjects, satire, religious argument in verse, and translated the Æneid and other works. Literary moderation and correctness marked the close of the century.

CHAPTER VII

Century XVIII

THE CENTURY OF PROSE

92. Coffee Drinking

Coffee drinking had a great deal to do with the development of literature in the eighteenth century. Some twenty years after Jonson's death, coffee became the fashionable drink, and coffee houses were opened by the hundred. These houses took the place of informal, inexpensive clubs; and gradually one became noted as headquarters for political discussion, another for social gossip, another for ship news, etc. "Will's" became the special meeting-place for literary men. Dryden was their chief, and around him circled several of those writers who were to do the best literary work of the early part of the eighteenth century.

Not long before Dryden's death, a boy of twelve slipped into the edge of the circle and stood gazing at the great man with dark, earnest eyes; for Dryden was the poet whom he most reverenced and admired. The boy was very small, he was badly deformed, and so helpless that he could not stand without supports; but his mind was wonderfully active, and he hoped to be able some day to write poems that would make him famous. He had already made some attempts that were amazingly good for a child.

93. Alexander Pope, 1688–1744

This boy's name was Alexander Pope. His father was a retired merchant who was exceedingly proud of his precocious son, while his mother looked upon him as the most marvellous boy that ever lived. The family

Alexander Pope
1688–1744

were Roman Catholics, and therefore he would not have been allowed to enter either of the universities even if he had been well; but he did a vast amount of reading and studying, though with very little formal instruction. Before he was twenty-one he had published several poems, he was well known among the literary men of the time, and associated with them upon equal terms. A dramatist four times his age had asked him for suggestions and criticisms. One suggestion which had come to him from William Walsh, a critic of the day, became the motto of his literary life. "Be correct," said

Walsh, "we have had great poets, but never one great poet that was correct." Pope set to work to be correct. He wrote and rewrote and polished and condensed and refined. In 1711, when he was only twenty-three, his *Essay on Criticism* came out. There is no originality in the poem; it is simply a combination of what Latin and French critics had said; but the thoughts are so clearly and concisely put that they seem new and fresh. For instance, there is no startling novelty in the statement that it is not well to use either obsolete words or recently formed, unauthorized words; but when Pope writes that—

In words, as fashions, the same rule will hold;
Alike fantastic, if too new or old:
Be not the first by whom the new are try'd,
Nor yet the last to lay the old aside,

we have a feeling that this is a most excellent way to express the thought. This feeling was what gave especial pleasure to the men of Queen Anne's day. Each separate thought of Pope's stands out like a crystal, and this clean-cut definiteness gave people the enjoyment that Shakespeare's perfect reading of men and his glowing imagination gave the people of his time.

Pope's next subject was even better suited to his talents. With the somewhat rough and ready manners of the age, a certain man of fashion had cut from the head of a maid of honor one of the—

Two locks which graceful hung behind
In equal curls, and well conspired to deck
With shining ringlets the smooth iv'ry neck.

The young lady was angry, and her family were angry. It was suggested to Pope that a mock-heroic poem about the act might help to pass the matter off with a laugh. This was the origin of *The Rape of the Lock,* one of the gayest, most sparkling little trifles ever written. Pope begins with a parody on the usual way of commencing an epic, and this comical air of importance is carried through the whole poem. The coming of the maid to adorn the heroine is expressed:—

Th' inferior priestess, at her altar's side,
Trembling begins the sacred rites of pride.

The adventurous baron resolves to gain the curl, and builds to Love an altar consisting of billets-doux, a glove, and gilt-edged French romances. The "fays, fairies, genii, elves, and demons" are propitious, and he sets out. He arms himself with a "little engine," a "two-edged weapon," that is, a pair of scissors.

The meeting points the sacred hair dissever
From the fair head, for ever and for ever!

A mimic war ensues and the lock vanishes. It takes its place among the stars and "adds new glory to the shining sphere."

Pope's next work was not a mock epic but a real epic, for he translated the *Iliad;* later, and with considerable assistance, the *Odyssey,* though his work can hardly be called a translation, for he knew very little Greek. It is rather a versification of the rendering of others. It is smooth, clear, and easy to read, but has not a touch of the old Greek simplicity or fire. Homer's *Iliad* comes from the wind-swept plain of Troy and the shore of the thundering sea; Pope's *Iliad* from a nicely trimmed garden. Nevertheless, gardens are not to be despised, and Pope's verses have the rare charm of a most exquisite finish and perfectness. Homer wrote, "The stars about the bright moon shine clear to see." Pope puts it:—

The moon, refulgent lamp of night!
O'er heaven's clear azure spreads her sacred light.

. . . . . .

Around her throne the vivid planets roll,
And stars unnumber'd gild the glowing pole.

It is no wonder that Richard Bentley, one of the greatest scholars of the day, said, "It is a pretty poem, Mr. Pope, but you must not call it Homer."

With the publication of these two works came not only fame but money. Pope made himself a home at Twickenham on the Thames, and with his widowed mother he spent there the rest of his life. He knew "everybody who was worth knowing," he was famous, and he was rich; on the other hand, he was such a sufferer that he spoke of his life as "one long disease." To his mother he was tenderness itself, and he was capable of a warm friendship, though one could not always count on its continuance; but to his enemies he was indeed just what they nicknamed him, "the wicked wasp of Twickenham," for he never hesitated to revenge in the most venomous verses any real or fancied slight. Even in *The Rape of the Lock* there are many scathing lines. At the severing of the curl the heroine cries out, and Pope says with an undertone of bitterness,—

Not louder shrieks to pitying heav'n are cast,
When husbands or when lap-dogs breathe their last;
Or when rich China vessels fall'n from high,
Inglitt'ring dust, and pointed fragments lie!

In 1728 Pope published a most malicious satire, *The Dunciad,* wherein every one who was so unfortunate as wittingly or unwittingly to have offended him was scourged most unmercifully, for he had forgotten his own words, "At every trifle scorn to take offence." Pope was the first literary man of his age, and he descended from his throne to chastise with his own hand every one who had not shown him due reverence. Men to whom he owed profound gratitude, but who had offended him in some trifle, and men who had been dead for years were attacked with equal spitefulness. Never was so great ability applied to so contemptible an object.

94. Pope's Later Years

The best work of Pope's later years was the *Essay on Man,* one of his *Moral Essays.* Didactic poetry can never have the winsome charm of imaginative; but whatever power to please the former may possess is shown in these *Essays.* There are scores of single lines and couplets that are as familiar as proverbs.

Worth makes the man, and want of it the fellow.
An honest man 's the noblest work of God.
Order is heaven's first law.
Man never is, but always to be blest.
And spite of pride, in erring reason's spite,
One truth is clear, Whatever is, is right.

Pope has given us the perfection of form and finish; but when we ask for "thoughts that breathe and words that burn," for thoughts so far beyond our own that we must bow in homage, they are lacking. Lofty imagination, sympathetic insight, humor, originality, depth, we do not find. Pope is great, but he is not of the greatest.

95. Addison and Steele

When Pope was a boy of twelve, there was living in a London garret a man just twice his age who was destined to become the best prose writer of Queen Anne's reign. He was dignified, reserved with strangers, and a little shy; but his ability to write had been so apparent that some time before this the Whigs had given him a pension of £300. This was not an infrequent act when the party in power wished to secure the adherence of a talented young writer. The king soon died, however, the Whigs were "out," and the young man, Joseph Addison, was left without resources. While he was living quietly in London, news came of the victory of Blenheim, and for perhaps the only time in the history of England, the government set out in quest of a poet. A friend recommended Addison, and he wrote a poem on the battle. One passage compared Marlborough to an angel who—

Pleased the Almighty's orders to perform,
Rides on the whirlwind and directs the storm.

These lines carried their author far on the road to success. One office after another was given to him, and the more he was known, the better he was liked. It was not easy to know him, for although with his friends he was the best companion in the world, the entrance of a stranger would silence him in a moment. Nevertheless, his kindness of heart could not be hidden, and this politician who could not make a speech was so warmly loved in Ireland, where he held a government position, that Dean Swift wrote him that the Tories and the Whigs were contending which should speak best of him.

Joseph Addison
1672–1719

While he was in Ireland a letter came to him from an old school friend, Richard Steele, which opened the way to a greater than political glory, though possibly when Addison read the letter, he only smiled and said to himself, "What will Dick do next!" "Dick" was one of Addison's worshippers. He had been a cheerful, warm-hearted boy, always getting into trouble, but so lovable that some one was usually ready to come to the rescue; and now that he was a man, he had changed very little.

He was married, but his "dearest Prue," his "prettiest woman," sometimes lived in luxury and sometimes was hard put to it to live at all in a house where food and fuel were so much a matter of chance. Steele had written some plays which were rather dull; and he had written a religious book which gave him considerable trouble, for his friends were always expecting him, he complained, to live up to his writings. Plainly, however, his mind turned toward literature, and as a reward for some pamphlets that he had produced, the position of Gazetteer had been given him, that is, the charge of the small sheet which published government news.

96. The Tatler, 1709–1711

These gazettes were exceedingly dull, and it occurred to Steele that to publish a small paper containing not only the news but a little interesting reading matter might be a successful undertaking. This paper was the famous *Tatler,* and it was of this that he wrote to Addison with so much enthusiasm. It was already well established, and instead of only being sent to the country by the tri-weekly post, as Steele had expected, it had been caught up by the London folk with the greatest eagerness. Its popularity was no marvel, for it was bright and entertaining. Steele wrote according to his mood; at one time a serious little sermon on ranking people according to their real merits and not according to their riches or honors; at another time a criticism of the theatre; at another, a half-jesting, half-earnest page on giving testimonials. This playful manner of saying serious things, with its opportunities for humor and pathos and character drawing, was exactly the mode of writing adapted to Addison, though he had never discovered it,—no great wonder, for this sort of essay was something entirely new. Bacon wrote "essays," but with him the word meant simply a preliminary sketch of a subject as opposed to a finished treatise. These light, graceful chats on politics, manners, literature, and art were meant for the day only, but they were so well done that they have become classics.

Suddenly Steele announced that the *Tatler* had come to its end. One reason that he gave for its discontinuance was that the previous numbers would make four volumes! He published them in book form with a whimsical and generous little acknowledgment of the help that he had received from Addison. "This good Office he performed with such Force of Genius, Humour, Wit, and Learning, that I fared like a distressed Prince, who calls in a powerful Neighbour to his Aid; I was undone by my Auxiliary; when I had once called him in, I could not subsist without Dependance on him."

97. The Spectator, 1711–1713

The *Tatler* had run for nearly two years. Two months after its closing number appeared, Steele and Addison united in publishing the *Spectator*, which came out every day but Sunday. This is even more famous than the *Tatler*, and its fame is due chiefly to "Sir Roger de Coverley," a character introduced by Steele and continued by Addison. Sir Roger is drawn as having been a gay young man of the town; but at the time of his appearance in the *Spectator* he is a middle-aged country gentleman, hale and hearty, loved by every one, believing himself to be the sternest of quarter-session justices, but in reality the softest-hearted man that ever sat on the bench. His servants and his tenants all love him. He has a chaplain whom he has chosen for good sense and understanding of backgammon, rather than for learning, as he did not wish to be "insulted with Latin and Greek" at his own table.

All through these essays there is kindly humor, vivacity, and originality; and all is expressed with exquisite simplicity and clearness in a style so perfectly suited to the thought that the reader often forgets to notice its excellence. The subjects, as in the *Tatler,* were anything and everything, and the essays themselves were the chat of refined, intelligent people; they were a kind of ideal coffee-house "extension."

98. Addison's Other Work

The *Spectator* came to an end as suddenly as the *Tatler.* A third paper, the *Guardian,* was begun after a short time; but between these two Addison brought out his drama *Cato.* It was a perfectly well-bred play,—dignified and cold. The *Spectator* represented Addison with his friends; *Cato* represented Addison with strangers. But, most unreasonably, this rather uninteresting drama was a distinct success; for both Tories and Whigs claimed to be described in its fine speeches, and every one wanted to see it. Addison probably thought it far superior to his essays; but neither that nor any other poetical work of his is of special value, except a few of his hymns. Addison's religion was sincere, and gave to his pen the inspiration which the theatre failed to furnish. His paraphrase of the twenty-third psalm, "The Lord my pasture shall prepare," is excellent; but in "The spacious firmament on high" there is a certain majesty and breadth that has rarely been excelled. He became the Secretary of State, but died when only forty-seven years of age. Merry Dick Steele became Sir Richard on the accession of George I. Before he was sixty, his health failed and he retired to the country. There is a tradition that in the feebleness of his last months he insisted on being carried out to see the villagers dance on the green and to give them prizes.

99. Jonathan Swift, 1667–1745

There were two men of the time of Queen Anne whose names are familiar to-day chiefly because each wrote a book that children like. The name of the first was Jonathan Swift, that of the second was Daniel Defoe. The first time that Addison saw Swift was at a coffee-house. A tall stranger in the garb of a clergyman stalked into the room, laid his hat on a table, and began to stride back and forth. After half an hour he paid the usual penny at the bar and walked away. This was the eccentric clergyman who had come from his home in Ireland to make a visit to England. He had been secretary to Sir William Temple, and he had written a book called the *Tale of a Tub*. This is an allegory wherein a dying father gives his sons Peter, Martin, and Jack (that is, the Church of Rome, the Lutherans, and the Calvinists) each a coat which will last throughout their lives if kept clean. The book describes the comical and sometimes unseemly acts of the three. Swift showed great ability to write clear, strong prose; but he used coarse mockery, reckless audacity, and cynical scorn, such unfit weapons for religious discussion that the clergyman author should have given up all hope of advancement in the church. His book, however, was so brilliant a satire that it gave him at once high rank as a wielder of the pen.

In 1704, the year of the publication of the *Tale of a Tub,* he also brought out the *Battle of the Books.* This had been written some time before to help Sir William Temple out of an embarrassing situation. Sir William had written an essay claiming that ancient literature was superior to modern, and had praised particularly a work which was soon afterward shown to be a modern forgery. The secretary dashed into the fray, treating the dispute with a sarcastic seriousness which soon became coarse and savage.

Swift had charge of a tiny parish not far from Dublin, but he went often to England, sometimes remaining several years. He wrote political pamphlets whose malignant ridicule delighted his politician friends. He cared little for money or for fame, but he longed for political power; and when he saw it dropped lightly into the hands of men who had not half his talents, he felt a savage scorn of those who would give authority so easily to men who held it so unworthily. He hoped to be given an English bishopric, but in view of the wrath which his *Tale of a Tub* had aroused, the utmost that his friends ventured to do was to make him Dean of St. Patrick's Cathedral in Dublin. Each piece of satire that Swift produced seemed more savage than what had preceded it. One of the most bitter is his *Modest*

Proposal, which suggested that the children of poor Irish parents should be served for food on the tables of the landlords, who, he says, "as they have already devoured most of the parents, seem to have the best title to the children." The cold, business-like method by which he arranges the details of his plan is as horrible as it is

Jonathan Swift
1667–1745

powerful. *Gulliver's Travels* was written as a satire, and expressed his hatred and scorn of men perhaps more fiercely than any other of his writings; but "Gulliver's" journeys to Lilliput and Brobdingnag are, forgetting the allegory and leaving out the occasional coarseness, most charming stories for children. Nothing could be more minutely accurate than his description of the little people of Lilliput, who are barely six inches high. They bring him a hogshead of wine, which holds just half a pint. They ascertain his height by the aid of a quadrant, and, finding its relation to theirs, they decide that he needs exactly 1724 times as much food as one of themselves. Swift makes no slip. From beginning to end, everything is consistent with the country of six-inch people. In Brobdingnag, matters are reversed, for Brobdingnag is a land of giants where Gulliver has a terrible encounter with a rat of the size of a large mastiff, has to swim for his life in a vast bowl of cream, and comes nearest to death when a year-old baby tries to cram him into its mouth. So perfectly is the illusion carried out that the hero is represented on his return to his own country as stooping to enter his house because the door seems to him so dangerously low.

If it were not for chance words and for Swift's letters, we should think of him as half mad with hatred and scorn; but two men as unlike as Pope and Addison cherished his friendship. Pope wrote that he loved and esteemed him, and Addison dedicated a book to him as "the most agreeable companion, the truest friend, and the greatest genius of his age." Somewhere in his nature there was a charm which held both the "wicked wasp of Twickenham" and the gentle, ever courteous Addison. His letters, too, written to "Stella," his pet name for a young girl whom he knew and taught at Sir William Temple's, are frankly affectionate; and even as she grew to mature womanhood, he still reported to her all the chat of the day and the little happenings to himself in which he knew she would be interested.

Be you lords or be you earls,
You must write to naughty girls,

he wrote to her. In 1728 Stella died, and this hater of his race and lover of individuals sorrowfully held for an hour the unopened letter that he knew announced her death. There was from the first a wild strain of insanity in this many-sided man, and for several years before his death his mind failed. He died in 1745.

100. Daniel Defoe, 1661?–1731

Swift would have looked upon it as the very irony of fate if he had known that his most bitter satire had become a book for children; but Daniel Defoe would have been pleased, though perhaps a little amused, to find that his *Robinson Crusoe,* which he published as a real account of a real man, had become not only a children's book but a work of the imagination. Defoe was educated to be a non-conformist clergyman, but he was little adapted to the profession. He was like Steele in his proneness to get into scrapes, but unlike Steele, he could usually find a way out. When "King Monmouth" made his attempt to gain the throne, Defoe was one of his adherents; but in some way he escaped punishment, and afterwards became a strong supporter of William and Mary. He soon showed that he could write most forcible English, and his *Shortest Way with Dissenters* proved him almost as much of a satirist as Swift himself. There is a vast difference, however, in the satire of the two men; for Defoe shows nothing of Swift's hatred of his race; and, earnest as he makes himself appear in his pamphlets, we always think of him as smiling wickedly over his pen to think how well he was befooling his readers. In this pamphlet he succeeded almost too well. He suggested that an excellent means of securing religious uniformity would be to hang dissenting ministers and banish their people. It was a time of severe laws and stern retribution, and the Dissenters were actually alarmed. Moreover, Parliament, too, persisted in taking the matter seriously, declared the pamphlet a libel on the English nation, and condemned its author to stand in the pillory. Most men would have been somewhat troubled, but Defoe and his pen were equal to the occasion; and while in prison awaiting his punishment, he wrote an *Ode to the Pillory,* which he called a state machine for punishing fancy. He closed with a message to his judges,—

Tell them: The men that placed him here
Are scandals to the Times!
Are at a loss to find his guilt,
And can't commit his crimes!

Defoe carried the day. He stood in the pillory; but flowers were heaped around him, he was cheered by crowds of admiring bystanders, and thousands of copies of his *Ode* were sold.

Defoe was the most inventive, original man of his age, and he even published an *Essay on Projects,* suggesting all sorts of new things. Among them was his plan for giving to women the education which was then limited to men. He said, "If knowledge and understanding had been useless additions to the sex, God Almighty would never have given them capacities; for he made nothing useless." Strikingly similar to these words of Defoe is the statement of Matthew Vassar a century and a half later in founding the first college for women: "It occurred to me that woman, having received from her Creator the same intellectual constitution as man, has the same right as man to intellectual culture and development."

Daniel Defoe
1659–1731

One of Defoe's projects came to more fame and importance than he dreamed. Every one was interested in a sailor named Alexander Selkirk, who had been abandoned on the island of Juan Fernandez, and who, after five years of loneliness, had been rescued and brought to England. Defoe went with the rest of the world to see the man and talk with him; but while others soon forgot his story, Defoe remembered, and a few years later he wrote *Robinson Crusoe,* an account of a man who was wrecked on a desert island with nothing except a knife, a pipe, a little tobacco in a box, and a hope of getting some articles from the wreck of the vessel. This book became a favorite at once. It was so realistic that every reader fancied himself in the sailor's place and planned with him what to do for safety and comfort. This is just where Defoe's unique power lies, in putting himself in the place of his characters. In *Robinson Crusoe* he imagined himself on the island and thought how he could get to the vessel, for instance, and how he should feel to find a footprint on the sand when he supposed that he was entirely alone. Having fancied what he should do, it was easy to put his thoughts into clear, simple English, never forgetting that his aim was to tell a story, not to ornament phrases. The book was so successful that Defoe wrote a continuation of the adventures of his hero. It was very like him to insert an aggrieved little preface, taking high moral grounds against the "envious people" who had called his work a romance, and saying that doing such deeds was "a Practice all honest Men abhor."

Three years after *Robinson Crusoe* appeared, Defoe produced his *Journal of the Plague Year,* which, was written, the title-page gravely asserts, "by a citizen who continued all the while in London." This was literally true, although the aforesaid citizen was but four or five years old at the time of the visitation. The book describes minutely all the details of the terrible season, from the piteous "Lord, have mercy upon us!" written on the houses to the coming of the horrible dead cart that sometimes carried away the dying with the dead. It is most impressive, and has more than once been quoted as authority on the events of the pestilence. Defoe wrote several picaresque stories, or stories having rascals for heroes, each tale expected, according to the preface of the author, to bring any wicked reader to repentance.

101. The Age of Queen Anne — The Novel

Taking a general view of the Age of Queen Anne, we see that it was marked, first, by the development of literary criticism; and, second, by the excellence of its prose and the beginning of the periodical. In poetry especially certain principles were tacitly adopted as producing the correctness which the age demanded. The five-beat line of Dryden and Pope, with the thought neatly enclosed within a well-polished rhymed couplet, became the generally accepted ideal of perfection. This did not tend to a free manifestation of poetical ability; but it did tend to produce prose so accurate, graceful, and agreeable as to become the glory of the Age of Anne. Its best manifestation was in the periodicals whose establishment was the second distinguishing mark of the age. They had been preceded by newspapers; but the *Tatler* and the *Spectator* were not bare chronicles of events, they were not the controversial weeklies of the Civil War, they were real literature, and their prose had not only usefulness but beauty.

Prose was soon to discover a new field, the novel. There had been Elizabethan romances, *The Pilgrim's Progress,* Dryden's translations, and the slender thread of narrative fiction in the *Spectator.* Then had come *Robinson Crusoe,* which, like *The Pilgrim's Progress,* was artistic enough to satisfy the most critical and simple enough to delight the most ignorant. The next step was the novel, that is, the story which pictures real life and deals with the passions, especially that of love. The novel must have a plot, it must have prominent and secondary characters; and, just as in a play, these characters must act naturally and must change as they are acted upon by incidents or by other characters.

102. Samuel Richardson, 1689–1761

The first book that fully answered these requirements was written by Samuel Richardson, a successful middle-aged printer. He had never written a book, but he had written letters by the score, and had written them so well that some one suggested his publishing a series of letters about every-day home life to serve as models for those who lacked his ability. The idea struck Richardson favorably, and it occurred to him that the interest would be increased if there were some thread of connection between the letters. The result was *Pamela*, or *Virtue Rewarded*, the first English novel. It came out in 1740, declaring on its title-page that its object was "to cultivate the Principles of Virtue and Religion." Pamela Andrews is a friendless young woman who is persecuted by the attentions of a fashionable

Samuel Richardson
1689-1761

reprobate. Finally, after being converted to honor and uprightness by her virtue, he offers her marriage, and she accepts him. The story goes on, volume after volume; but the fiction-hungry people of 1740 were sorry when it came to an end.

103. Henry Fielding, 1707–1754

Everybody was interested in *Pamela,* but a writer of comic plays named Henry Fielding was not only interested but amused; for the sentimentality of the book and its rather patronizing tone of giving good moral advice struck him as being ludicrous. Straightway he seized his pen and began in caricature *Joseph Andrews.* Joseph is Pamela's brother, and he is as much tormented by the devotion of a certain widow as was Pamela by the attentions of her persecutor. Fielding had more ability to make his characters seem real than Richardson, but he was not the superior of the publisher in delicate strokes and careful attention to details.

Within thirteen years after the appearance of *Pamela,* Richardson wrote two more novels, *Sir Charles Grandison* and his best work, *Clarissa Harlowe.* There were eight volumes of *Clarissa,* and after the appearance of the first four, Richardson was besieged by letters without number, telling him how their writers had wept over his pathos, and beseeching him to give the story a happy ending. Fielding, too, produced other novels, and of these, *Tom Jones* is his best work. Fielding is strong and robust. His novels are as breezy as if they had been written on a mountain top and as true to life as if they had come from the very heart of a London crowd. Unfortunately, they as well as, in varying degree, all the novels of the time, are marked by what seems to the present age a revolting coarseness.

104. Tobias Smollett, 1721–1771

Two other novelists were soon added to the company, Tobias George Smollett and Laurence Sterne. Smollett studied medicine and went to sea as a ship doctor, but his real interest was literature, and in 1748 he wrote *Roderick Random,* which pictures many scenes from his own life, with here and there a bit of tenderness or whimsicality. Several other works followed this, animated and interesting, but without Fielding's accurate character drawing.

105. Laurence Sterne, 1713–1763

Sterne was an Irish clergyman with a good income and an irregular talent. His three works are as inconsistent as the man himself, for one is a collection of sermons; one, *Tristram Shandy,* a whimsical delineation of home life with one or two delightful characters; and one, *The Sentimental Journey.* In this Sterne is sometimes frankly immoral; sometimes he gives us beautiful little descriptions; sometimes his sentiment is ridiculously affected; sometimes he gives such passages as the following meditation on the Bastile:—

> *And as for the Bastile—the terror is in the word.—Make the most of it you can, said I to myself, the Bastile is but another word for a tower;—and a tower is but another word for a house you can't get out of.—Mercy on the gouty! for they are in it twice a year—but with nine livres a day, and pen and ink and paper and patience, albeit a man can't get out, he may do very*

well within,— at least for a month or six weeks; at the end of which, if he is a harmless fellow, his innocence appears, and he comes out a better and wiser man than he went in.

After thus moralizing himself into satisfaction, suddenly he hears a starling in a cage who has learned to say the one sentence, "I can't get out." Sterne's mood changes. He writes a glowing address to liberty, pictures one captive and his sorrows, and sends his servant away, "not willing he should see anything upon my cheek which would cost the honest fellow a heartache."

106. Samuel Johnson, 1709–1784

The decade marked by the beginning of the novel was from 1740 to 1750. The chief place of literary honor during the thirty years following 1750 is given to a man whose essays are not so good as those of Addison and Steele, whose dictionary was antiquated long ago, whose principal story is voted dry, whose edition of Shakespeare is worthless, and whose *Lives of the Poets* alone is of any special value today. This man was Samuel Johnson. He was the sickly, nervous son of a Lichfield bookseller. He made his way to the university, pitifully poor, but too independent to accept help. A few years later, he opened a private school for boys. He was very large and awkward; he rolled from side to side when he walked; he grumbled and muttered, and his face, seamed and scarred by disease, trembled and twitched. The wonder is not that the school was a failure, but that even one pupil ventured to attend it. After the failure Johnson went to London with a capital of twopence half-penny and a partly completed tragedy. His aim was to find literary work; and for some time he did whatever there was to do. After ten years or more of drudgery, he was little richer than at first; but he had become so well known that several booksellers united in offering

Dr. Johnson
1709–1784

him fifteen hundred guineas to prepare a dictionary of the English language. Seven or eight years of hard work passed, and the book was completed. It shows that its author knew nothing of etymology,—but in those days comparatively little was known of the science by any one,—its definitions are sometimes exceedingly good, and sometimes based upon the whims of the writer; for instance, he hated the Scotch, and therefore he defined oats as "grain which in England is generally given to horses, but in Scotland supports the people." It was still the feeling in England that a book of such importance should be dedicated to a "patron," who was expected to return the honor by an interest in the work and generous assistance. The plan of the dictionary had been addressed to Lord Chesterfield, and this dainty nobleman at first encouraged its author; but he soon tired of the uncouth scholar, whom he called "a respectable Hottentot, who throws his meat anywhere but down his throat," and was "not at home" to his calls.

When it was known that the dictionary was about to appear, Chesterfield became interested, and hoped, in spite of his neglect, to secure the dedication to himself. He published letters recommending it, but they were too late. Johnson published in return a reply which was calm and dignified, but so scathing that it practically ended literary patronage save that of the public. The book came out. It was infinitely better than anything preceding, and it was received with an enthusiasm which in this age of dictionaries can hardly be imagined.

In the course of the seven years that Johnson spent on the dictionary, he published the *Rambler,* a periodical made up of essays written after the fashion of Addison's, but lacking Addison's light touch and graceful humor. Neither these nor the dictionary added any large amount to the author's finances; and when, in 1759, the death of his mother occurred, he had not money for the funeral expenses. To raise it, he wrote in the evenings of one week, *Rasselas, Prince of Abyssinia.* This is usually called a story, but the characters serve only as mouthpieces for the various reflections of the author. "Abyssinia" is simply a convenient name for an imaginary country.

Three years after the publication of the dictionary the government offered Johnson a pension of £300. Even in his poverty the independent lexicographer hesitated to accept it; and well he might, for in his dictionary he had defined a pension as "pay given to a state hireling for treason to his country;" but he was finally made to see that the offered gift was not a bribe but a reward for what he had already accomplished. He accepted it, and then life became easier.

107. James Boswell, 1740–1795

It was about this time that he met a Scotchman named Boswell, who became his humble worshipper. Wherever Johnson went, Boswell followed. Boswell asked all sorts of questions, both useful and idle, just to see what reply his oracle would make. The great man snubbed the little man, and the little man hastened home to write in his journal what a superb snub it was. Mrs. Boswell was not pleased. "I have seen a bear led by a man," she said, "but never before a man led by a bear." Johnson once wrote her, "The only thing in which I have the honour to agree with you is in loving him;" for the young worshipper had at last won a return of affection from his idol. For twenty years he wrote at night every word that he could remember of Johnson's conversation through the day. It was well worth noting, for Johnson was the best talker of the age. Now that his pension relieved him of want, he had little inclination to make the effort required by writing, but he was ever ready to talk. Much of his best talking was done at the famous Literary Club, which he, Sir Joshua Reynolds, and Edmund Burke founded. He always seemed to feel that literary composition required the use of long words and a ponderous rolling up of phrases; but his conversation was direct and simple. He argued, he spoke of history, of biography, of literature or morals. His scholarship, his powerful intellect, and his colloquial powers gave value to whatever he said. When a new book came out, the first question asked by the public was, "What does the Club say of it?" Johnson was the great man of the Club, and for years he was really, as he has so often been called, the literary dictator of England.

108. Johnson's Later Work

During the last twenty years of his life he did a comparatively small amount of literary work. He edited Shakespeare, an undertaking for which his slight knowledge of the sixteenth century drama had given him but an ill preparation. He journeyed to Scotland, and was treated so kindly that much of his prejudice against the Scotch melted away. His letters about this journey, written to a friend, were easy and natural; but when he made them into a book, *The Journey to the Hebrides,* they were translated into the ceremoniously elaborate phraseology which alone he regarded as worthy of print. His best work was his *Lives of the Poets,* a series of sketches prepared for a collection of English poetry. These were intended to be very short, but Johnson became interested in them, and did far more than he had agreed. The result is not only brief "lives" of the authors but criticisms of their writings. These criticisms are not always just, for sometimes Johnson's strong prejudices and sometimes his lack of the power to appreciate certain qualities stood in the way of fairness; but, fair or unfair, they are the honest expression of an independent, powerful mind, and every one is well worth reading. This was Johnson's last work. He died in 1784.

109. Oliver Goldsmith, 1728–1774

One of Johnson's special friends at the Club was the poet Oliver Goldsmith, a genial, gay-hearted Irishman, a boy all his life. What to do with him was always a puzzling question to his friends. His bishop would not accept him as a clergyman, either because of his pranks at the university or because of the scarlet breeches which he insisted upon wearing. A devoted uncle sent him to London to study law; but on the way he was beguiled into gambling and did not reach the city. He began to study medicine at Edinburgh; made his way to Leyden for further instruction; borrowed money to go to Paris, but spent it on rare tulip bulbs for his uncle; and finally set out to travel over the Continent "with but one spare shirt, a flute, and a single guinea." He took his degree probably at Padua, went to London, read proof for Richardson, acted as tutor in an academy, wrote children's books—possibly *Goody Two Shoes.* He thought of going to India as a physician, of exploring central Asia, of journeying to Aleppo to study the arts of the East. He had no special longing to become a knight of the quill, but he needed money and he wrote. *Letters from a Citizen of the World* brought him a small sum; an agreeable little *History of England* brought more; but Goldsmith had no more providence than a sparrow, and soon Johnson, like his early friends in Ireland, began to wonder what to do with "Noll." His careless fashion of living was entirely different from Johnson's sturdy uprightness; but Johnson's heart was big enough to sympathize with him, and when a message came one morning that Goldsmith was in great trouble, Johnson guessed what the matter was and sent him a guinea, following it himself as soon as possible.

Goldsmith had not paid his rent, and his landlady had arrested him. The two men discussed what could be done, and Goldsmith produced the manuscript of a novel ready for the press. Johnson carried it to a bookseller and sold it for £60. This was the manuscript of the *Vicar of Wakefield;* but the publisher did not realize what a prize he had won, and was in no haste to bring the book out. In the mean time, Goldsmith's *Traveller* appeared. Then there was a sensation at the Club; for, save by Johnson, Reynolds, Burke, and perhaps a few others, Goldsmith has been looked upon as a mere literary drudge. He had felt the unspoken contempt, and had been awkward and ill at ease. Now that the Club and the other literary folk of the day declared that the *Traveller* was the best poem that had appeared since the death of Pope, Goldsmith's peculiarities were no longer called awkwardness, but the whims of a man of genius. Then came out the *Vicar of Wakefield* with its ridiculous plot, its delightful humor, its gentleness, its comical situations, and the exquisite grace of style that marked the work of Goldsmith's pen, whether poem or novel or history. Again the literary world was delighted; but the £60 received for the manuscript had long ago been spent. His next work was a comedy, *The Good-Natured Man.* This gave him £500; and straightway he began to live as if he were to have £500 a month. Soon his pockets were empty, and the much praised Dr. Goldsmith was again at the beck and call of the booksellers. He wrote history,

Oliver Goldsmith
1728–1774

natural history, whatever they called for; one thing was as easy as another. In 1770 he wrote *The Deserted Village.* Like almost all of Pope's work, this is written in the rhymed heroic couplet, but here the resemblance ends. Pope's writings were polished; Goldsmith's were marked by an inimitable natural charm, the charm of a graceful style, of a tenderness and delicate humor of which Pope never dreamed. The idea of the poem is pathetic; but the parts that come to mind oftenest are the sympathetic description of the village pastor who was "passing rich with forty pounds a year," and the picture of the schoolmaster:—

In arguing, too, the parson owned his skill,
For, even tho' vanquished, he could argue still;
While words of learned length and thundering sound
Amazed the gazing rustics ranged around;
And still they gazed, and still the wonder grew,
That one small head could carry all he knew.

Once more Goldsmith wrote a play, *She Stoops to Conquer.* This was founded upon his own adventures when first possessed of a guinea and a borrowed horse. "Where is the best house in the place?" he had demanded in a strange village with all the airs that he fancied to be the mark of an experienced traveller. The home of a wealthy gentleman was mischievously pointed out, and the young fellow rode up to the door, gave his orders right and left, and finally invited his host and family to join him in a bottle of wine. The host had discovered that the consequential youngster was the son of an old friend, and he carried on the mistake till the boy was about to take his leave.

This play was Goldsmith's last work. His income had become sufficient for comfort; but he had no idea how to manage it, and he was always in debt. He died when not yet forty-six years of age, the same careless, generous, lovable boy to the end. His bust was placed in Westminster Abbey by the Club. Johnson wrote the inscription, which said that he "left scarcely any style of writing untouched, and touched nothing that he did not adorn."

110. Edmund Burke, 1729–1797

This period, already so rich in essays and novels and poetry, was also marked by oratory and history. Its greatest orator was Edmund Burke, an Irishman, who made his way to England and began his literary work by publishing essays about the time when Johnson's dictionary came out, the most famous being *On the Sublime and Beautiful.* Johnson admired him heartily, and felt that in him he had an opponent worthy of his steel. "That fellow calls forth all my powers," he said. At another time he declared that a stranger could not talk with Burke five minutes in the street without saying to himself, "This is an extraordinary man."

Burke entered Parliament and was one of the most prominent figures of the House in the stormy days preceding the American Revolution. Then it was that he made his famous *Speech on Conciliation with America.* On the part of the government he was the most prominent prosecutor of Warren Hastings for abuse of power in India. The Reign of Terror in France called forth his *Reflections on the French Revolution.* Burke was not merely a politician; he was a thinker and orator and poet who devoted himself to politics. The thought is always first with him, but in the expression of the thought he is generous in his use of poetical adornment; and yet his adornment is vastly more than a mere decoration. In his *Conciliation,* for instance, no statistics would have given his audience nearly so good an idea of the energy and enterprise of the colonists as his picturesque description of the manner in which they had carried on the whale fishery:—

> *Whilst we follow them among the tumbling mountains of ice, and behold them penetrating into the deepest frozen recesses of Hudson's Bay and Davis's Straits, whilst we are looking for them beneath the Arctic Circle, we hear that they have pierced into the opposite region of polar cold, that they are at the antipodes, and engaged under the frozen Serpent of the north.*

111. William Robertson, 1721–1793

The historians of the eighteenth century are represented by William Robertson, David Hume, and Edward Gibbon. Robertson was a Scotch clergyman who wrote of three different countries, *A History of Scotland during the Reigns of Queen Mary and James the Sixth,* in 1759; then *The History of Charles V. of Germany;* and finally, *A History of America.*

112. David Hume, 1711–1776

David Hume was also a Scotchman, a man of such indomitable perseverance that his energy was not conquered even by years of unsuccessful effort. At twenty-three he determined to devote himself to literature. His first book was a failure, but he struggled on with many failures and small success. He was not the kind of man to be discouraged, and with the utmost composure he set to work on a *History of England.* The first volume failed. He wrote a second. That failed. He wrote a third. It was received with some slight interest. He continued, and at last the reading world began to appreciate what he had done. They discovered that whatever was narrated was told vividly, that Hume recognized a great event when he saw it, and took pains to trace not only its effect but the causes which led up to it; and that he was interested not only in great events but in the people and their ways. One fault was common to both Hume and Robertson, or possibly in some degree to their age, a lack of historical accuracy, the most unpardonable fault in a writer of history.

113. Edward Gibbon, 1737–1794

No such charge can be made against the writings of Edward Gibbon. He was an Englishman with whom, even as a boy, the love of history was a passion. The idea of writing the *History of the Decline and Fall of the Roman Empire* came to him in Rome in 1764, but the first volume did not appear until 1776. The labor involved in preparing this work was enormous. It was not the simple story of a single people, but a complicated narrative involved with the history of all Europe. Merely to collect the necessary knowledge was a gigantic task. It demanded a most powerful intellect to arrange the facts, and to show their proper connection; a remarkable literary ability to present them clearly and attractively. All this Gibbon did, a little ponderously sometimes, but vividly and eloquently. He is by far the greatest of the eighteenth century historians.

114. New Qualities in Literature

In the literature of the last quarter of the century certain qualities were seen which were new chiefly in that they were much more strongly manifested than before. First, there was more interest in man simply because he was man, and not because he was rich or of noble birth. The revolution in America and the early part of the revolution in France emphasized the idea that every one, no matter of how lowly a position, possessed rights. Second, there was a genuine love of real nature, not nature made into clipped hedges and gravelled walks. Third, there was a certain impatience of restraint, an unwillingness to accept the conclusions of others. Subjects were chosen that were of personal interest to the author and were therefore treated with warmth of feeling.

115. Thomas Gray, 1716–1771

These qualities were the marks of what is known as the romantic revival, a revolt against the artificial formality of Pope and his followers. Even while Pope was alive and at the height of his fame, poets in both Scotland and England began to manifest a sincere love for nature and to break away from the rhymed couplet. In 1751, seven years after the death of Pope, a notable poem was produced by Thomas Gray, a quiet, sensitive scholar who spent more than half his life in Cambridge. Here he wrote his famous *Elegy in a Country Churchyard.* For eight years he kept the *Elegy* by him, adding, taking away, polishing, and refining, until it had become worthy, even in form, to be named among the great poems of the world. Its fame, however, is due less to its polish than, first, to its genuine interest in the lives of the poor, to its sympathy with their pleasures and realization of their hardships; and, second, to its observation of the little things of nature, the "moping owl," the "droning flight" of the beetle, "the swallow twittering from the straw-built shed." Nature, according to the school of Pope, was rude and perhaps a little vulgar until smoothed and trimmed and made into lawns and gardens. Pope might have brought a swan or a peacock into a poem, but he would hardly have thought it fitting to introduce beetles or swallows, save the swallows that "roost in Nilus' dusty urn." Neither would Pope have thought a ploughman who "homeward plods his weary way" a proper subject for poetry. To Pope a ploughman was simply a part of the world's machinery, and he would no more have written about him than about a bolt or a screw. All Gray's poems can be contained in one thin volume, but their significance, especially that of the *Elegy,* can hardly be overestimated.

116. Percy's Reliques, 1765

Interest in romanticism was greatly strengthened by the appearance in 1765 of a book called *The Reliques of Ancient English Poetry,* but better known as "Percy's *Reliques.*" This was a collection of old ballads made by Bishop Percy. Unfortunately he felt that in their original form they were too rude to be presented to the literary world; and therefore he smoothed and polished them to some extent, substituting lines of his own for such as were missing or such as appeared to him unworthy. The timid editor was astounded to find that these old ballads received a hearty welcome, and that their very simplicity and rude directness were their great charm to people who were tired of couplets and criticism.

117. William Cowper, 1731–1800

Thus the *Elegy,* the *Reliques,* and even Goldsmith's *Deserted Village,* written in couplets as it was, helped on the new romanticism. So did the work of William Cowper, who began to write soon after the death of Goldsmith, and who resembled Goldsmith in love of nature and in writing straight from the heart. As a boy Cowper was the shyest of children, and it is no wonder that the timid little fellow suffered agonies when at the age of six he was sent to boarding school. From time to time throughout his life his mind was unbalanced, often because the gentle, conscientious man feared that his sins were unpardonable. His later years were spent in the quiet villages of Weston and Olney; and he sent to his friends most charming letters about his pets, his garden, his long walks about the country, and the merry thoughts and witty fancies that were continually coming into his mind. Every one knew him and every one loved him. He was as happy as was possible to him. Here it was that he wrote. Many of his hymns, such as *God moves in a mysterious way,* and *Oh! for a closer walk with God,* are familiar; but equally well known are *The Diverting History of John Gilpin* with its rollicking fun, and *The Task.* "What shall I write on?" the poet once asked his friend Lady Austen. "The sofa," she replied jestingly. He obeyed, and named his poem *The Task.* He wrote first and with mock dignity about the evolution of the sofa. Then he slipped away from parlors and cities and wrote of the country that he loved.

God made the country, and man made the town,

he said. Here he is at his best. Every season was dear to him. He writes of winter:—

I love thee, all unlovely as thou seemest,
And dreaded as thou art.

He sympathizes with the horses dragging a heavy wagon in the storm; he notes the robin,—

Flitting light
From spray to spray, where'er he rests he shakes
From many a twig the pendant drops of ice
That tinkle in the withered leaves below.

He says indignantly:—

I would not enter on my list of friends
(Though graced with polished manners and fine sense,
Yet wanting sensibility) the man
Who needlessly sets foot upon a worm.

All this was quite different from the earlier poetry of the century. Pope's influence had not disappeared by any means, and Cowper could write such balanced lines as—

Knowledge is proud that he has learned so much;
Wisdom is humble that he knows no more;

but this frank love of nature and simple things was not in the least like Pope; and there was more and even better poetry of this sort to be done before the close of the century by a Scotchman named Robert Burns.

118. Robert Burns, 1759–1796

Burns was the son of an intelligent, religious farmer. His years of school were few, but he was by no means an ignorant man, for he had a shelf of good books, and he had long evenings of conversation with his father, a man of no common mould. Another thing was of the utmost value to him who was to become the poet of Scotland, and that was his mother's familiarity with the ballads and songs of the olden time, and the fairy tales and legends with which the mind of one Betty

Davidson, a member of the family, was stocked.

When Burns was sixteen, he met a pretty girl, and wrote a poem to her, *Handsome Nell.* This was the beginning, and from that time until he was twenty-eight, his life was full of song-writing, of hard work, and of the rather wild merry-making of one or two clubs. He had no model for his poetry except the poems of Allan Ramsay, who wrote in the early part of the century, and Robert Fergusson, who wrote about the middle. When Burns discovered Fergusson's work, he was delighted, for here was a poet who wrote in Scotch, who loved nature, who had a turn for satire keen and kindly, and a touch of humor. Burns felt that he had found a master, and for some time he meekly followed Fergusson's ways of writing and imitated his metres without apparently the least idea that he himself was far greater than his predecessor.

When Burns was twenty-five, his father died. He and his brother tried hard to make some profit from the farm, but it seemed hopeless. Robert's own wildness had brought him into difficulties, and he determined to go to Jamaica. One thing must be had first, and that was the money for his outfit and his passage. Some of his friends suggested that printing the poems which he had written might help to fill his empty purse. In 1786 the little volume was published, and the poet felt rich with his twenty guineas. He bought his outfit, paid his passage, and wrote what he supposed was the last song he should ever compose in Scotland. The vessel was not quite ready to sail, and while he waited, a letter came which suggested that it might be worth while to publish an edition of his poems in Edinburgh. For the glory and gain of such a possibility, the poet set out for Edinburgh and the ship sailed without him. He had no letters of introduction to the great folk of the capital city, but none were needed, for his poems had gone before him; and he, the young peasant fresh from his unsuccessful farming, found himself the social and literary lion of the day. The new edition of his poems came out, and he was fêted and flattered until many a brain would have turned.

Robert Burns
1759–1796

The farmer poet, however, was perfectly self-possessed. He was not in the least overpowered by the attention shown him. His only mistake was in not realizing that the people who praised him so heartily would forget all about him in a month. He hoped that some of those men of rank and wealth who claimed to be his friends and admirers would help to secure for him some position in which he could have part of his time free for poetry. He was disappointed, for nothing came of his visit but a little money, a little fame, and the restless, unhappy feeling that there was a world of intellect, of cultivation, of association with the most brilliant men of his country, and that he was shut out from this by nothing but the want of money. He was not strong enough to put the thought away from him.

He had one more winter in Edinburgh; but while there was quite as much admiration of his poems, the novelty was gone, and the lovers of novelty were not so attentive. Burns made no complaint. He secured a position as an excise man, rented a little farm, married Jean Armour, and set out to live on his small income. Scotland's poet was disciplining smugglers, working on a farm, and incidentally writing such poems as *Tam O' Shanter, Bannockburn,* and *The Banks o' Doon.*

The farm was not a success, and he moved to a tiny house in Dumfries. The years were hard. Burns's readiness to please and be pleased led him into whatever company chose him, not the company which he should have chosen. He wrote to a friend that he was "making ballads, and then drinking and singing them." He was keenly sensitive to right and wrong, but lacked the power to choose the right and refuse the wrong. The end came very soon, for he was only thirty-seven when he died.

119. Burns's Most Notable Work

The songs of Burns have been sung wherever English is spoken. They are so simple and sincere that they go straight to the heart, so musical that they almost make their own songs of melody. Songs of such intense feeling as "My luve is like a red, red rose," of such tenderness as "O wert thou in the cauld blast" cannot go out of fashion. Burns's tenderness is not for human beings alone, but for the tiny field mouse whose "wee bit housie" has been torn up by the plough, and whom he comforts,—

But, Mousie, thou art no thy lane,[*]
In proving foresight may be vain:
The best-laid schemes o' mice an' men
Gang aft a-gley.[†]

Closely allied to his tenderness is his charity, a charity which is often delightfully combined with humor, as in his *Address to the Deil,* which closes,—

But fare you weel, auld Nickie-ben![‡]
O wad ye tak a thought an' men'!
Ye aiblins[§] *might—I dinna ken—*
Still hae a stake.[¶]

Two of Burns's longer poems of contrasting character are, next to his songs, his most famous works,—*Tam o' Shanter* and *The Cotter's Saturday Night.* The first is one of the most fascinating poems ever written. The good-for-nothing Tam, the long-suffering, scolding wife, the night at the inn where "ay the ale was growing better," the furious storm, Tam's setting out for home "fou and unco happy," but with prudent glances over his shoulder "lest bogles catch him unawares,"—these are all put before us, sometimes with a touch of humor, sometimes with uproarious fun; but always fascinating, always impossible to read without a smile.

The second poem, *The Cotter's Saturday Night,* is a picture of the poet's own childhood home on Saturday evening when—

[*] not alone.
[†] go oft amiss.
[‡] A nickname of Satan.
[§] perhaps.
[¶] chance.

The elder bairns come drapping in,
At service out, amang the farmers roun'.

Everything is simple and homely.

The mother, wi' her needle an' her sheers,
Gars[*] auld claes[†] look amaist as weel 's the new;
The father mixes a' wi' admonition due.

We can almost hear the knock of the bashful "neebor lad" who has come to call on the oldest daughter. We see them all sitting down to the porridge that forms their supper. We watch the gray-haired father as he takes the Bible,—

And "Let us worship God!" he says with solemn air.

A Scotchman asked to read in public said, "Do not ask me to give *The Cotter's Saturday Night.* A man should read that on his knees as he would read his Bible." Love of his childhood's home, love of country, love of the right were in Burns's heart when he wrote—

From scenes like these old Scotia's grandeur springs,
That makes her lov'd at home, rever'd abroad.
Princes and lords are but the breath of kings,
"An honest man's the noblest work of God."

The eighteenth century began and ended with poetry, but it produced no poet of the first rank. It was the age of prose, and it is famous for essayists, novelists, writers on ethics and politics, and historians—a proud record for one short century.

[*] makes.
[†] clothes.

SUMMARY

Century XVIII

THE CENTURY OF PROSE

Early prose writers:
- Joseph Addison.
- Richard Steele.
- Jonathan Swift.

Forerunner of the novelists:
- Daniel Defoe.

Novelists:
- Samuel Richardson.
- Henry Fielding.
- Tobias Smollett.
- Laurence Sterne.
- Oliver Goldsmith (romantic poet).

Artificial poet:
- Alexander Pope.

Writers on ethics and politics:
- Samuel Johnson.
- Edmund Burke.

Historians:
- William Robertson.
- David Hume.
- Edward Gibbon.

Romantic poets:
- Thomas Gray.
- Oliver Goldsmith.
- Robert Burns.

Coffee houses became important factors in literature.

Pope was the greatest poet of the first half of the century. His influence for correctness, conciseness, and clearness has never ceased to affect literature. Even his metre, the heroic couplet, prevailed for many years.

The best prose writers of the early part of the century were:—

1. Addison, who won political success by a couplet.

2. Steele, who founded the *Tatler.* These two men wrote the best parts of the *Tatler,* the *Spectator,* famous for the *Sir Roger de Coverley* papers, and the *Guardian;* and this was the beginning of periodical literature.

3. Swift, the many-sided, was famous for his bitter satire, and the warmth of his friendship. His best known book is *Gulliver's Travels.*

Defoe, too, was a many-sided man. His satire was written with such apparent sincerity that it was more than once taken in earnest. His best work is *Robinson Crusoe.*

The Age of Queen Anne as a whole was marked by the development of literary criticism, by the excellence of its prose, and by the beginning of the periodical.

In 1740 prose discovered a new field, the novel. The first, *Pamela,* was written by Richardson. This was followed by Fielding's *Joseph Andrews,* Smollett's *Roderick Random,* Sterne's *Tristram Shandy,* and many others.

Between 1750 and 1780 the chief place of honor was held by a man of powerful intellect, Johnson, who wrote *Lives of the Poets* and many other works, compiled a dictionary, put an end to "patronage" in literature, was famous for his conversational ability, and was the literary oracle of his day. His life was written by his admirer Boswell.

One of Johnson's special friends was Oliver Goldsmith, to whom the writing of children's books, history, novels, poetry, and plays was equally easy and the results almost equally excellent.

The period was also marked by the eloquence of Edmund Burke, and by the work of three historians: Robertson, who wrote of Scotland, Germany, and America; Hume, who wrote of England; and Gibbon, who wrote of the Roman Empire.

The "romantic revival," a revolt against the artificial formality of Pope, was increasing in power. It was marked by three qualities: interest in man as man, love of nature, independence of thought. This revolt was apparent in Gray's *Elegy* and in Goldsmith's poems, was strengthened by the appearance of Percy's *Reliques,* and was carried on by the works of Cowper; but its best manifestation was in the writings of Burns, who is famous for poems of such contrasting character as his songs, *Tam O'Shanter,* and *The Cotter's Saturday Night.*

The eighteenth century is famous for poets, essayists, novelists, writers on ethics and politics, and historians.

CHAPTER VIII

Century XIX

THE CENTURY OF THE NOVEL

120. The "Lake Poets"

The three qualities that were so clearly manifested in the poetry of Burns, namely, interest in man, love of nature, and impatience of restraint, become even more apparent in the writings of the nineteenth century. Individuality increased. It is less easy to label writers as belonging to a certain "school." The three poets of the first of the century who are usually classed together as the "Lake School" have little in common except their friendship and the fact that they lived in the Lake Country. These three were William Wordsworth, Samuel Taylor Coleridge, and Robert Southey.

When Wordsworth was twenty-one he went to France to study. Those were the Revolutionary days; and the young student sided with the Girondists so vigorously that he would surely have fallen into political trouble if his friends had not stopped his allowance in order to compel him to return. When the Revolution became only a wild orgy of slaughter, he was disappointed and doubtful of everything; but his beloved sister Dorothy came to live with him, and, as he said, gave him an exquisite regard for common things and preserved the poet in him.

After three or four years of quiet country life, a brilliant, sympathetic man became a visitor at the Wordsworth cottage. This was Coleridge. He was a man who was interested in everything by turns. His brain was full of visions and schemes. He was in the army for a while. He planned to found a model republic on the Susquehanna. He was a wonderful talker on politics, philosophy, theology, poetry—whatever came uppermost. Together he and Wordsworth discussed what ideal poetry should be. Wordsworth believed that a poet should write on everyday subjects in everyday language. Coleridge believed that lofty or supernatural subjects might be so treated as to seem simple and real.

William Wordsworth
1770–1850

121. Lyrical Ballads, 1798

The two men agreed to bring out a little book, *Lyrical Ballads*, and go to Germany with its proceeds; and this was done. Coleridge's chief contribution to the volume was *The Rime of the Ancient Mariner*, that weird and marvellous tale of the suffering that must follow an act not in loving accord with nature. This poem is like the old ballads in its simplicity and directness, but very unlike them in the fulness of its harmony. Coleridge was a master of sound. Here is his sound picture of a brook:—

A noise like of a hidden brook
In the leafy month of June,
That to the sleeping woods all night
Singeth a quiet tune.

The breaking up of the ice is thus described:—

It cracked and growled, and roared and howled,
Like noises in a swound.

The similes of the poem are of the kind that not only adorn a statement but illuminate it; the mariner passes, "like night," from land to land. The vessel in a calm is

As idle as a painted ship
Upon a painted ocean.

Wordsworth's contributions to the book were many, and of widely differing value. When he remembered his theories, he was capable of such stuff as—

But yet I guess that now and then
With Betty all was not so well;
And to the road she turns her ears,
And thence full many a sound she hears,
Which she to Susan will not tell.

Here, too, was his *We are Seven.* The treatment is quite as simple as in the preceding poem; but while the first seems like the awkward attempt of a man to be childlike, the simplicity of the second is appropriate because the poem is a conversation with a child. In this same volume was the beautiful *Tintern Abbey*, wherein all theories were forgotten. It is hardly colloquial language when the author says,—

> *The sounding cataract*
> *Haunted me like a passion;*

or when he bids—

> *Therefore let the moon*
> *Shine on thee in thy solitary walks;*
> *And let the misty mountain-wind be free*
> *To blow against thee.*

122. Robert Southey, 1774–1843

After their visit to Germany, both poets settled in the Lake Country. Near them was the home of the poet Southey, who had been one of Coleridge's converts to the Susquehanna scheme.

These were the three who were best known as poets when the nineteenth century began. Southey wrote weird, strange epics: *The Curse of Kehama,* a Hindoo tale and *Thalaba,* the story of a young Arabian who sets out to avenge his father. Southey was always attracted by the strange and distant; and yet he took delight in the simplest things, and made the best of whatever came. In 1813 he was chosen Laureate; but only a few years later he discovered that the public did not care for more poetry from him, and he said with the utmost composure, "I have done enough to be remembered among poets, though my proper place will be among the historians, if I live to complete the works upon yonder shelves." For twenty years longer Southey worked industriously on prose. He wrote histories and biographies, an excellent life of Nelson among the latter. Here was his true field, for his prose is charmingly clear and sturdy; and while making no apparent attempt at formal description, he nevertheless contrives to leave a strongly outlined picture in the mind of the reader.

123. Coleridge's Best Work

Coleridge's best poetry was written about the time of the publication of *Lyrical Ballads.* It was then that he composed *Christabel,* the mystic tale of the innocent

Samuel Taylor Coleridge
1772–1834

maiden who is enthralled by the power of magic. Then, too, he wrote the dazzling fragment, *Kubla Khan,* part of a poem which, he said, came to him while he slept. The rest of it was driven from his memory by an interruption. Whatever Coleridge touched with his poetic gift was rich and splendid; but nearly everything was incomplete. So it was in prose. No one can read a single page of his writings without realizing that their author was a man of deep and original thought and of rarely equalled ability; and yet here, too, all was unfinished. Coleridge said that he trembled at the thought of the question, "I gave thee so many talents; what hast thou done with them?" His excuse was a certain weakness of the will. This was increased by the use of opium, which he began to take to quiet pain, and which was for many years his tyrant. This great man, who influenced every one that heard him speak or that read his written words, was utterly without ability to command his own powers, to govern his own mind. He has left little save fragments,—but they are magnificent fragments.

124. Wordsworth's Life

Wordsworth's life was quite unlike that of Coleridge. He married in 1802, and, as he said, was "conscious of blessedness" in his marriage. A sum of money which had been due to his father was at last paid to him, and he lived on happily and tranquilly in his beloved Lake Country, making many trips abroad or to different parts of the British Isles. He was a keen lover of beauty, but the beauty of nature rather than that of art. He fell asleep before the Venus de Medici, but he wrote one of his best sonnets on the beach at Calais. His finest poems were written during the early years of the century.

Appreciation was slow in finding Wordsworth, partly because first Scott and then Byron were coming before the public, and there was nothing in Wordsworth's writings to arouse the wild enthusiasm with which people welcomed their productions. Another reason was that Wordsworth's utter lack of humor permitted him in pursuit of his theories to put absurd doggerel into poems that were otherwise fine. The critics ridiculed the doggerel and passed by what was really worthy. "Heed not such onset," the poet said to himself, and serenely continued to write. Slowly one after another began to see that no one else could describe the every-day sights of nature like Wordsworth, or could interpret so well the feelings that they aroused in one who loved them. Other poets could write of tempests and crags and precipices; but Wordsworth alone could picture a "common day" and an "ordinary" landscape. He could do more than picture; he could make the reader feel that in nature was a mysterious life, the thought of its Creator, half expressed and half revealed. Long before 1830 Scott had ceased to write poetry, Byron and Shelley and Keats were dead. Men began to turn back a score of years, to see that in Wordsworth's poems there was an excellence that they had overlooked. They passed by the imbecilities of *Peter Bell*, they read the charming little daffodil poem, they began to appreciate the grandeur of the *Ode on the Intimations of Immortality*, with its magnificent sweep of poetry:—

There was a time when meadow, grove, and stream,
The earth, and every common sight,
To me did seem
Apparelled in celestial light,
The glory and the freshness of a dream.

Little by little Wordsworth's noble office was recognized,

and he was known as the faithful interpreter of nature and of God in nature. In 1842 a complete edition of his works was called for. On the death of Southey during the following year, he was made Laureate with the good-will of all lovers of true poetry.

Those first thirty years of the century were glorious times for literature. Besides the Lake Poets, there were the romantic writers, Scott and Byron; the lovers of beauty, Shelley and Keats; the essayists, Charles Lamb and De Quincey; the magazine critics; and the realist, Jane Austen.

125. Walter Scott, 1771–1832

The first that we know of Walter Scott, he was a little lame, sickly child who had been sent away from Edinburgh to his grandfather's farm in the hope that he might grow stronger. Fortunately for all that love a good story, this hope was realized, and it was not long before he was galloping wherever a pony could carry him and scrambling wherever the pony could not go. The two things that he liked best were this wild roaming over the country and listening to the old ballads and legends that his grandmother recited to him by the score. When he was older, he was sent to school in Edinburgh. He was not the leader of his class by any means; but out of school there was not a boy who would not gladly follow him to some wild, romantic spot to listen to his stories of the border warfare. One day he came across a book half a century old which delighted his heart. It was Bishop Percy's *Reliques.* This was happiness. The hungry schoolboy forgot his dinner and lay out under the trees

Sir Walter Scott
1771–1832

reading over and over again of Douglas and Percy and Robin Hood and Sir Patrick Spens. This book settled the question of what his life-work should be, though it was some years before he found his place.

After leaving the university he studied law and was admitted to the bar. He married, held various public offices, and was financially comfortable. In 1799, when he was twenty-eight, he made his first appearance in literature with some translations from German poetry. A little later he wrote a border ballad, *The Eve of St. John.* Great numbers of border ballads were still remembered, though they had never been put into print. Scott determined to collect these, and somewhat in the fashion of Fuller, he roamed over the country, taking down every scrap of the old balladry, every bit of legend that he could get from any one who chanced to remember the ancient lore. In 1802 he published *Minstrelsy of the Scottish Border*, and in 1805, *The Lay of the Last Minstrel.* Then there was enthusiasm indeed. Men had wandered into distant lands for the new, the strange, the romantic; but the *Lay* revealed their own country as its home.

Here was a poem which was song, description, dialogue, legend, superstition, chivalry, every-day life,—and all blended into a story told by an ideal story-teller. Scott's listeners were as intent as those of his schooldays had been. There was no more thought of courts and law books. The teller of stories had found his place. He planned a romantic novel, but laid it aside. During the next three years he edited various works, and in the third year he published *Marmion.* Large sums of money were coming in from his poems and also from the publishing business, in which he had engaged with some old school friends, and he was free to carry out his dearest wish, to buy the estate of Abbotsford and become one of the "landed gentry."

126. Scott Abandons Poetry

In 1812, the year of his removal to Abbotsford, *Childe Harold,* a brilliant poem in a new vein, came out, written by Lord Byron. The crowd had found a new idol, and Scott's next poem, published the following year, had much smaller sales than his previous works. Scott brought out another poem, but evidently the fickle public did not care for more of his poetry, and he began to think about the romance which he had planned several years earlier. The result of this thinking was that in 1814 the reading world went wild with delight over *Waverley,* by an unknown writer; for Scott, no one knows just why, did not wish to be known as its author. Story after story followed,—one, two, even three, in a single year. "Walter Scott is the only man in the land who could write them," was the general belief; but the secret was kept for some time.

Scott was happy in his home. Abbotsford was the very hearthstone of Scotland for a joyous hospitality. Great folk and little folk, rich and poor, lords and ladies, scientific men, artists, authors, admirers from across the sea, old school friends, relatives even to the twentieth degree—they were all welcomed to Abbotsford. Sir Walter—for George IV had made him a baronet—usually worked three or four hours before breakfast, which was between nine and ten, and perhaps two hours afterwards; but when noon had come, he was ready for any kind of amusement, provided it was out of doors,—a long walk or ride with his pet dogs, hunting or fishing, or whatever might suggest itself.

It is a pity that this happy life should have been clouded; but in 1826 the publishers with whom Scott was connected failed. The romancer might easily have freed himself from all claims; but instead he quietly set to work to pay with his pen the $650,000 that was due. Novels, histories, a nine-volume life of Bonaparte, editorial work, translations, were undertaken in rapid succession. Paralysis attacked him; still he struggled on. In 1831 the government loaned him a frigate to carry him to Italy for rest and change.

The might
Of the whole world's good wishes with him goes,

wrote Wordsworth; but rest had come too late. In 1832 he returned to Abbotsford, and there he died. "Time and I against any two," he had said bravely when he took the enormous debt upon himself. Time had failed him, but he had paid more than half, and the royalties on his books finally paid the rest.

Scott's best work was his Scottish romances, wherein he aimed chiefly at telling a romantic story and laid the scene in the past in order to add to the romantic effect. In such stories as *Kenilworth,* however, he shows himself the real inventor of the historical novel, that fascinating combination of old and new, of customs and manners that are strange practised by men and women with loves and hates and instincts like our own. His power lies, first, in his knowledge of the past, a knowledge so full and so ready that of whatever age he wrote he seemed to be in his own time; second, in his imagination, his ability to invent incidents and picture scenes; third, in his power of humorous perception and characterization, especially in Scottish characters. There have been more profound students than Scott, and there have been better makers of plots; but no man, either before or after him, has ever combined such familiarity with the past and such ability to tell a story.

127. Lord Byron, 1788–1824

George Gordon, Lord Byron, whose *Childe Harold* brought Scott's narrative poetry to an end, was the son of a worthless profligate and a mother who sometimes petted him, sometimes abused him, and was capable of flying into storms of anger at a moment's warning. He was so sensitive about his lameness that as a tiny child he struck fiercely with his whip at a visitor who ventured to express some pity for him. When he was ten years of age, he became Lord Byron, and was so fond of alluding to his rank that the schoolboys called him "the old English baron." At nineteen he published his first book of poems, *Hours of Idleness.* It was only a boy's work, but the position of this boy made it conspicuous, and the Edinburgh critics reviewed it sharply. Byron was angry, and two years later he blazed out with *English Bards and Scotch Reviewers,* wherein he not only attacked the reviewers, with his scornful couplet,—

> *A man must serve his time to every trade*
> *Save censure—critics all are ready made,—*

but struck fiercely at his innocent fellow authors. Wordsworth he pronounced an idiot, Coleridge the laureate of asses, Scott a maker of stale romance, and the mighty Jeffrey, writer of the article, he declared to be "the great literary anthropophagus." His own critical judgments were of small value, and he was afterwards exceedingly sorry for his foolish lines; but evidently this boy was not to be suppressed even by the great folk of the *Edinburgh Review.*

Byron went abroad, and in 1812 he produced the first part of *Childe Harold's Pilgrimage,* and then, he said, "I awoke one morning and found myself famous." He continued to write. Scott's *Lay of the Last Minstrel* and *Marmion* began to seem tame when compared with the turbulent characters and the novel manners of the East, where most of Byron's scenes were laid. England and the Continent bowed down before this new genius. He married, but soon his wife left him, giving no reason for her desertion. Public sympathy was with her, and Byron became a wanderer, tossing back to England poems of scorn and satire and affection and pathos; sometimes living simply and quietly, sometimes sinking to the depths of dissipation; in his writings sometimes low and vulgar, but always brilliant. He wrote wild, romantic tales in poetry,—*The Bride of Abydos, The Corsair,* and others; he wrote equally wild and lurid dramas; and, last of all, *Don Juan,* the story of a vicious man and his life; often revolting, but, as Scott said, containing "exquisite morsels of poetry." Byron was capable of tender sympathy with suffering and warm appreciation of heroism, as he shows in *The Prisoner of Chillon;* but, as a general thing, there were but two subjects that interested him deeply, himself and nature. His poems have one and the same hero, a cynical young man, weary of life, scornful and melancholy. This is the poet's somewhat theatrical notion of himself. He once objected to a bust of himself on the ground that the expression was "not unhappy enough." There is nothing theatrical, however, about his love of nature when he writes such lines as—

The big rain comes dancing to the earth.

Oh, night
And storm and darkness, ye are wondrous strong,
Yet lovely in your strength.

This stormy cynic could also write, and with most exquisite delicacy of touch, of a quiet summer evening:—

It is the hush of night, and all between
Thy margin and the mountains, dusk, yet clear,
Mellow'd and mingling, yet distinctly seen,
Save darken'd Jura, whose capt heights appear
Precipitously steep; and drawing near,
There breathes a living fragrance from the shore,
Of flowers yet fresh with childhood; on the ear
Drops the light drip of the suspended oar,
Or chirps the grasshopper one good-night carol more.

In 1823 the Greeks were struggling to win their freedom from the Turks. Byron determined to play a part in the war, and set out for Missolonghi. The misanthropic poet suddenly became the practical commander; but before he could take the field, he died of fever at the age of thirty-six.

128. Percy Bysshe Shelley, 1792–1822

The works of two poets of this time, Percy Bysshe Shelley and John Keats, are so strongly marked by their love of beauty and their ability to express it as to separate them from the others. Shelley's whole life was a revolt against restraint. After five months at Oxford he wrote a pamphlet against the Christian religion, and was promptly expelled. At nineteen he married a young girl, three years his junior, because he thought she was tyrannized over in being required to obey the rules of her school.

Shelley loved the world, and he longed to have all things pure and beautiful; but he fancied that the one change needed to bring about this state of purity and beauty was to abolish the laws and the religion in which men believed. It is hard for ordinary mortals to understand his way of looking at matters; but those who knew him best were convinced of his honesty, *Prometheus Unbound* is one of his best long poems. He pictures the hero as rebelling against the gods, indeed, but as loving man. The longer works are very beautiful, but there are three or four of his shorter poems that every one loves. One is *The Cloud,* beginning,—

I bring fresh showers for the thirsting flowers,
From the seas and the streams;
I bring light shade for the leaves when laid
In their noonday dreams.

Another favorite is his *Ode to the West Wind*, and yet another is *To a Skylark:*—

Hail to thee, blithe spirit—
Bird thou never wert—
That from heaven or near it
Pourest thy full heart
In profuse strains of unpremeditated art.

There is a wonderful upspringing in this poem; it hardly seems to touch the ground, but to be made of light and music. In even so earthly a simile as his comparison between the lark and a glow-worm, he lightens and lifts it by a single word:—

Like a glow-worm golden
In a dell of dew,
Scattering unbeholden
Its AERIAL *hue*
Among the flowers and grass which screen it from the view.

Another simile which surely would never have come to the mind of any one but Shelley, or perhaps Donne, was,

Like a poet HIDDEN
IN THE LIGHT OF THOUGHT,
Singing hymns unbidden,
Till the world is wrought
To sympathy with hopes and fears it heeded not.

Shelley was drowned while yachting in the Bay of Spezzia. The quarantine law required that his body should be burned, and this was done in the presence of Byron and two other friends. His ashes were laid in the little Protestant burying-ground at Rome, not far from Keats, who had died only a year before. It was in grief for the loss of Keats that he had written his lament, *Adonais,* in which he had said of the poet,—

Peace, peace! he is not dead, he doth not sleep!
He hath awakened from the dream of life.

A little volume of Keats's poems was with Shelley on the yacht and was washed up with his body.

129. John Keats, 1795–1821

For Keats life was not easy, though he had nothing in him of revolt against the established order of things. At school he was a great favorite and also a great fighter. A small thing made him happy and a small thing made him miserable. At fifteen he was apprenticed to a London surgeon; but long before then he had begun to dream golden dreams of what had been when the world was younger. His inspiration came from the past, from the Middle Ages as drawn by Spenser, and from the graceful fancies and depths of the Greek mythology.

In 1818, when he was twenty-three years of age, Keats published his *Endymion.* It was savagely criticised by the *Quarterly Review* and *Blackwood's Edinburgh Magazine,* but the young poet was not to be suppressed. He made no bitter reply, as Byron had done, but he quietly wrote on, and two years later published some of his best work. Here were *The Eve of St. Agnes, Lamia,* and others of his longer poems, absolutely overflowing with beauty and glowing with light and color:—

John Keats
1795–1821

Rose-bloom fell on her hands, together prest,
And on her silver cross soft amethyst,
And on her hair a glory like a saint.

If all Keats's poems but one were to be destroyed, most of those who love him would choose the *Ode to a Grecian Urn* to be saved. This poem is silver-clear, there is not a touch of color. About the urn is a graceful course of youths and maidens and gods with pipes and timbrels and leafy boughs. The poet writes:—

Heard melodies are sweet, but those unheard
Are sweeter; therefore, ye soft pipes, play on;
Not to the sensual ear, but, more endeared,
Pipe to the spirit ditties of no tone;
Fair youth, beneath the trees, thou canst not leave
Thy song, nor ever can those trees be bare;

Bold Lover, never, never canst thou kiss,
Though winning near the goal—yet, do not grieve;
She cannot fade, though thou hast not thy bliss,
For ever wilt thou love, and she be fair.

Keats was only twenty-four when he died, in Italy, where he had gone in the hope of saving his life. His ideals were so high that he felt as if what he had done was nothing. "If I should die," he said, "I have left no immortal work behind me;" but the lovers of poetry have thought otherwise and have ranked him among the first of those who have loved beauty and have created it.

130. Charles Lamb, 1775–1834

While Keats and Shelley were in Italy, while Byron and Scott were at the height of their literary glory, while Wordsworth and Southey and Coleridge were revelling in the beauties of the Lake Country, Charles Lamb, the most charming of essayists, was adding and subtracting at his desk in the East India House, until, as he said, the wood had entered into his soul.

When Lamb was a little boy, he was sent to the Blue-Coat School. He longed to go on to the university, but his aid was needed at home. A few years later his sister Mary, in a sudden attack of insanity, killed her mother. The young man of twenty-one, with some literary ambition and a keen appetite for enjoyment, bravely laid aside his own wishes, reckoned up his little income of £120 a year, and took upon him the care of his father and his sister. Mary Lamb recovered, but as the years went on, attacks came with increasing frequency. Yet it was not, save for this constant dread, an unhappy life for either of them. There was never money enough for thoughtless expenditure, but there was enough for their simple way of living. Their circle of friends widened; and what a company it was that used to meet in those little brown rooms! There were Wordsworth, Coleridge, Southey, Leigh Hunt, De Quincey, and others without number. There was the sister Mary in her gray silk gown and white muslin kerchief and quaintly frilled cap. Every one of that brilliant company respected and admired her, valued her opinion, and never failed of her sympathy. In the midst of them all was Charles Lamb, seeing nothing but good in every one of them, often pouring out the wildest fun, but always mindful of his sister, lest too eager a discussion or a jest too many might lead on to an attack of insanity. It was when she was "ill," as he tenderly phrased it, that he planned to dedicate to her his little volume of poems, because, as he said, people living together "get a sort of indifference in the expression of kindness for each other."

The best of his time and strength went to the endless adding and subtracting, but the evenings were often given to writing, so far as the friends would permit. "I am never C.L.," Lamb groaned half in jest and half in earnest, "but always C.L. and Co." Yet in the work done in these fragments of his life he has left us a rich legacy. For ten years, from 1797 to 1807, his pen attempted all sorts of things. He wrote several poems, among them *The Old Familiar Faces,* with its depth of tender affection and longing; and *Hester,* most graceful of all memorials. He wrote a story or two; he was actually

Charles Lamb
1775–1834

under agreement to provide six witty paragraphs a day for one of the papers; he wrote prologues and epilogues for his friends' plays, and finally he wrote a play of his own. It was acted; but it was such an evident failure that the author himself, sitting far up in front, hissed it louder than any one else.

In 1807, the *Tales from Shakespeare* came out, and that was a success. Mary wrote the comedies and Charles the tragedies, "groaning all the while," his sister said, "and saying he can make nothing of it, which he always says till he has finished, and then he finds out he has made something of it."

During the following year he published *Specimens*

of Dramatic Poets Contemporary with Shakespeare. Here he gives, as he says, "sometimes a scene, sometimes a song, a speech, or a passage, or a poetical image, as they happened to strike me,"—and to know how they struck the mind of Charles Lamb is the delightful part of it, for no one else has ever gone so directly to the heart of a play as this unassuming clerk of the East India House—and then he talks a little in a friendly, informal way. His crowning work is the *Essays of Elia,* short, delightful little chats about whatever came into his mind. He writes about the Blue-Coat School in the days of his boyhood, about *Witches and Other Night Fears;* he muses about *Dream Children;* he complains whimsically of the *Decay of Beggars in the Metropolis;* he presents with a merry mockery of profound learning a grave *Dissertation upon Roast Pig;* and describes with pathetic humor the feelings of *The Superannuated Man* who after many years of faithful work is given a pension by his employers, and is at liberty to live his own life. This was a page from Lamb's experience, for in 1825 his employers gave him a generous pension, and at last he was free. This is what he says of his freedom:—

"I have indeed lived nominally fifty years, but deduct out of them the hours which I have lived to other people, and not to myself, and you will find me still a young fellow. For that is the only true Time, which a man can properly call his own—that which he has all to himself; the rest, though in some sense he may be said to live it, is other people's Time, not his. The remnant of my poor days, long or short, is at least multiplied for me threefold. My ten next years, if I stretch so far, will be as long as any preceding thirty. 'T is a fair rule-of-three sum. . . . I have worked task-work and have all the rest of the day to myself." The "rest of the day" was short, for after only nine years of freedom, the most genial, delicate, charming of humorists passed away.

131. Thomas De Quincey, 1785–1859

"Charming" is the word that best describes the essays of Charles Lamb, but "fascinating" ought always to be saved for those of Thomas De Quincey. The man himself is intensely interesting. As a boy he was a great favorite with the other boys because of his never-failing good-nature and his willingness to help them with their lessons; and with the teachers because he was such a brilliant scholar. When he was fifteen, he could chatter away in Greek as easily as in English. Two years later he went on a ramble to Wales, then slipped away to London, and came near dying of starvation. After being at Oxford, he visited Wordsworth. They became friends and were neighbors for twenty-seven years. Whoever met De Quincey was delighted with him. To the Wordsworth children he was their beloved "Kinsey," and he was equally dear to John Wilson, who was to become the great "Christopher North" of *Blackwood's Magazine.* He was always ready to join in any light chat, but if left to himself, he had a fashion of gliding away in his talk to all sorts of profound and mysterious themes which only he knew how to make delightful.

During those years in the Lake Country too great generosity and the failures of others had lessened his little fortune. He had a wife and children to support, and he began to write for the magazines; he even edited a local newspaper at a salary of one guinea a week. In 1821 he went to London. He was thirty-six years old, older than Byron or Shelley or Keats had been when their fame was secure; but with De Quincey there had been for seventeen years an enemy at court in the shape of opium, which among other effects weakened his will so that only the pressure of necessity could drive him to action. The necessity had come. Charles Lamb was writing his essays for the *London Magazine*, and he introduced De Quincey to the editors. Not long after this introduction the readers of the *Magazine* were deeply interested by an article called *Confessions of an English Opium-Eater.* It might well arouse interest, for it was a thrilling account of the experiences that come from the use of opium. It sounded so honest that the critics were half decided that it must be a work of imagination. This was the real beginning of the one hundred and fifty magazine articles written by De Quincey.

Sorrows came upon him. His wife and two of his sons died, and he was helpless. In all practical matters he was the most ignorant of men. With a large draft in his pocket, he once lived for a number of days in the cheapest lodgings he could find, because he did not know that the draft, payable in twenty-one days, could be cashed at once. Now with six motherless children, he was more of a child than any of them. His oldest daughter quietly planned for him to have a home at Lasswade, near Edinburgh, and there he was loved and cared for. Caring for this gentle, erratic man must

Thomas De Quincey
1785–1859

have been somewhat of a "worriment," for he was quite capable of slipping out in the evening for a walk, lying down under a tree or a hedge, and sleeping calmly all night long. His books and papers accumulated like drifts in a snowstorm, and only his daughter's gentle control prevented him from filling room after room with them, and so driving the family out of doors.

Two of his best-known essays are *The Flight of a Tartar Tribe* and *Murder Considered as One of the Fine Arts.* The inspiration of the first seems to have been a few sentences in a missionary report. From these and his own wide reading, he made the flight of the Tartars across Asia as vivid as any actual journey of his readers. The second essay is written with a delightful air of mock gravity, and with verifying quotations from various languages. He declares his firm belief "that any man who deals in murder, must have very incorrect ways of thinking, and truly inaccurate principles." In a later article he carries his jest further and declares that "If once a man indulges himself in murder, very soon he comes to think little of robbing; and from robbing he comes next to drinking and Sabbath-breaking, and from that to incivility and procrastination. Once begin upon this downward path, you never know where you are to stop. Many a man has dated his ruin from some murder or other that perhaps he thought little of at the time."

So De Quincey goes on. He can be dreamy and gentle, strikingly vivid, or whimsical, or he can give a plain, straightforward narrative, and in every case adapt his style perfectly to the mood of the hour. His published works fill sixteen volumes, "full of brain from beginning to end."

132. The Reviews

Almost all of De Quincey's work was done for some one of the magazines that were established in the first twenty years of the century. The earliest was the *Edinburgh Review.* It began in 1802 with very decided principles. One was that articles must be written by men of standing; second, that they must be paid for; third, that reviews and criticisms should be absolutely independent. Francis Jeffrey soon became its editor, and was its ruling spirit for a quarter of a century. This magazine was so strongly Whiggish in tone that an opposition Tory magazine, the *Quarterly Review,* was soon founded. Then came *Blackwood's Magazine,* whose great man was John Wilson, or "Christopher North." These periodicals were so partisan and so bent upon being "independent" that many authors, like Keats and Wordsworth, suffered most unfairly at their hands; but, however hard their reviews were for individual writers, they were certainly good for literature, for the very savageness of their criticism aroused discussion and interest in literary matters.

133. Jane Austen, 1775–1817

In the midst of the poems and romances and essays and reviews, the novel of home life held a little place, but an important one. Immediately after the days of Richardson, Fielding, and Smollett, there was much story-writing, but these stories were generally romances. The best and almost the only real novels of the earliest years of the nineteenth century were written by a young girl named Jane Austen, who lived in a quiet village rectory. In 1796, when she was twenty-one, she wrote *Pride and Prejudice,* and during the next few years several other works followed. She kept her authorship a secret, and, indeed, did not publish a book until 1811, three years before the coming out of *Waverley.*

In some ways, these novels of the beginning of the century are very different from those written at its end. For one thing, Miss Austen often tells in long conversations what in later books is expressed by a hint.

Her pictures give the minutest details of thought and feeling and action. In *Emma,* for instance, it requires several pages to make it clear that an elderly gentleman is afraid of a drive through the snow, but finally decides to attempt it. The same character in a later novel would glance anxiously out of the window and order his carriage. Miss Austen had a keen but most delicate sense of humor. In her own line she was almost as much of a realist as Defoe. She has a fashion of choosing several characters so nearly alike that we feel sure she "can make nothing of it;" but in her bits of description and her long conversations characteristics come out amazingly well; and suddenly we realize that she "has made something of it," that these monotonous people who seemed to have been created by the dozen have become thoroughly real and individual and interesting. Miss Austen died in 1817. The romantic poetry of Byron and what Scott called "the big bow-wow strain" of his own novels were filling the minds of readers, and it was not until long after her death that her work received the attention and admiration that it deserved.

Occasionally in the history of literature we come to what seems a natural boundary. Such a boundary was reached in 1832. Before the close of that year, Byron, Shelley, Keats, and Scott were dead; the literary work of Lamb and Coleridge was practically complete; Wordsworth wrote little more that was of value; only De Quincey and Southey were still active. The condition of the country was rapidly changing. In political history, too, 1832 was a natural boundary, for in that year a Reform Bill was passed, giving for the first time to many thousand people in England the right to be represented in Parliament. Education became more general, not only the education of schools, but that of books and papers. Books became cheaper, the circulation of papers increased. Cheap magazines were established. Scientific discoveries and inventions overthrew former ways of living and working and forced people to think, whether they would or not. The audience makes the author, and the author makes the audience. The half-century following 1832 was to see—among other marks of literary progress—a remarkable development of the novel, the essay, and the poem.

The three novelists of the Victorian Age whose writings are looked upon as modern classics are Charles Dickens, William Makepeace Thackeray, and Mary Ann Evans Cross, or "George Eliot."

134. Charles Dickens, 1812–1870

The first nine years of Charles Dickens's life were very happy; but his father's salary was cut down, and before long he was imprisoned for debt. The rest of the family established themselves in the prison, and there the little boy spent his Sundays. Through the week he was left to work all day in a cellar and spend his nights in an attic. It is no wonder that throughout his life he had deep sympathy for lonely children. After a while came a few years of prosperity, and the boy was sent to school. His father became a parliamentary reporter for one of the papers; and when Charles was seventeen, he set out to learn shorthand. He was wise enough to realize that a good reporter must know much more than shorthand; and he read, read hard hour after hour, whenever he had the hours.

There were two things that the young man liked to do better than all else. One was to act and the other was to write; and one day he was too happy to keep the tears from his eyes, for the *Monthly Magazine* had published a paper of his, known afterwards as *Mr. Minns and his Cousin* in *Sketches by Boz.* "Boz" was his little sister's pronunciation of Moses, a nickname which Charles had given to his brother in memory of "Moses" in *The Vicar of Wakefield.* Other sketches followed. By and by they came out in book form. Then a publishing firm asked if he would write a series of humorous articles. He agreed, and this was the origin of the *Pickwick Papers.* Dickens was now twenty-five; his fame and his bank account were increasing rapidly. The following year he wrote *Oliver Twist,* and his other novels appeared in quick succession. He edited several periodicals, he wrote sketches of travel, and in 1850 he published *David Copperfield,* the work that he loved best, and a book that those who love its author cannot help finding most pathetic in the pictures that it gives of his own younger days. For twenty years longer his work went on. The public were more and more charmed with each story; and well they might have been, for every page was sparkling with merriment or throbbing with a pathos that came so straight from the writer's own heart that it could not fail to move his readers. When his characters blunder, they blunder delightfully. When they are sad, we sympathize with them; but when they are merry, then comes a full tide of rollicking fun that "doeth good like a medicine."

Dickens never seemed happier than when he was acting in amateur theatricals. This taste is evident in his novels. They often lack the drama's completeness of plot, but many of the characters have a touch of "make-up" which sometimes gives the reader a sense of their unreality, a feeling that they are figures on a stage rather than real men and women. Moreover, Dickens almost always fixes upon some special trick of expression or some one prominent quality, and by it he labels the character. Uriah Heep is always " 'umble," Mr. Micawber is always "waiting for something to turn up." This is not character drawing; it is caricature. Nevertheless, no one who reads Dickens can help being grateful to the man whose work not only gives us amusement but is all aglow with good will and kindliness.

Charles Dickens
1812–1870

Dickens was an intense and constant worker. "I am become incapable of rest," he said. Not only did he do a vast amount of work, but he threw his whole self into every book. Little Nell was so real to her creator that after writing of her death, he walked the streets of London all night, feeling as if he had really lost a beloved child friend. Long lives do not go with such work as this, and Dickens died, almost at his desk, at the age of fifty-eight.

135. William Makepeace Thackeray, 1811–1863

In 1836, when Dickens had just begun the *Pickwick Papers,* the artist who was to illustrate them died, and a young man offered himself as a substitute, but was not accepted. This was William Makepeace Thackeray, who was to be counted as one of the three great novelists of the Victorian Age. His early life was unlike that of Dickens, for, born in India, he was sent to England to be educated, and had all the advantages of school and university. Just what he should do with himself was not easy to decide; but he had artistic ability and he concluded to study art. About the time when he came to the decision that he had not the talent to be as great an artist as he had hoped, his fortune was lost. Then he began to contribute to several magazines; and as if laughing at himself for having even thought of being a famous artist, he signed his articles "Michael Angelo Titmarsh."

William Makepeace Thackeray
1811–1863

Thackeray's fame was of slower growth than Dickens's. People read his *Great Hoggarty Diamond* in *Fraser's Magazine* and his *Book of Snobs* in *Punch;* they were amused and interested, but they did not lie awake nights longing for the next number. Publishers did not contend wildly for his manuscripts, and he was sometimes asked to shorten those that he presented. Dickens had an unfailing good nature and cheerfulness and a healthy confidence in himself almost from the first that swept his readers along with him. Thackeray was not so cheery, and he was not quite so sure of himself or of his audience. Again, people like to be amused. When Dickens made fun of his characters, he laughed at them with the utmost frankness, and every one laughed with him. When Thackeray disapproved, he wrote satirically; and satire is not so easy to see and not so amusing to every one as open ridicule. Dickens's pathos, too, was much more marked than Thackeray's. For these reasons Thackeray's fame grew slowly. In 1847–1848 he wrote *Vanity Fair.* Now Thackeray greatly admired Fielding, and oddly enough, this book had somewhat the same relation to Dickens's novels that Fielding's *Joseph Andrews* had to *Pamela.* Dickens always had heroes and heroines, and they were always good. They might be thrown among wicked people, but they were never led astray by bad company. Thackeray declared that *Vanity Fair* had no hero. Its heroine, Becky Sharp, is distinctly bad. Her badness and cleverness stand out in bolder relief from contrast with Amelia's goodness and dulness. The book is a satire on social life, but it is a kindly satire. Like Shakespeare, Thackeray has charity for every one; and even in the case of Becky, he does not fail to let us see how much circumstances have done to make her what she is.

Besides novels Thackeray also wrote lectures on *The English Humourists* and on *The Four Georges.* He wrote some merry burlesques, one on *Ivanhoe* called *Rebecca and Rowena,* wherein Rowena marries Ivanhoe but makes him wretched by her jealousy of Rebecca. His best novel is *Henry Esmond,* a historical romance of the eighteenth century; but in *The Newcomes* is the character that comes nearest to every one's heart, the dear old Colonel who loses his fortune and is obliged to live on the charity of the Brotherhood of the Gray Friars. If Thackeray had written nothing else, his picturing of the exquisite simplicity and self-respecting dignity with which Colonel Newcome accepts the only life that is open to him, would have been enough to prove his genius. This is the way he describes the Colonel's death:—

"Just as the last bell struck, a peculiar sweet smile shone over his face, and he lifted up his head a little, and quickly said 'Adsum' and fell back. It was the word we used at school when names were called; and, lo, he whose heart was as that of a little child had answered to his name, and stood in the presence of his Maker."

136. "George Eliot," 1820–1881

Mary Ann Evans Cross, much better known as "George Eliot," was only a few years younger than Dickens and Thackeray; but the mass of their work was done before she wrote her earliest novel. Her first thirty-two years were spent in Shakespeare's country of Warwickshire. She was always a student; and, although she left school at sixteen, she went on with French and German and music. She also studied Greek and Hebrew. When she was twenty-seven years old she translated a German work. This was so well done that it brought her much praise. She began to write essays, and in 1851 she left the house that had been made lonely by the death of her father and went to London as assistant editor of the *Westminster Review.* It was six years longer before she attempted fiction; and even then the attempt was not an idea of her own. She felt very doubtful of her ability to succeed, and probably hesitated longer about sending her *Scenes from Clerical Life* to *Blackwood's* than about forwarding her first essay to a publisher. She could hardly believe her own eyes when she read the admiring notices that appeared from all directions. There was no question that she was no longer to be a writer of essays, but of novels; and two years later *Adam Bede* came out. Then there was not only increased admiration but a curiosity that was determined to be gratified, for no one knew who was the author of either book. Carlyle was convinced that it was a man, but Dickens was one of the first to believe that it was a woman. Her next volume, *The Mill on the Floss,* tells us much of her life as a child. Not at all like Maggie of the *Mill* is the little heroine of her following book, *Silas Marner,* the story of a miser who is brought back to love and happiness by the tiny golden-haired child who made her way into his lonely cottage.

George Eliot wrote no more books about her

childhood, and we never again come as near her own life as in *The Mill on the Floss.* She wrote now a historical novel, *Romola;* now a story of English life, *Middlemarch,* and other works. In one way her novels may be said to have the same theme; the chief character longs for a nobler and better life than he has, and at last, after many efforts, he finds it. He who does wrong is punished; but with all her exactness of justice, she never fails to make us see that the temptations to which one yields are real to him, however feeble they may be to others. "When I had finished it," said Mrs. Carlyle of *Adam Bede,* "I found myself in charity with the whole human race." George Eliot's characters grow. Scott's Ivanhoe and Rebecca and Rowena are exactly the same at the end of the book as at the beginning; but Maggie Tulliver and Adam and Silas are altered by years and events. We must admit that her later novels have less freshness and beauty and humor than the earlier; but the novelist who pictures even one phase of human life as exactly, as thoughtfully, and as sympathetically as George Eliot must ever be counted among the greatest.

137. Thomas Babington Macaulay, 1800–1859

The most prominent essayists between 1832 and 1900 were Macaulay, Carlyle, Ruskin, and Arnold.

Thomas Babington Macaulay must have been as interesting when a small boy as he was when a man. He was hardly more than a baby when he read anything and everything, and his memory was so amazing that he could repeat verbatim whatever he had read. He was the busiest of children; for before he was eight, he had written an epitome of general history, and an essay on Christian religion which he hoped would convert the heathen, besides epics, hymns, and various other poems. He was always able to talk in grown-up fashion. The story is told that when he was only four years of age, some hot tea was spilled over his legs. After various remedies had been applied, he was asked if he felt better. "Thank you, madam," the little fellow replied gravely, "the agony is abated." The great charm of the wonderful boy was that he never seemed to notice that he was any brighter than other boys. He fancied that older people knew everything, and was inclined to feel humble because he did not know more. He had delightful rambles with the other children over a great common broken by ponds and bushes and hillocks and gravel pits, for every one of which he had a name and a legend. To go away to school and leave all these good times and his eight brothers and sisters was a severe trial, and he begged most piteously to come home for just one day before the vacation.

As he grew older, he no longer learned by heart without the least effort; but even then, a man who could recite the whole of *Pilgrim's Progress* and *Paradise Lost* had small reason to complain of a poor memory, and he seemed to read books by simply turning the pages. After taking his degree, he studied law, wrote a few articles for the magazines, and in 1825, when he was just twenty-five years of age, published in the *Edinburgh Review* his *Essay on Milton.* Before the next number of the *Review* was out, the young contributor was a famous man. He had done something that no one else had succeeded in doing; he had written in a style that was not only clear and

Lord Macaulay
1800–1859

strong and interesting, but was brilliant. Every sentence seemed to be the crystallization of a thought. Every sentence was so closely connected with what preceded it that the reader could almost feel that he was thinking along with the writer and that his own thoughts were being put into words.

Just as in Addison's day, each political party was on the watch for young men of literary talent, and Macaulay soon had an opportunity to enter Parliament. A few years later he was given a government position in India with a salary that enabled him to return within three years with means sufficient to justify him in devoting himself to literature. Through the years between the publication of his *Essay on Milton* and 1849, his literary fame was on the increase. He wrote a most valuable work on Indian law, he wrote a number of essays, the famous ones on Johnson and on Warren Hastings among them. He wrote his spirited *Lays of Ancient Rome,* and he read, read English, Greek, Latin, but especially English history; for he had planned no less a work than a history of England from 1688 to the French Revolution. In 1848 his first volume came out, and then Macaulay learned what popularity meant.

Novels were forgotten, for every one was reading the *History of England.* Edition after edition was issued. Within a few weeks after its publication in England, six different editions were published in the United States, and one firm alone sold 40,000 copies. As other volumes followed, the sales became even greater. In 1856, his publishers gave him a check for £20,000, "part of what will be due me in December," he wrote in his journal. Brilliant as the work is, it is severely criticised, for Macaulay was too intense in his feelings and too "cock-sure of everything," as was said of him, to be impartial; but it is a wonderful succession of the most vivid pictures and as interesting as a romance. Honors came to him thick and fast, and soon the queen raised him to the peerage. He worked away industriously, hoping to complete his history; but before the fifth volume had come to its end he died, sitting at his library table before an open book.

138. Thomas Carlyle, 1795–1881

Never were four writers more unlike than our four essayists; and the second, Thomas Carlyle, was unlike everybody else; he was in a class by himself. His father was a Scotchman, a sensible, self-respecting stone mason who had high hopes for his eldest son. When the boy had entered the University of Edinburgh, the way seemed to lie open for him to become a clergyman; but before the time came for him to take his degree, he decided that the pulpit was not the place for him. His friends must have felt a little out of patience, for he seemed to have no very definite idea of what he did want. After teaching a while, he concluded that he did not want *that* in any case, and set to work to win his living from the world by writing. The world gave no sign of caring particularly for what he wrote or for his translations from the German; and when he was thirty-one years of age, he seemed little further advanced on the road to literary glory than when he was twenty-five. In his thirty-first year he married Jane Welsh, a witty, clever young lady who was not without literary ability of her own. She had strong confidence in her husband's powers and a vast ambition for him to succeed. There was little income, and the only course seemed to be to go to her small farm of Craigenputtock; and there they lived for six years a most lonely life. Out of the solitude and dreariness came *Sartor Resartus,* "The Tailor Retailored." The foundation of the book is the notion that as man is within clothes, so the thought of God is within man and nature. The work did not meet a warm reception. "When is that stupid series of articles by the crazy tailor going to end?" asked one of the subscribers to *Fraser's,* the magazine in which it was published; and many people agreed with him, for while the pages were glowing with poetical feeling and sparkling with satire, the style was harsh and jagged and exasperating. Carlyle manufactured new words, and he used old ones in a fashion that seemed to his readers unpardonably ridiculous. It was very slowly that one after another found that the book had a message, a ringing cry to "Work while it is called To-day," and that its earnestness of purpose was arousing courage and breathing inspiration.

Carlyle decided that it was best for him to live in

London, and in 1834 Craigenputtock was abandoned. Three years later, his *History of the French Revolution* was published,—not a clear story by any means, but a series of flashlight pictures, so vivid and realistic that at last recognition came to him. For nearly thirty years he continued to write. Such keen, powerful sentences as these came from his pen:—

"No man, it has been said, is a hero to his valet; and this is probably true; but the fault is at least as likely to be the valet's as the hero's."

"No mortal has a right to wag his tongue, much less to wag his pen, without saying something."

Here are some of his definitions:—

"A dandy is a clothes-wearing man,—a man whose trade, office, and existence consist in the wearing of clothes."

"Genius means the transcendent capacity of taking trouble, first of all."

These sentences show Carlyle in his simplest style; but he was capable of such expressions as this:—

"The all of things is an infinite conjugation of the verb—'To do.'"

London he called "That monstrous tuberosity of civilized life."

His *Heroes and Hero-Worship* appeared first as lectures. Fifteen years of hard labor gave the world his *History of the Life and Times of Frederick II, commonly called Frederick the Great.* Then came honors that would have rejoiced the heart of the father who had believed in his boy. Carlyle never forgot that father, and of him he wrote, "Could I write my Books as he built his Houses, walk my way so manfully through this shadow-world, and leave it with so little blame, it were more than all my hopes." What Carlyle looked upon as his greatest honor was his being chosen Lord Rector of the University at Glasgow; but the joy was taken away from him almost before he had tasted it, for he had barely finished his inaugural address before word was brought of the death of his wife. He lived until 1881, fifteen years after meeting with this loss. During the year before his death, a cheap edition of *Sartor Resartus* was issued, and thirty thousand copies were sold within a few weeks. Carlyle had found his audience.

139. John Ruskin, 1819–1900

John Ruskin was a quiet, gentle little lad, who was brought up with books and pictures and travel and comforts of all sorts, watched over by the most loving of parents, but instantly punished for the slightest disobedience. His parents, like Carlyle's, expected their son to be a clergyman. He grew up with the thought that he should be a preacher, and a preacher he was all his life, though he did not talk in pulpits but in books. His earliest books were about art. *Modern Painters* was their name, and the first volume came out soon after he had taken his degree at Oxford. His text was the landscape painting of Turner, whom he declared to be "the greatest painter of all time." However that might be, there was no question that the young man of twenty-four was the greatest art critic of his time. For nearly twenty years he worked on the five volumes of *Modern Painters,* writing also during that time several books on architecture. He almost always gave fanciful titles to his writings, and one of his earliest architectural works he called *Stones of Venice.* Ruskin was eager to have all, even the humblest of the workingmen, enjoy art and beauty; but he found that it was very hard for a man to produce works of art or even to enjoy beauty when he was not sure of his next meal. Such thoughts as these led Ruskin to write *Unto This Last* and *Munera Pulveris,* wherein he discussed fearlessly the relations between rich and poor, employer and employed, etc. His ideas were looked upon as revolutionary, and the magazine in which *Unto This Last* was coming out refused to continue publishing the chapters. In Ruskin's time there were better opportunities to make fortunes than there had been before, and therefore the struggle for wealth was increasingly eager. He preached that not competition but Christian thoughtfulness was the proper spirit of trade; that idleness was guilt, but that labor should be made happy by the pleasures of art and the joy that comes from the ability to appreciate nature. These are the thoughts that leaven all his subsequent books, though he wrote on many different subjects, ever giving whimsically poetical titles; for example, *Deucalion* treats of "the lapse of waves and the life of stones;" *Sesame and Lilies* treats of "Kings' Treasuries," by which he means books and reading, and of "Queens' Gardens," that is, the education and rightful work of women. His final book, an autobiography, is called *Prœterita.*

Even the people who did not agree with Ruskin's theories could not help admiring his style and the wealth of imagination with which he beautified his simplest statements. His richness of imagery is not like Spenser's, however,—so overpowering that the thought is lost. With Ruskin the thought is always present, always easy to find, and very often made beautiful. All this he accomplishes with the simplest Saxon words, for a generous share of his vocabulary came from the Bible, which in his childhood days he was required to read over and over, and long passages of which he was made to learn by heart. This is the way he describes the river Rhone:—

> *There were pieces of waves that danced all day as if Perdita were looking on to learn; there were little streams that skipped like lambs and leaped like chamois; there were pools that shook the sunshine all through them, and were rippled in layers of overlaid ripples, like crystal sand; there were currents that twisted the light into golden braids, and inlaid the threads with turquoise enamel; there were strips of stream that had certainly above the lake been mill-streams, and were looking busily for mills to turn again; there were shoots of streams that had once shot fearfully into the air, and now sprang up again laughing that they had only fallen a foot or two; and in the midst of all the gay glittering and eddied lingering, the noble bearing by of the midmost depth, so mighty, yet so terrorless and harmless, with its swallows skimming instead of petrels, and the dear old decrepit town as safe in the embracing sweep of it as if it were set in a brooch of sapphire.*

People might well admire such a manner of writing;

and Ruskin once said half sadly, "All my life I have been talking to the people, and they have listened, not to what I say, but to how I say it." This is not true, however, for in art, in ethics, even in sociology, he has found a large audience of thoughtful, appreciative listeners.

140. Matthew Arnold, 1822–1888

Matthew Arnold was the son of Dr. Arnold, Head Master of Rugby, the "Doctor" of *Tom Brown at Rugby.* Ruskin was free to lead his life as he would. Arnold was a busy public official, for from his twenty-ninth year till three years before his death he was inspector of schools and could give to literature only the spare bits of his time. Yet from those broken days came forth both poetry and prose that give him a high rank. He loved the Greek literature, and in his poems there is much of the Greek restraint which does for his poetry what high-bred courtesy does for manners. In his *Forsaken Merman,* for instance, one of his most original and most exquisite poems, there is not a word of outspoken grief; but all the merman's loneliness and longing are in the oft-repeated line,—

Children, dear, was it yesterday?

Some readers are chilled by this reserve; but to those who sympathize, it suggests rather a strength of feeling that cannot weaken itself to words. The poem that he wrote in memory of his father after a visit to Rugby Chapel fairly throbs with love and suppressed sorrow, but he writes bravely:—

O strong soul, by what shore
Tarriest thou now? For that force
Surely has not been left vain!
Somewhere, surely, afar,
In the sounding labour-house vast
Of being, is practised that strength,
Zealous, beneficent, firm!

As a writer of prose, Matthew Arnold's special work is criticism of books and of life. His trumpet gives no uncertain sound. As he says, "We must accustom ourselves to a high standard and to a strict judgment." It is he who tells us that if we keep in mind lines and expressions of the great masters, they will serve as a touchstone to show us what poetry is real. This he says in his essay *On the Study of Poetry,* and it shows what clear, definite, helpful thoughts he has for those who go to him for advice or for pleasure.

In this latest age of English literature, many poets have written well, but two only are counted as of the first rank, Robert Browning and Alfred Tennyson.

141. Robert Browning, 1812–1889

One of the most interesting of Robert Browning's writings is a letter which says, "I love your verses with all my heart, dear Miss Barrett." Miss Barrett was the author of several volumes of poems, many of them full of sympathy, of tender sentiment, and of religious trust,—poems of the sort that sink into the hearts of those who love a poem even without knowing why. One of these is *The Cry of the Children,* meaning the children who were toiling in mills and in mines. It pictures their sadness and weariness, and closes with the strong lines,—

But the child's sob in the silence curses deeper
Than the strong man in his wrath.

Another favorite is *The Rhyme of the Duchess May*, which ends with a good thought expressed with the poet's frequent disregard of rhyme:—

And I smiled to think God's greatness flowed
around our incompleteness,
Round our restlessness, His rest.

The author had been an invalid for years, and she was able to see only a few people. She replied to Mr. Browning's letter, "Sympathy is dear—very dear to me; but the sympathy of a poet, and of such a poet, is the quintessence of sympathy!" It was four months before Miss Barrett was able to receive a call from Mr. Browning, but at last they met. Some time later they were married; and until the death of Mrs. Browning, in 1861, they made their home in Italy,—a home which was ideal in its love and happiness. Mr. Browning had written much poetry, but it was not nearly so famous as that of his wife. It was harder to understand; for some of it was on philosophical subjects, and some of it was dramatic. Sometimes it is not easy to tell how to classify a poem; his *Paracelsus*, for instance, is called a drama, but it is almost entirely made up of monologue. The simplest of his dramas is *Pippa Passes*. The young girl Pippa is a silk-winder who has but one holiday in the year. When the joyful morning has come, she names over the "Four Happiest" in the little town and says to herself,—

I will pass each and see their happiness
And envy none.

She "passes," first, by the house wherein is one of the "Happiest;" but Pippa does not know that this one and her lover have just committed a murder. As Pippa sings,

God's in his heaven—
All's right with the world,

the horror of their crime comes over them, and they repent of their evil. So the song of the pure little maiden touches the life of each one of the "Four Happiest;" but the child goes to sleep wondering whether she could ever come near enough to the great folk to "do good or evil to them some slight way."

After their marriage both Mr. and Mrs. Browning continued to write. Mrs. Browning's most conspicuous work was *Aurora Leigh,* a novel in verse which discusses many sociological questions,—too many for either a novel or a poem,— and her beautiful *Sonnets from the Portuguese,* which were in reality not from the Portuguese, but straight from her own heart, and which tell with most exquisite delicacy the story of her love for her husband. Browning published two volumes before the death of his wife, *Christmas Eve and Easter Day,* and *Men and Women.* In 1868–1869 and more than thirty-five years after he began to write, he published *The Ring and the Book.* This is the story of an Italian murder, which in the course of the poem is related by a number of different persons. It met with a hearty reception, partly because it is not only a poem and a fine one but also a wonderful picturing of the impression made by one act upon several unlike persons; and partly because in those thirty-five years Browning's admirers, consisting for a long time of one reader here and another one there, had increased until now his audience was ready for him. Indeed, it was growing with amazing rapidity, partly because of his real merit, and partly because he sometimes wrote in most involved and obscure fashion. People who liked to think were pleased with the resistance of the more difficult poems; they liked to puzzle out the meaning. People who did not like to think but who did wish to be counted among the thinkers hastened to buy Browning's poems and to join Browning clubs.

Robert Browning
1812–1889

The best way for most people to enjoy these poems is not to struggle with some obscure and unimportant difficulty of phrase or of thought, but to read first what they like best, and find little by little what he has said that belongs to them especially. Read some of the shorter lyrics: *Prospice, The Lost Leader, The Pied Piper of Hamelin,* that weird and fascinating rhyme for children, and *Rabbi Ben Ezra,* with its magnificent—

Grow old along with me!
The best is yet to be.

Those last two lines are the keynote of Browning's inspiration, his cheerful courage in looking at life and his robust confidence in the blessedness of the life that lies beyond. One cannot have too much of Browning.

142. Alfred Tennyson, 1809–1892

Neither is it possible to have too much of Tennyson, who, far more than Browning, was the representative poet of the Victorian Age. Two stories have been saved from Tennyson's childhood. One is of the five-year old child tossing his arms in the blast and crying, "I hear a voice that's speaking in the wind." The other is of an older brother's reading a slateful of the little Alfred's verses and declaring judicially, "Yes, you can write." There were twelve of the Tennyson children. "They all wrote verses," said a neighbor; and when Alfred was seventeen and one of his brothers a year older, they published a little book of verse. Two years later Alfred entered college, and while in college he published *Poems, Chiefly Lyrical.* These seem less like completed works than like the first sketches of an artist for a picture. They are glimpses of the poet's talent, experiments in sound rather than expressions of thought. In 1832 he brought out a little volume which ought to have convinced whoever glanced at it that a true poet had arisen, for here were not only such poems as *The May Queen* and *Lady Clara Vere de Vere,* which were sure to strike the popular fancy, but also *The Dream of Fair Women, The Lotus-Eaters,* and *The Lady of Shalott.* Nevertheless, the critics were severe; and this was perhaps the best thing that could have happened to the young poet, for he set to work to study and think. Ten years later he brought out two more volumes, and then there was no question that he was the first poet of his time. The best known of these poems are his thrilling little song,—

Break, break, break,
On thy cold gray stones, O Sea!
And I would that my tongue could utter
The thoughts that arise in me,

and *Locksley Hall.* The latter has been read and recited and quoted and parodied, but it is not even yet worn out. Here are the two stanzas that were Tennyson's special favorites:—

Love took up the glass of Time and turn'd it in his glowing hands;
Every moment, lightly shaken, ran itself in golden sands.

Love took up the harp of Life, and smote on all the chords with might;
Smote the chord of Self, that, trembling, pass'd in music out of sight.

In these volumes, too, were *Morte d'Arthur* and snatches of poems on Galahad and Launcelot,—enough to show that Tennyson had found old Malory, and that the stories of King Arthur and the Round Table were haunting his mind. When *The Princess* came out, there was some criticism of the impossible story in a probable setting, of the mingling of the earnest and the burlesque, which the poet had not entirely forestalled by calling the poem a *Medley.* It is a very beautiful medley, however, and the songs which were interspersed in the later edition are most exquisite. Here are "Sweet and Low," "The splendor falls on castle walls," and others.

The year 1850 was a marked season for Tennyson. It was the year of his marriage to the lady from whom financial reasons had separated him for twelve years; it was the year of publication of *In Memoriam* and of his appointment as Laureate. *In Memoriam* was called forth by the death of Arthur Henry Hallam, Tennyson's best-loved college friend, which took place seventeen years earlier. It is a collection of short poems, gleams of his thoughts of his friend, changing as time passed from "large grief," from questioning, "How fares it with the happy dead?" from tender memories of Hallam's words and ways—from all these to the hour when he who grieved could rest—

And hear at times a sentinel
Who moves about from place to place,
And whispers to the worlds of space,
In the deep night, that all is well.

The duties of the Laureate have vanished, but there is a mild expectation that he will manifest some interest in the greater events of the kingdom by an occasional poem. Tennyson fulfilled this expectation generously, and his Laureate poems have a clear ring of sincerity. They range all the way from his welcome to the present queen of England,—

Sea-kings' daughter from over the sea,

to his superb *Ode on the Death of the Duke of Wellington:*

Bury the Great Duke
With an empire's lamentation,
Let us bury the Great Duke
To the noise of the mourning of a mighty nation.

Not only sincerity, but tender respect and sympathy, unite in his dedication of the *Idylls of the King* to the memory of Prince Albert:—

These to His Memory—since he held them dear,
Perchance as finding there unconsciously
Some image of himself.

Alfred, Lord Tennyson
1809–1892

To the queen in her sadness he says:—

Break not, O woman's heart, but still endure;
Break not, for thou art Royal, but endure.

In the *Idylls* Tennyson had come to his kingdom; for the "dim, rich" legends were after his own heart. Here was a thread of story which he could alter as he would; here were love, valor, innocence, faithlessness, treachery, religious ecstasy, an earthly journey with a heavenly recompense. Here were opportunities for the brilliant and varied ornament in which he delighted, for all the beauties of description, and for a character drawing as strong as it was delicate.

In the *Idylls* Tennyson shows his power to present the complex in character; but in *Enoch Arden* he draws with no less skill a simple fisherman who through no fault of his own meets lifelong sorrow and loneliness. Enoch, is wrecked on a desert island, and his wife, believing him dead, finally yields and marries his friend. After many years Enoch finds his way home, but his home is his no more, and he prays:—

Uphold me, Father, in my loneliness
A little longer! aid me, give me strength
Not to tell her, never to let her know.
Help me not to break in upon her peace.

So simply, so naturally is the story told that the whole force of the silent tragedy, of the greatness of the fisherman hero, is not realized till the triumph of the closing words,—

So past the strong, heroic soul away.

Yielding to the fascination which the drama has for men of literary genius, Tennyson wrote several historical plays, but this was not his field. The characters are not lifelike, and, though the plays read well, they do not act well.

Among his last work was *Crossing the Bar.* Every true poet has a message. His was of faith and trust, and nothing could be more fitting as his *envoy* than the closing stanza of this lyric:—

For though from out our bourne of Time and Place
The flood may bear me far,
I hope to see my Pilot face to face
When I have crost the bar.

143. The Age of the Pen

The nineteenth century has been called the age of steam and electricity; but perhaps a better name would be the age of the pen, for almost every one writes. In this mass of literary work there is much excellence; but, leaving out the greatest authors, only a prophet could select "the few, the immortal names that were not born to die." The historical value of these many writers is unknown, their intrinsic value is undecided; criticism is variable, and is prejudiced by their nearness. Nevertheless, it is hard to pass over the "Pre-Raphaelite Brotherhood," such a group of poets as William Morris with his *Earthly Paradise,* Dante Gabriel Rossetti with the weird charm of his *Blessed Damozel;* and Algernon Charles Swinburne, whose verses, ever strong and intense, reveal the touch of a master of all music.

Aside from the historians already named, the greater number of writers of history have taken England for their theme. John Richard Green, in his *Short History of the English People,* gave new life to the men of the olden times; Edward Augustus Freeman, ever accurate and painstaking, wrote of the *Norman Conquest;* James Anthony Froude was, like Macaulay, a partisan, and therefore not always to be trusted in his estimates of men, but, like Macaulay, he possessed the "historical imagination," which is, after all, little more than the ability to remember that men of the past were as human as men of the present.

Among scientific writings Charles Darwin's *Origin of Species,* Sir Charles Lyell's *Principles of Geology,* and the works of Tyndall and Huxley have been most widely read. The names of essayists and critics are many. Walter Pater with his harmonious sentences, John Henry Newman with his exquisitely polished diction, are well

Cardinal Newman

known and are well worthy of honor. Especially hopeless is the effort to make a satisfactory choice among the novelists. Not every one would dream of attempting a scientific treatise or a volume of even second-rate poetry; but who is there, from Disraeli, the British premier, to the young girl whose graduation gown is still fresh, that does not feel the longing to produce a novel? Edward Bulwer Lytton, Lord Lytton, won fame by his *Last Days of Pompeii;* Elizabeth Cleghorn Gaskell was the author of *Cranford,* that little masterpiece of delineation of village life; Charles Reade wrote *Put Yourself in His Place* and other stories, many of which aimed vigorous blows at some social injustice. Within the last twenty years novels have made their appearance by the score. Who can say whether the excellence which we see in many of them is really enduring excellence or only some quality so especially congenial to our own times that it seems excellent to us? Whether these later works are strong and lasting currents in the stream of England's literature or whether they are only eddies and ripples, it is too early to decide.

The Poets' Corner, Westminster Abbey

For twelve hundred years or longer this stream has flowed, now narrowed, now broadened, but ever moving onward. The epic has swept on from the simple thought and primeval virtues of Beowulf to the harmonious organ tones of Paradise Lost. The drama, beginning with the mystery play, has come to its height under the magic touch of Shakespeare, and presents not only action but that intangible thing, thought, and development of character. The early lyric is known to us in a single poem, *Widsith*. To-day lyric poetry means the glorious outburst of song of the Elizabethan times; it means such poems as Browning's *Prospice*, wherein the physical courage of the viking has become the religious courage of the Christian; and it means such delicate, thoughtful, sympathetic love of nature and such exquisiteness of expression as are shown in the works of Burns and Wordsworth and Tennyson. Prose, at first as heavy and rough and clumsy as a weapon of some savage tribe, has become through centuries of hammering and filing and tempering as keen as a Damascus blade. History, which was at first the bare statement of certain occurrences, has become a vivid panorama of events, combined with profound study of their causes and their results. Biography is no longer the throwing of a preternatural halo around its subject; the ideal biography of to-day is that which, uncolored by the prejudice of the writer, presents the man himself as interpreted by his deeds and words. The novel is the form of literary expression belonging especially to the present age; and because of its very nearness to us in time and in interest, the judgment of its merits is difficult. Of two points, however, we may be sure: first, that to centre in one character of a book all interest and all careful workmanship is a mark of degeneracy; second, that to picture life faithfully, but with the faithfulness of the artist and not of the camera, is a mark of excellence. It is this requirement of faithfulness to truth which is after all the most worthy literary "note" of our age. The history must be accurate; the biography must be unprejudiced; the reasoning of the essay must be without fallacy; the poem must flash out a genuine thought; and the novel that would endure must be true to life. Whatever the future of England's literature may be, it has at least the foundation of honest effort and an inexorable demand for sincerity and truth.

SUMMARY

Century XIX

CENTURY OF THE NOVEL

Before 1832

The "Lake Poets:"
- William Wordsworth.
- Samuel Taylor Coleridge.
- Robert Southey.

The romantic poets:
- Walter Scott (historical novelist).
- Lord Byron.

Lovers of beauty:
- Percy Bysshe Shelley.
- John Keats.

Essayists:
- Charles Lamb.
- Thomas De Quincey

The realist:
- Jane Austen.

During the first thirty years of the century the principal authors were:—

1. The "Lake Poets,"—Wordsworth, Coleridge, and Southey. Wordsworth believed that poetry should treat of simple subjects in every-day language. Coleridge

believed in treating lofty subjects in a realistic manner. These theories were illustrated by *We Are Seven* and *The Ancient Mariner.* Southey wrote weird epics whose scenes were laid in distant lands, and also many histories and biographies. Coleridge had universal talent, but left everything incomplete. Wordsworth quietly wrote on, and slowly his power to describe and interpret nature was recognized.

2. The romantic writers, Scott and Byron. Scott's first work was ballad writing and ballad collecting. Then came the *Lay of the Last Minstrel, Marmion*, etc. Byron's poetry won the attention of the crowd, and Scott then devoted himself to the *Waverley* novels. He undertook also histories, biographies, and translations; and the inventor of the historical novel died of overwork.

Byron's first poetry was savagely reviewed, and he replied fiercely. *Childe Harold* made him famous. He wrote many cynical, romantic narrative poems and many beautiful descriptions of nature. He died while trying to help the Greeks win freedom from the Turks.

3. The lovers of beauty, Shelley and Keats. Shelley's life was a continual revolt against established law. His poems are marked not only by beauty but by a certain light and airy quality which makes them unlike other poems.

Keats's first poem, *Endymion*, was criticised as savagely as Byron's early work. He made no reply and continued to write. Although he died at the age of twenty-four, he is ranked among the first of those who have loved beauty and created it.

4. The essayists, Lamb and De Quincey. Lamb could give to literature only fragments of his time. He attempted poems, stories, and plays; but had no special success till the publication of *Tales from Shakespeare*. His best work was his *Essays of Elia*, wherein he shows himself the most graceful and charming of humorists.

De Quincey's first work, *Confessions of an English Opium-Eater*, won much attention and was the first of his one hundred and fifty magazine articles; wherein he is dreamy, whimsical, or merely the teller of a plain story, as the mood seizes him; but is always interesting.

5. The magazine critics. *The Edinburgh Review*, edited by Jeffrey; the *Quarterly Review;* and *Blackwood's*, edited by John Wilson, were all founded during the first twenty years of the century.

6. The realist, Jane Austen, who wrote quiet novels of home life with exceedingly good delineation of character.

After 1832

Novelists:
- Charles Dickens.
- William Makepeace Thackeray.
- "George Eliot."

Poets:
- Robert Browning and Mrs. Browning.
- Alfred Tennyson.

Essayists:
- Thomas Babington Macaulay (historian).
- Thomas Carlyle.
- John Ruskin.
- Matthew Arnold.

In 1832, nearly all these authors were dead or had ceased to write. There were changes in government; education became more general; reading matter was cheaper; scientific discoveries aroused thought. During the half-century following 1832, there was a remarkable development of:—

1. The novel, in the hands of Dickens, Thackeray, and "George Eliot." The *Pickwick Papers* made Dickens famous. During twenty years he published novel after novel, merry, pathetic, but always charming; even though the characters often seem unreal and are usually labelled by some one quality.

Thackeray was less amusing and won fame more slowly. He was a satirist, but a kindly one. He wrote not only novels but lectures, literary and historical, and historical novels.

"George Eliot" did not attempt fiction till she was thirty-seven, but her first work was so successful that after its publication she devoted herself to novel writing. Even aside from their literary merit, the justice and charity of her novels can hardly fail to make them lasting.

2. The essay, in the hands of Macaulay, Carlyle, Ruskin, and Arnold. Macaulay wrote at twenty-five his essay on Milton, the brilliant style of which brought him recognition. He wrote many essays, some poetry, and then his *History of England*. This was not impartial by any means, but was intensely interesting and sold in enormous numbers.

Carlyle had reached middle age before his talent was recognized, chiefly because he often wrote in a harsh and disagreeable style. His *Life of Frederick II*, published when he was between sixty and seventy, brought him wide fame and honors of all kinds.

Ruskin at the age of twenty-four was recognized as the greatest art critic of his time. His love of beauty and his wish that workingmen should enjoy it led him to a fearless discussion of the relations between rich and poor, and thereby he aroused severe criticism. His style, however, was admired by all.

Arnold, like Lamb, could give to literature only spare minutes. His poems are marked by a Greek restraint. His prose was in great degree made up of criticism of books and life; in both of which he insisted upon a high standard.

3. In poetry, Browning and Tennyson are counted as of the first rank. Browning's wife was famous as a poet in her early years, but appreciation came to him slowly. For thirty-five years he found only scattered admirers. Then he published *The Ring and the Book*, and at last his audience was ready. His writings are often involved in thought and in phrase; but they are of a high order of poetry and are marked by courage and faith.

Tennyson was the representative poet of the Victorian Age. His first work seems like experiments in sound. Excellent as it is, it met severe criticism. Twelve years after the publication of his first volume he was recognized as the first poet of his time. His most popular works are *In Memoriam, The Idylls of the*

King, and *Enoch Arden*, three poems of utterly different character. His Laureate poems have an unusual ring of sincerity. His attempts at drama were not successful. His message, like Browning's, was one of faith and trust.

Besides those mentioned, the century has been rich in poets, novelists, historians, scientists, and essayists, many of whom in almost any other age would have been looked upon as men of the highest genius.

Tracing the course of English literature for twelve hundred years, we see the development of both poetry and prose from the simplest beginnings to a high degree of excellence. The novel is the special form of literary expression characteristic of this age. In it, as in all other literary work of the time, the first demand is for faithfulness to truth.

William Cullen Bryant — Edgar A. Poe — Walt Whitman

J. R. Lowell — Henry W. Longfellow — Oliver Wendell Holmes

R. Waldo Emerson — Sidney Lanier — John G. Whittier

A SHORT HISTORY OF AMERICA'S LITERATURE

PREFACE

We are so near to even the beginning of our American literature that to write its history is an especially difficult undertaking. Too little time has passed to trace influences and tendencies, perhaps even to estimate justly the value of the work whose strongest appeal is not to the present. During the last century, our world has moved so swiftly that the light has flashed now upon one writer, now upon another. Who can foretell upon which the noontide of to-morrow will shine most brilliantly? Who can say whether our realism will not seem unworthy triviality, whether the closely connected sentences of our best prose may not present the repellent formality of conscious art? In every decade many writers have come forward whose names it seems ungracious to omit. Wherever the lines are drawn, they will appear to some one an arbitrary and unreasonable barrier. A single slender volume can make no pretensions to completeness; but if this one only leads its readers to feel a friendship for the authors mentioned on its pages, and a wish to know more of them and their writings, its object will have been accomplished.

CHAPTER I

1607–1765

THE COLONIAL PERIOD

1. Literary Work in England

In the early part of the seventeenth century England was all aglow with literary inspiration. Shakespeare was writing his noblest tragedies. Ben Jonson was writing plays, adoring his friend Shakespeare, and growling at him because he would not observe the rules of the classical drama. Francis Bacon was rising swiftly to the height of his glory as Chancellor of England and incidentally composing essays so keen and strong and brilliant that he seems to have said the last word on whatever subject he touches. There were many lesser lights, several of whom would have been counted great in any other age.

2. Early American Histories

In all the blaze of this literary glory colonists began to sail away from the shores of England for the New World. They had to meet famine, cold, pestilence, hard work, and danger from the Indians. Nevertheless, our old friend, John Smith, wrote a book on Virginia, and George Sandys completed on Virginian soil his translation of Ovid's *Metamorphoses.* These men, however, were only visitors to America; and, important as their writings may be historically or poetically, they have small connection with American literature. It was on the rockbound coast of Massachusetts that our literature made its real beginning. The earnest, serious Pilgrims and Puritans disapproved of the plays and masques that were flourishing in England; pastoral verse was to them a silly affectation; the delicate accuracy of the sonnet showed a sinful waste of time and thought. They were striving to make an abode for righteousness, and whatever did not manifestly conduce to that single aim, they counted as of evil. Writing their own history, however, was reckoned a most godly work. "We are the Lord's chosen people," they said to themselves with humble pride. "His hand is ever guiding us. Whatever happens to us then must be of importance, and for the glory of God it should be recorded." With this thought in mind, Governor William Bradford of Plymouth, the "Father of American History," wrote his *History of Plymouth Plantation,* "in a plaine stile," as he says, and "with singuler regard unto ye simple trueth in all things." He tells about the struggles and sufferings of his people in the Old World, about that famous scene in Holland when "their Revẽ^{d} pastor falling downe on his knees, (and they all with him,) with watri cheeks comended them with most fervent praiers to the Lord and his blessing. And then with mutuall imbrases and many tears, they tooke their leaves one of an other; which proved to be ye last leave to many of them." Governor Bradford could picture well such a scene as this, and he could also write spicily of the lordly salt-maker who came among them. "He could not doe anything but boil salt in pans," says the Governor, "and yet would make them y[t] were joynd with him beleeve there was so great misterie in it as was not easie to be attained, and made them doe many unnecessary things to blind their eys, till they discerned his sutltie."

A second history, that of New England, was also written by a governor, John Winthrop of the Massachusetts Bay Colony. Among his accounts of weightier matters he does not forget to tell of the little, everyday occurrences,—of the chimney that took fire, of the calf that wandered away and was lost, of the two young men on shipboard who were punished for fighting by having their hands tied behind them and being ordered to walk up and down the deck all day, of the strange visions and lights that were seen and the strange voices that were heard. It is such details as these that carry us back to the lives of our ancestors, their fears and their troubles.

3. The Bay Psalm Book, 1640

While these two histories were being written, three learned men in Massachusetts set to work to prepare a version of the *Psalms* to use in church. A momentous question arose: Would it be right to use a trivial and unnecessary ornament like rhyme? "There is sometimes rhyme in the original Hebrew," said one, "and therefore it must be right to use it." Thus established, they took their pens in hand, and in 1640 the famous *Bay Psalm Book* was published in America, the first book printed on American soil. This was the version of Psalm xxxv, 5:—

As chaffe before the winde, let them
be, & Gods Angell them driving.
Let their way dark and slippery bee,
and the Lords Angell them chasing.

The "Admonition to the Reader" at the end of the book declares that many of these psalms may be sung to "neere fourty common tunes," and indeed there seems no reason why a hymn like this should not be sung to one tune as well as another. Now these struggling poets were scholars; two of them were university graduates. They had lived in England during the noblest age of English poetry. Why, then, did they make the *Psalms* into such doggerel? The reason was that they were in agonies of conscience lest they should allow the charm of some poetical expression to lure them away from the seriousness of truth; and they declared with artless complacency and somewhat unnecessary frankness that they had "attended Conscience rather than Elegance, fidelity rather than poetry."

A generous amount of verse was written in the colonies even in the early days. Many of the settlers were educated men, fully accustomed to putting their thoughts on paper, and they seemed to feel that it dignified a thought to make it into verse. Religion was the all-absorbing subject, and therefore they have left us many thousand lines of religious hopes and fears. Unfortunately, it takes more than study to make a man a poet, and hardly a line of all the accumulation can be called poetry.

4. Michael Wigglesworth, 1631–1705

The most lengthy piece of this early colonial rhyme was produced by the Reverend Michael Wigglesworth of Malden. It was called *The Day of Doom, or, A Poetical Description of the Great and Last Judgment.* It painted with considerable imaginative power the Last Judgment as the Reverend Michael thought it ought to be. After the condemnation of the other sinners, the "reprobate infants," the children who had died in babyhood, appear at the bar of God and plead that they are not to blame for what Adam did. They say:—

Not we, but he ate of the Tree
whose fruit was interdicted:
Yet on us all of his sad Fall,
the punishment 's inflicted.

The answer is:—

A Crime it is, therefore in bliss
you may not hope to dwell;
But unto you I shall allow
the easiest room in Hell.

The early colonists bought this book in such numbers that it may be looked upon as America's first and greatest literary success. The first year 1800 copies were sold; and it is estimated that with our increased population this would be equivalent to a sale of 2,000,000 copies to-day.

5. Anne Bradstreet, 1612 or 1613–1672

The praise of Michael Wigglesworth was as naught when compared with the glory of one Mistress Anne Bradstreet, who abode with her husband and

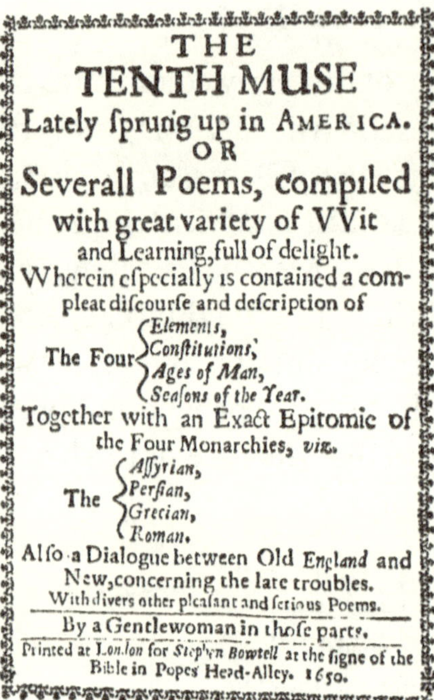

THE
TENTH MUSE
Lately ſprung up in AMERICA.
OR
Severall Poems, compiled
with great variety of VVit
and Learning, full of delight.
Wherein eſpecially is contained a com-
pleat diſcourſe and deſcription of
The Four *Elements*, *Conſtitutions*, *Ages of Man*, *Seaſons of the Year*.
Together with an Exact Epitomie of
the Four Monarchies, *viz.*
The *Aſſyrian*, *Perſian*, *Grecian*, *Roman*.
Alſo a Dialogue between Old *England* and
New, concerning the late troubles.
With divers other pleaſant and ſerious Poems.
By a Gentlewoman in thoſe parts.
Printed at *London* for *Stephen Bowtell* at the ſigne of the
Bible in Popes Head-Alley. 1650.

The Title-Page of Anne Bradstreet's Book of Poems

eight children in the wilderness of Andover and therein did write much poetry. People were in ecstasies over her compositions, and they did not accuse her publisher of exaggeration when he wrote on the title-page of her book, "Severall Poems, compiled with great variety of Wit and Learning, full of delight." She was called "The Tenth Muse, lately sprung up in America." Learned Cotton Mather declared that her work "would outlast the stateliest marble." However that may be, it was certainly the nearest approach to poetry that the colonies produced during their first century, and now and then we find a phrase with some little poetic merit. In her poem *Contemplations,* for instance, are the lines:—

I heard the merry grasshopper then sing,
The black-clad cricket bear a second part;
They kept one tune and played on the same string,
Seeming to glory in their little art.

6. The Children's Book

One cannot help wondering a little what the

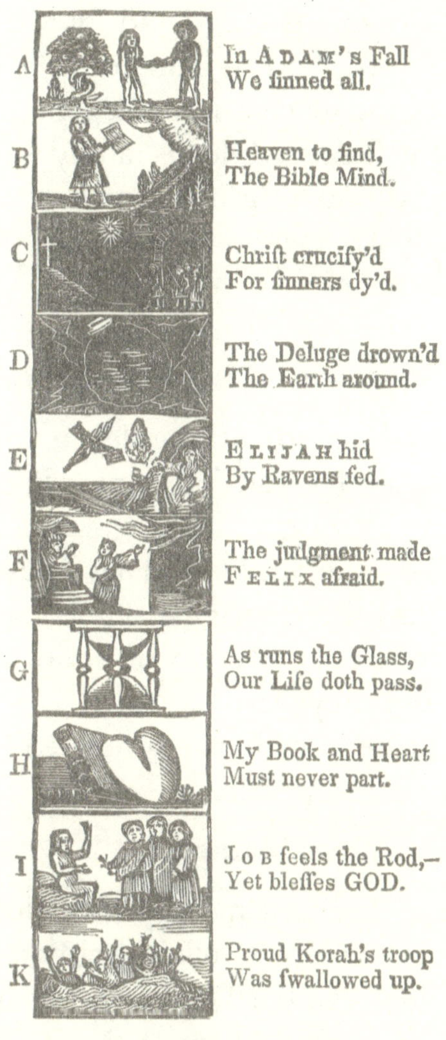

The Alphabet in the New England Primer

children found to read in colonial days, for the youngest baby Pilgrim was an old man before it occurred to any one to write a child's book. Even then, it was a book that most of the boys and girls of to-day would think rather dull, for it was a serious little schoolbook called the *New England Primer.* No one knows who wrote it, but it was published by one Benjamin Harris at his coffee-house and bookstore in Boston, "by the Town-Pump near the Change," some time between 1687 and 1690. It contained such knowledge as was thought absolutely necessary for children. After the alphabet came a long list of two-letter combinations, "ab, eb, ib, ob, ub; ac, ec, ic, oc, uc," etc.; then a list of words of one syllable; and at last the child had worked his way triumphantly to "a-bom-i-na-tion" and "qual-i-fi-ca-tion." There were several short and simple prayers, and there was a picture of the martyr, John Rogers, standing composedly in the flames while his family wept around him, and the executioner grinned maliciously. There was a second alphabet with a rhyme and a picture for every letter. It began:—

In Adam's Fall
We sinnéd all.

In the course of countless reprints, many changes were made. It is said that in one edition or another the couplet for every letter in the alphabet was changed except that for A; but the Puritan never gave up his firm grasp upon the belief in original sin. For a century these two lines were a part of every orthodox child's moral equipment, and they were the keynote of the greater part of the prose and rhyme produced in America during the colonial period.

7. Cotton Mather, 1663–1728

Even if almost all the colonial books were written for the grown folk, the children and their future were not forgotten. How to make sure of educated ministers for them and for their children's children was the question. It was settled by the founding of Harvard College in 1636, only sixteen years after the little band of Pilgrims landed at Plymouth. One of its most famous graduates during the colonial days was the Reverend Cotton Mather. He took his degree at fifteen, and three years later he was already so famous for his learning that he received an urgent call to become a pastor in far-away New Haven. He refused, became his father's assistant at the North Church in Boston; and at the North Church he remained for more than forty years. Preaching, however, was but a small part of his work. He had the largest library in the colonies, and he knew it thoroughly. He could write in seven languages; he was deeply interested in science; he kept fasts and vigils innumerable. He was grave and somewhat stern in manner, and people were seldom quite at ease with him; but he had a tender spot in his heart for boys and girls, and whenever he passed through a village, he used to beg a holiday for the children of the place. He was horrified at the severity shown in the schools of the day; and among his own flock of fifteen there was rarely any punishment more severe than to be forbidden to enter his presence. One of his sons wrote that their father never rose from the table without first telling them some entertaining story, and that when a child had done some little deed that he knew would please the stately minister, he would run to him, and say, "Now, father, tell me some curious thing."

With all his other occupations, he did an immense amount of writing. Nearly four hundred books and pamphlets have been published, and there are still thousands of pages in manuscript. His best-known book is his *Magnalia Christi Americana,* or *The Ecclesiastical History of New England.* Like Bede's *Ecclesiastical History,* it is much more entertaining than one would think from its ponderous title. Cotton Mather's aim was to record the dealings of God with his chosen people, and the character of those people. He followed the fashion of dropping in bits of Latin and Greek, and making intricate contrasts and comparisons that sometimes remind the reader of John Donne—without Donne's genius. He begins the book with an imitation of the Æneid, which he and his early readers probably thought extremely effective. But there is much besides a Virgilian preface in his work. There are enthusiastic descriptions of the men whom he admired, written with many a touch of beauty and sincere tenderness. Then, too, the book is a perfect storehouse of all sorts of wonder-tales: the story of the "ship in the air" which Longfellow made into a rhyme, using often the very words of the old chronicler; that of the two-headed snake of Newbury, of which Whittier wrote; and many others. Among the pages that bristle with august phrases from the dead languages, we find here and there some simple story like the following, which is told of Winthrop, and which makes us feel that Mather in his wig and bands and Winthrop in his exasperatingly untumbled ruff are not so unlike men of to-day, and would be exceedingly interesting people to know:—

> *In a hard and long Winter, when Wood was very scarce at Boston, a Man gave him a private Information, that a needy Person in his Neighbourhood stole Wood sometimes from his Pile; whereupon the Governour in a seeming Anger did reply, Does he so? I'll take a Course with him; go, call that Man to me, I'll warrant you I'll cure him of stealing! When the Man came, the Governour considering that if he had Stoln, it was more out of Necessity than Disposition, said unto him, Friend, It is a severe Winter, and I doubt you are but meanly provided for Wood; wherefore I would have you supply yourself at my Wood-Pile till*

this cold Season be over. And he then Merrily asked his Friends, Whether he had not effectually cured this Man of Stealing his Wood?

8. Samuel Sewall, 1652–1730

During the greater part of Cotton Mather's life an interesting diary was being written by Judge Samuel Sewall. He tells of being comfortable in the stoveless meeting-house, though his ink froze by a good fire at home; of whipping his little Joseph "pretty smartly" for "playing at Prayer-time and eating when Returne Thanks;" of the lady who cruelly refused to bestow her hand upon the eager widower, even though wooed with prodigal munificence by the gift of "one-half pound of sugar almonds, cost three shillings per pound." Though the writings of the honest old Judge cannot strictly be called literature, their frank revelation of everyday life presents too excellent a background for the writings of others to be entirely forgotten.

9. Jonathan Edwards, 1703–1758

In 1730 Judge Sewall died. In that year a young man of twenty-seven was preaching in Northampton who was to become famous for his original, clear, and logical thought and his power to move an audience. He had been a wonder all the days of his life. When he ought to have been playing marbles, he was reading Greek and Latin and Hebrew. He was deeply interested in natural philosophy, and even more deeply in theology. When he was fourteen, he read Locke's *Essay on the Human Understanding,* and declared that it inexpressibly entertained and pleased him.

Such was Jonathan Edwards. He was the greatest clergyman of the first half of the eighteenth century, and some have not feared to call him the "most original and acute thinker yet produced in America." He was quite different from the earlier colonial pastors like Cotton Mather, men who were gazed upon by their flocks with wonder and humble reverence as recognized leaders in religion, learning, and politics. His time was devoted to theology. After twenty-four years in Northampton he went to the little village of Stockbridge and became a missionary to the Indians. Then there was such poverty in the Edwards family that fresh, whole sheets of paper were a rare luxury, and the thoughts of the keenest mind in the land were jotted down on the backs of letters or the margins of pamphlets. By and by these thoughts were published in book form. This book was *The Inquiry into the Freedom of the Will.* Then the modest missionary to the Indians became famous among metaphysicians the world over, for in acute, powerful reasoning he had no superior. It is small wonder that Princeton hastened to send a messenger to the little village in the wilderness to offer him the presidency of the college. He accepted the offer, but died after only one month's service.

Jonathan Edwards
1703–1758

Unfortunately, the passage of Edwards's writings that is oftenest quoted is from his sermon on "Sinners in the hands of an angry God," wherein even his clearsightedness confuses God's pitying love for the sinner with his hatred of sin. More in harmony with Edwards's natural disposition is his simple, frank description of his boyhood happiness when after many struggles he first began to realize the love of God. He wrote:—

> *The appearance of everything was altered; there seemed to be, as it were, a calm, sweet cast or appearance of divine glory in almost everything. God's excellency, his wisdom, his purity and love, seemed to appear in everything: in the sun, moon, and stars; in the clouds and blue sky; in the grass, flowers, trees; in the water and all nature; which used greatly to fix my mind. I often used to sit and view the moon for a long time; and in the day spent much time in viewing the clouds and sky, to behold the sweet glory of God in these things: in the mean time, singing forth, with a low voice, my contemplations of the Creator and Redeemer. And scarce anything, among all the works of nature, was so sweet to me as thunder and lightning; formerly nothing had been so terrible to me. Before, I used to be uncommonly terrified with thunder, and to be struck with terror when I saw a thunder-storm rising; but now, on the contrary, it rejoiced me. I felt God, if I may so speak, at the first appearance of a thunder-storm; and used to take the opportunity, at such times, to fix myself in order to view the clouds, and see the lightnings play, and hear the majestic and awful voice of God's thunder.*

10. Minor Writers

Such was the literature of our colonial days. Few names can be mentioned, but there were scores of minor writers. There was Roger Williams, that lover of peace and arouser of contention; John Eliot, one of the three manufacturers of the *Bay Psalm Book*, whose Indian Bible is a part of literature, if not of American literature. There was the witty grumbler, Nathaniel Ward, the "Simple Cobler of Agawam;" William Byrd, who described so graphically the dangers and difficulties of running a surveyor's line across the Dismal Swamp. There was John Woolman, the Quaker, so tender of conscience that he believed it wasteful and therefore wrong to injure the wearing qualities of cloth by coloring it; and of such charming frankness that he confesses how uneasy he felt lest his fellow Friends should think he was "affecting singularity" in wearing a hat of the natural color of the fur. Some of the paragraphs of his journal might almost have come from the pen of Whittier, so full are they of the poet's sensitiveness and shyness and his boldness in doing right. There were newspapers, the *Boston News Letter* the first of all. There were almanacs, the first appearing at Cambridge almost as soon as Harvard College was founded.

The colonial days passed swiftly, and the time soon came when the country was aroused and thrilled by an event that changed the aim and purpose of all colonial writings. In 1765 the Stamp Act was passed; and after that date, when men took their pens in hand, their compositions did not belong to the Colonial Period;

for, consciously or unconsciously, they had entered into the second period of American literature, the literature of the Revolution.

SUMMARY

1607–1765

THE COLONIAL PERIOD

William Bradford	*"The New England Primer"*
John Winthrop	*Cotton Mather*
"The Bay Psalm Book"	*Samuel Sewall*
Michael Wigglesworth	*Jonathan Edwards*
Anne Bradstreet	

In the early part of the seventeenth century England was aglow with literary inspiration. American literature began in Massachusetts, in the histories written by Bradford and Winthrop. The *Bay Psalm Book* was the first book published in America. Much verse of good motive but small merit was written, the longest piece being Wigglesworth's *Day of Doom.* Anne Bradstreet wrote the best of the colonial verse. The only book for children was the *New England Primer.* Cotton Mather was the last of the typical colonial ministers. Sewall's diary pictures colonial days. Edwards was the greatest preacher of the first half of the eighteenth century. He won world-wide fame as a metaphysician. Among the minor writers were Williams, Eliot, Ward, Byrd, and Woolman. The passage of the Stamp Act in 1765 marked the beginning of the second period of American literature, the literature of the Revolution.

CHAPTER II

1765–1815

THE REVOLUTIONARY PERIOD

11. Benjamin Franklin, 1706–1790

The Stamp Act was an electric shock to the colonists. They expected to be ruled for the benefit of the mother country, for that was the custom of the age; but this Act they believed to be illegal, and it aroused all their Anglo-Saxon wrath at injustice. There was small inclination now to write religious poems or histories of early days. Every one was talking about the present crisis. As time passed, orations and political writings flourished; and satires and war songs had their place, followed by lengthy poems on the assured greatness and glory of America.

At the first threat of a Stamp Act, Pennsylvania had sent one of her colonists to England to prevent its passage if possible. This emissary was Benjamin Franklin, a Boston boy who had run away to Philadelphia. There he had become printer and publisher, and was widely known as a shrewd, successful business man, full of public spirit. He spent in all nearly eighteen years in England as agent of Pennsylvania and other colonies. On one of his visits home he signed the Declaration of Independence. Almost immediately he was sent to France to secure French aid in our Revolutionary struggles. Then he returned to America, and spent the five years of life that remained to him in serving his country and the people about him in every way in his power.

Benjamin Franklin
1706–1790

Such a record as this is almost enough for one man's life, but it was only a part of Franklin's work. He specialized in everything. His studies of electricity gained him honors from France and England. Harvard, Yale, Edinburgh, and Oxford gave him honorary degrees. He invented, among other things, the lightning-rod and the Franklin stove. He founded the Philadelphia Library, the University of Pennsylvania, and the American Philosophical Society. He it was who first suggested a union of colonies, and he was our first postmaster-general. His motto seems to have been, "I will do everything I can, and as well as I can."

When he was a boy in Boston, he wrote a ballad about a recent shipwreck, which sold in large numbers. "Verse-makers are usually beggars," declared his father; and the young poet wrote no more ballads, for he intended to "get on" in life. A little later, he came across an odd volume of *The Spectator*, and was delighted with its clear, agreeable style. "I will imitate that," he said to himself; so he took notes of some of the papers, rewrote the essays from these, and then compared his work with his model. After much of this practice, he concluded that he "might in time come to be a tolerable English writer."

The hardworking young printer had but a modest literary ambition, but it met with generous fulfilment; for if he had done nothing else, he would have won fame by his writings. These consist in great part of essays on historical, political, commercial, scientific, religious, and moral subjects. He had studied *The Spectator* to good purpose, for he rarely wrote a sentence that was not strong and vigorous, and, above all, clear. Whoever reads a paragraph of Franklin's writing knows exactly what the author meant to say. His first literary glory came from neither poem nor essay, but from *Poor Richard's Almanac*, a pamphlet which he published every autumn for twenty-five years. It was full of shrewd, practical advice on becoming well-to-do and respected and getting as much as possible out of life. The special charm of the book was that this advice was put in the form of proverbs or pithy rhymes, every one with a snap as well as a moral. "Be slow in choosing a friend, slower in changing." "Honesty is the best policy." "Great talkers are little doers." "Better slip with foot than tongue." "Doors and walls are fools' paper." Such was the tone of the famous little *Almanac.* Another of his writings, and one that is of interest to-day, is his *Autobiography*, which he wrote when he was sixty-five years of age. In it nothing is kept back. He tells us of his first arrival in Philadelphia, when he walked up Market Street, eating a great roll and carrying another under each arm; of his scheme for attaining moral perfection by cultivating one additional virtue each week, and of his surprise at finding himself more faulty than he had supposed! The self-revelation of the author is so honest and frank that the book could hardly help being charming, even if it had been written about an uninteresting person; but written, as it was, about a man so learned, so practical, so shrewd, so full of kindly humor as Benjamin Franklin, it is one of the most fascinating books of the century.

12. Revolutionary Oratory

Franklin's *Autobiography* was never finished, perhaps because the Revolution was at hand and there was little time for reminiscences. The minds of men were full of the struggles of the present and the hopes of the future. Most of the oratory of the time is lost. We can only imagine it from the chance words of appreciation of those who listened to it. There was Otis, whom John

Patrick Henry Making his Tarquin and Cæsar Speech

Adams called "a flame of fire." There was Richard Henry Lee, the quiet thinker who blazed into the eloquence of earnestness and sincerity, the man who dared to move in Congress, "that these united colonies are, and of right ought to be, free and independent states." There was Patrick Henry, that other Virginian, who began to speak so shyly and stumblingly that a listener fancied him to be some country minister a little taken aback at addressing such an assembly. But soon that assembly was thrilled with his ringing "I know not what course others may take, but as for me, give me liberty or give me death!"

13. Political Writings

Those writers who favored peace and submission to England are no longer remembered; those who urged resistance even unto war will, in the success of that war, never be forgotten. Prominent among them was Thomas Paine, an Englishman whom the wise Benjamin Franklin met in England and induced to go to America in 1774. Two years later he published the most famous of his writings, *Common Sense.* This pamphlet told why its author believed in a separation from the mother country. Its clear and logical arguments were a power in bringing on the war. And when the war had come, his *Crisis* gave renewed courage to many a disheartened patriot. Thomas Jefferson was the author not only of the *Declaration of Independence,* but of many strong pamphlets that aroused men's souls to the inevitable bloodshed. It was he who, only a few days after the adoption of the *Declaration of Independence,* suggested the motto for the seal of the United States, *E pluribus unum;* and it is hard to see how a better one could have been found. George Washington would have smiled gravely to see himself written down as one of the lights of literature; but his *Farewell Address,* his letters, and his journals are not without literary value in their clearness and strength and dignity, in their noble expression of ennobling thoughts.

At the close of the Revolution, the question of the hour was how the Republic should be organized

Madison *1751–1836* | *Jay* *1745–1829* | *Hamilton* *1757–1804*

The Authors of The Federalist

and governed. A number of political pamphlets had been written during the war; and now such writings became the main weapons of those into whose hands the formation of the Constitution had fallen. The best-known of these papers were written by Alexander Hamilton, John Jay, and James Madison. They were collected and published as *The Federalist* in 1788–1789, the time when the country was hesitating to adopt the Constitution. Here is an example of the straightforward, dignified, self-respecting manner in which they laid before the young nation the advantages of the proposed method of electing a President:—

> *The process of the election affords a moral certainty that the office of President will never fall to the lot of any man who is not in an eminent degree endowed with the requisite qualifications. Talents for low intrigue, and the little arts of popularity, may alone suffice to elevate a man to the first honors in a single State; but it will require other talents, and a different kind of merit,*

to establish him in the esteem and confidence of the whole Union, or of so considerable a portion of it, as would be necessary to make him a successful candidate for the distinguished office of President of the United States. It will not be too strong to say, that there will be a constant probability of seeing the station filled by characters pre-eminent for ability and virtue.

14. The "Hartford Wits"

The poets of Revolutionary times chose the same subject as the prose writers. The poem might be a ballad on some recent event of the war, a satire, or a golden vision of the greatness which, in the imagination of the poet, his country had already attained; but in one form or another the theme was ever "Our Country." A piece of literary work that falls in with the spirit of the times wins a contemporary fame whose reflection often remains much longer than the quality of the work would warrant. Among the writers of such poetry were the "Hartford Wits," as they were called, a group of Connecticut authors whose principal members were Timothy Dwight, John Trumbull, and Joel Barlow.

Timothy Dwight was a grandson—and a worthy one—of Jonathan Edwards. In 1777 he was studying law, but his patriotism, and perhaps his inherited tastes, turned him into a minister; for the army needed chaplains. He was licensed to preach, and joined the Connecticut troops. Then it was that he wrote his *Columbia*, a patriotic song which predicted in bold, swinging metre a magnificent future for the United States. He says:—

As the day-spring unbounded, thy splendor shall flow,
And earth's little kingdoms before thee shall bow:
While the ensigns of union, in triumph unfurled,
Hush the tumult of war and give peace to the world.

He wrote an epic, called *The Conquest of Canaan;* which is long, dull, and forgotten. He left many volumes and much manuscript; but the one piece of his work that has any real share in the life of to-day is his hymns, particularly his version of Psalm cxxxvii, beginning:—

I love thy kingdom, Lord,
The house of thine abode.

John Trumbull's merry, good-natured face does not seem at all the proper physiognomy for a man who began life as an infant prodigy and ended it as a judge of the superior court. When he was five years old, he listened to his father's lessons to a young man who was preparing for college, and then said to his mother, "I'm going to study Latin, too." The result was that when he was seven, he passed his entrance examinations for Yale, sitting upon a man's knee, so the tradition says, because he was too little to reach the table. He was taken home, however, and did not enter college until he was thirteen. He wrote the best satire of the Revolutionary days, *M'Fingal.* His hero is a Tory.

From Boston in his best array
Great Squire M'Fingal took his way.

The poem is a frank imitation of *Hudibras*, and, either luckily or unluckily for Trumbull's fame, some of his couplets are so good that they are often attributed to Butler. Among them are:—

No man e'er felt the halter draw
With good opinion of the law.

But optics sharp it needs, I ween,
To see what is not to be seen.

The third of this group was Joel Barlow. In 1778 he graduated from Yale. His part in the Commencement programme was a poem, *The Prospect of Peace.* He was well qualified to write on such a subject, for he had had a fashion of slipping away to the army when his vacations came around, and doing a little fighting. Two years later, he followed the example of his friend Dwight, and became an army chaplain. After the war was over, he produced a poem, *The Vision of Columbus,* afterwards expanded into an epic, *The Columbiad.* People were so carried away with its patriotism and its sonorous phrases that they forgot to be critical, and the poem made its author famous. He is remembered now, however, by a merry little rhyme which he wrote on being served with hasty pudding in Savoy. He takes for the motto of his poem the dignified Latin sentiment, "Omne tulit punctum qui miscuit utile dulci," and translates it delightfully, "He makes a good breakfast who mixes pudding with molasses." He thus apostrophizes the delicacy:—

Dear Hasty Pudding, what unpromised joy
Expands my heart, to meet thee in Savoy!
Doom'd o'er the world through devious paths to roam,
Each clime my country and each house my home,
My soul is soothed, my cares have found an end,
I greet my long-lost, unforgotten friend.

Poor Barlow! aspiring to a national epic and remembered by nothing but a rhyme on hasty pudding!

15. Philip Freneau, 1752–1832

In the midst of these writers of unwieldy and long-forgotten epics was one man in whom there abode a real poetic talent, Philip Freneau, born in New York. His early poems were satires and songs, often of small literary merit, indeed, but with a ring and a swing that made them almost sing themselves. The boys in the streets, as well as the soldiers in the camps, must have enjoyed shouting:—

When a certain great king, whose initial is G,
Forces Stamps upon paper, and folks to drink Tea;
When these folks burn his tea and stampt paper, like stubble—
You may guess that this king is then coming to trouble.

When the war was over, verse that was neither epic, war song, nor satire had a chance to win appreciation. Freneau then published, in 1786, a volume of poems. In some of them there is a sincere poetic tenderness and delicacy of touch; for instance, in his memorial to the soldiers who fell at Eutaw Springs, he says:—

Stranger, their humble graves adorn;
You too may fall, and ask a tear;
'Tis not the beauty of the morn
That proves the evening shall be clear.

The lyric music rings even more melodiously in his *Wild Honeysuckle,* which ends:—

From morning suns and evening dews
At first thy little being came;
If nothing once, you nothing lose,

For when you die you are the same;
The space between is but an hour,
The frail duration of a flower.

This year 1786 was the one in which Burns published his first volume, and the year in which he wrote of his "Wee, modest, crimson-tippéd flower." Freneau was as free as Burns from the influence of Pope and his heroic couplet which had so dominated the poets of England for the greater part of the eighteenth century. He was no imitator; and he had another of the distinctive marks of a true poet,—he could find the poetic where others found nothing but the prosaic. Before his time, the American Indian, for instance, had hardly appeared in literature; Freneau was the first to see that there was something poetic in the pathos of a vanishing race. In all the rhyming of the two centuries immediately preceding 1800, there is nothing that gave such hope for the future of American poetry as some of the poems of Philip Freneau.

16. Charles Brockden Brown, 1771–1810

There was hope, too, for American prose, and in a new line, that of fiction; for the Philadelphia writer, Charles Brockden Brown, published in 1798 a novel entitled *Wieland.* It is full of mysterious voices, murders, and threatened murders, whose cause and explanation prove to be the power of a ventriloquist. The book was called "thrilling and exciting in the highest degree;" but the twentieth-century reader cannot help wondering why the afflicted family did not investigate matters and why the tormented heroine did not get a watch-dog. Then, too, comes the thought of what the genius of Poe could have done with such material. Nevertheless, there is undeniable talent in the book, and unmistakable promise for the future. Some of the scenes, especially the last meeting between the heroine and her half-maniac brother, are powerfully drawn. Brown published several other novels, one of which, *Arthur Mervyn,* is valued for its vivid descriptions of a visitation of the yellow fever to Philadelphia. Like Freneau, Brown saw in the Indian good material for literature; but to him the red man was neither pathetic nor romantic,—he was simply a terrible danger of the western wilderness.

During the fifty years of the Revolutionary period, the literary spirit had first manifested itself in the practical, utilitarian prose of Franklin and the writers of *The Federalist* and other political pamphlets; then in the patriotic satires and epics of the Hartford Wits. Finally, in the work of both Freneau and Brown there was manifest a looking forward to literature for literature's sake, to a poetry that dreamed of the beautiful, to a prose that reached out toward the imaginative and the creative.

SUMMARY

1765–1815

THE REVOLUTIONARY PERIOD

Benjamin Franklin
Thomas Paine
Thomas Jefferson
George Washington
"The Federalist"
Timothy Dwight
John Trumbull
Joel Barlow
Philip Freneau
Charles Brockden Brown

The passage of the Stamp Act turned the literary activity of the colonists from history and religious poetry toward oratory, political writings, satire, war songs, and patriotic poems. Franklin was the most versatile man of his times. His work in politics, science, and literature deserved the honor which it received. His most popular publication was *Poor Richard's Almanac.* His work of most interest to-day is his *Autobiography.* The leading orators were Otis, Lee, and Henry. Some of the political writers were Paine, Jefferson, and Washington. *The Federalist* contains many political essays by Hamilton, Jay, and Madison. Among the "Hartford Wits" were Dwight, the author of *The Conquest of Canaan,* but best known by his hymns; Trumbull, whose *M'Fingal* was the best satire of the Revolution; and Barlow, who wrote an epic, *The Columbiad,* but is best known by his rhyme, *The Hasty Pudding.* Freneau wrote poems that rank him above all other poets of the period. Brown's *Wieland* was the forerunner of the nineteenth-century novel.

CHAPTER III

THE NATIONAL PERIOD — EARLIER YEARS

1815–1865

A. THE KNICKERBOCKER SCHOOL

17. National Progress

The last fifteen years of the Revolutionary period, from 1800 to 1815, were marked by great events in America. New States were admitted to the Union; the Louisiana Purchase made the United States twice as large as before; the expedition of Lewis and Clark revealed the wonders and possibilities of the West; Fulton's invention of the steamboat brought the different parts of the country nearer together; the successes of the War of 1812, particularly the naval victories, increased the republic's self-respect and sense of independence. This feeling was no whit lessened by the conquest of the Barbary pirates, to whom for three hundred years other Christian nations had been forced to pay tribute. Just as the great events of the sixteenth century aroused and inspired the Elizabethans, so the growth of the country, the victories, discoveries, and inventions of the first years of the nineteenth century aroused and inspired the Americans. There was rapid progress in all directions, and no slender part in this progress fell to the share of literature.

18. The Knickerbocker School

During the Revolutionary period the literary centre had gradually moved from Massachusetts to Philadelphia. When the nineteenth century began, a boy of seventeen was just leaving school whose talents were to do much to make New York, his birthplace and home, a literary centre. Moreover, the name of one of his characters, Diedrich Knickerbocker, has become a literary term; for just as three English authors have been classed together as the Lake Poets because they chanced to live in the Lake Country, so the term Knickerbocker School has been found convenient to apply to Irving, Cooper, Bryant, and the lesser writers who were at that time more or less connected with New York.

19. Washington Irving, 1783–1859

This boy of seventeen was Washington Irving. He first distinguished himself by roaming about in the city and neighboring villages, while the town crier rang his bell and cried industriously, "Child lost! Child lost!" After leaving school, he studied law; but he must have rejoiced when his family decided that the best way to improve his somewhat feeble health was to send him to Europe, far more of a journey in 1800 than a trip around the world in 1900. He wandered through France, Italy, and England, and enjoyed himself everywhere. When he returned to New York, nearly two years later, he was admitted to the bar; but he spent all his leisure hours on literature. *The Spectator* had the same attraction for him that it had had for Franklin. When he was nineteen, he had written a few essays in a somewhat similar style;

and now he set to work with his brother William and a friend, James K. Paulding, to publish a *Spectator* of their own. They named it *Salmagundi*, and in the first number they calmly announced:—

> *Our purpose is simply to instruct the young, reform the old, correct the town, and castigate the age; this is an arduous task, and therefore we undertake it with confidence.*

The twenty numbers of this paper that appeared were bright, merry, and good-natured. Their wit had no sting, and they became popular in New York. The law practice must have suffered some neglect, for Irving had another plan in his mind. One day a notice appeared in the *Evening Post* under the head of "Distressing." It spoke of the disappearance of one Diedrich Knickerbocker. Other notices followed. One said, "A very curious kind of a written book has been found in his room in his own handwriting." The way was thus prepared, and soon *Knickerbocker's History of New York* was on the market. It was the most fascinating mingling of fun and sober history that can be conceived of, and was mischievously dedicated to the New York Historical Society. Everybody read it, and everybody laughed. Even the somewhat aggrieved descendants of the Dutch colonists managed to smile politely.

Knickerbocker's History brought its author three thousand dollars. His talent was recognized on both sides of the Atlantic, but for ten years he wrote nothing more. Finally he went to England in behalf of the business in which he and his brother had engaged. The

Washington Irving
1783–1859

business was a failure, but still he lingered in London. A government position in Washington was offered him, but he refused it. Then his friends lost all patience. He had but slender means, he was thirty-five years old, and if he was ever to do any literary work, it was time that he made a beginning. Irving felt "cast down, blighted, and broken-spirited," as he said; but he roused himself to work, and soon he began to send manuscript to a New York publisher, to be brought out in numbers under the signature "Geoffrey Crayon." His friends no longer wished that he had taken the government position, for this work, the *Sketch Book,* was a glowing success. Everybody liked it, and with good reason, for among the essays and sketches, all of rare merit, were

Rip Van Winkle and *The Legend of Sleepy Hollow.* Praises were showered upon the author until he felt, as he wrote to a friend, "almost appalled by such success." Walter Scott, "that golden-hearted man," as Irving called him, brought about the publication of the book in England by Murray's famous publishing house. Its success there was as marked as in America, for at last a book had come from the New World that no one could refuse to accept as literature. The Americans had not forgotten the sneer of the English critic, "Who reads an American book?" and they gloried in their countryman's glory. The sale was so great that the publisher honorably presented the author with more than a thousand dollars beyond the amount that had been agreed upon.

An enthusiastic welcome awaited Irving whenever he chose to cross the Atlantic, but he still lingered in Europe. In the next few years he published *Bracebridge Hall* and *Tales of a Traveller.* The latter was not very warmly received, for the public were clamoring for something new. Just as serenely as Scott had turned to fiction when people were tired of his poetry, so Irving turned to history and biography. He spent three years in Spain, and the result of those years was his *Life of Columbus, The Conquest of Granada, The Companions of Columbus,* and, last and most charming of all, *The Alhambra.*

Irving had now not only fame but an assured income. He returned to America, and there he found himself the man whom his country most delighted to honor. Once more he left her shores, to become minister to Spain for four years; but, save for that absence, he spent the last

Sunnyside

twenty-seven years of his life in his charming cottage, Sunnyside, on the Hudson near Tarrytown. He was not idle by any means. Among his later works are his *Life of Goldsmith* and *Life of Washington.* In these biographies he had two aims: to write truly and to write interestingly. His style is always clear, marked by exquisite gleams of humor, and so polished that a word can rarely be changed without spoiling the sentence. To this charm of style he adds in the case of his *Life of Goldsmith* such an atmosphere of friendliness, of comradeship, of perfect sympathy, that one has to recall dates in order to realize that the two men were not companions. No man's last years were ever more full of honors than Irving's. The whole country loved him. As Thackeray said, his gate was "forever swinging before visitors who came to him." Every one was welcomed, and every one carried away kindly thoughts of the magician of the Hudson.

20. James Fenimore Cooper, 1789–1851

About the time that the New York town crier was finding Irving's wanderings a source of income, a year-old baby, named James Fenimore Cooper, was taking a much longer journey. He travelled from his birthplace in Burlington, New Jersey, to what is now Cooperstown, New York, where his father owned several thousand acres of land and proposed to establish a village. The village was established, a handsome residence was built, and there, in the very heart of the wilderness, the boy spent his early years. He was used to the free life of the forest; and it is small wonder that after he entered Yale, he found it rather difficult to obey orders and was sent home in disgrace.

His next step was to spend four years at sea. Then he married, left the navy, and became a country gentleman, with no more thought of writing novels than many other country gentlemen. One day, after reading a story of English life, he exclaimed, "I believe I could write a better book myself." "Try it, then," retorted his wife playfully; and he tried it. The result was *Precaution*. Unless the English novel was very poor, this book can hardly have been much of an improvement, for it is decidedly dull. Another fault is its lack of truth to life, for Cooper laid his scene in England in the midst of society that he knew nothing about. The book was anonymous. It was reprinted in England and was thought by some critics to be the work of an English writer. Americans of that day were so used to looking across the ocean for their literature that this mistake gave Cooper courage. Moreover, his friends stood by him generously. "Write

James Fenimore Cooper
1789–1851

another," they said, "and lay the scene in America." Cooper took up his pen again. *The Spy* was the result. Irving's *Sketch Book* had come out only a year or two earlier, and now American critics were indeed jubilant. A novel whose scene was laid in America and during the American Revolution had been written by an American and was a success in England. The bolder spirits began to whisper that American literature had really begun. Two years later, Cooper published *The Pioneers,* whose scene is laid in the forest, and also *The Pilot,* a sea tale.

There was little waiting for recognition. On both sides of the ocean his fame increased. He kept on writing, and his eager audience kept on reading and begged for more. His books were translated into French, German,

Norwegian, even into Arabic and Persian. Among them was his *History of the United States Navy,* which is still an authority. Some of his books were very good, others were exceedingly poor. The *Leatherstocking Tales* are his best work. The best character is Natty Bumppo, or Leatherstocking, the hunter and scout, whose achievements are traced through the five volumes of the series.

Cooper spent several years abroad. When he returned, he found that the good folk of Cooperstown had long been using a piece of his land as a pleasure ground. Cooper called them trespassers, and the courts agreed with him. The matter would have ended there had it not been a bad habit of Cooper's to criticise things and people as boldly as if he were the one person whose actions were above criticism. Of course he had not spared the newspapers, and now they did not spare him. He sued them for libel again and again. In one suit of this kind, the court had to hear his two-volume novel, *Home as Found,* read aloud in order to decide whether the criticisms in question were libellous or not. He often won his suits, but he lost far more than he gained; for, while Irving was loved by the whole country, Cooper made new enemies every day. Before his death he pledged his family to give no sight of his papers and no details of his home life to any future biographer who might ask for them. This is unfortunate, for Cooper was a man who always turned his rough side to the world; but at least we can fall back upon the knowledge that the people who knew him best loved him most.

Cooper's success was so immediate that he hardly realized the need of any thought or special preparation for a book; therefore he wrote carelessly, often with most shiftless inattention to style or plot or consistency. Mark Twain is scarcely more than just when he declares that the rules governing literary art require that "when a personage talks like an illustrated, gilt-edged, tree-calf, hand-tooled, seven-dollar Friendship's Offering in the beginning of a paragraph, he shall not talk like a negro minstrel in the end of it. But this rule is flung down and danced upon in the *Deerslayer* tale." On the other hand, something must be pardoned to rapid composition, to the wish for an effect rather than accuracy of detail; and it is at best a most ungrateful task to pour out harsh criticism upon the man who has given us so many hours of downright pleasure, who has added to our literature two or three original characters, and who has brought into our libraries the salt breeze of the ocean and the rustling of the leaves of the forest.

21. William Cullen Bryant, 1794–1878

America had now produced a writer of exquisite prose and a novelist of recognized ability, but had she a poet? The answer to this question lay in the portfolio of a young man of hardly eighteen years, who was named William Cullen Bryant.

He was born in Cummington, Massachusetts, the son of a country doctor. He was brought up almost as strictly as if he had been born in Plymouth a century and a half earlier. Still, there was much to enjoy in the quiet village life. There were occasional huskings, barn-raisings, and maple-sugar parties; there were the woods and the fields and the brooks and the flowers. There were books, and there was a father who loved them. There was little money to spare in the simple country home, but good books had a habit of finding their way thither, and the boy was encouraged to read poetry and to write it. Some of this encouragement was perhaps hardly wise; for when he produced a satirical poem, *The Embargo*, the father straightway had it put into print.

When Bryant was sixteen, he entered Williams College as a sophomore. His reputation went before him, and it was whispered among the boys, "He has written poetry and some of it has been printed." His college course was short, for the money gave out. The boy was much disappointed, but he went home quietly and began to study law. He did not forget poetry, however, and then it was that *Thanatopsis*, the poem in the portfolio, was written. Six years later, Dr. Bryant came upon it by accident and recognized its greatness at a glance. Without a word to his son, the proud father set out for Boston and left the manuscript at the rooms of the *North American Review*, which had recently been established. Tradition says that the editor who read it dropped the work in hand and hurried away to Cambridge to show his colleagues what a "find" he had made; and that one of them, Richard Henry Dana, declared there was some fraud in the matter, for no one in America could write such verse. The least appreciative reader of the poem could hardly help feeling the solemn majesty, the organ-tone rhythm, the wide sweep of noble thought. *Thanatopsis* is a masterpiece. It went the country over; and wherever it went, even in its earlier and less perfect form, it was welcomed as America's first great poem. Meanwhile, its author was practising as a lawyer in a little Massachusetts village. He was working conscientiously at his profession; but fortunately he was not so fully employed as to have no spare hours for poetry, and it was about this time that he wrote his beautiful lines, *To a Waterfowl.* This poem came straight from his own heart, for he was troubled about his future, and, as he said, felt "very forlorn and desolate." The last stanza,—

> *He who, from zone to zone,*
> *Guides through the boundless sky thy certain flight,*
> *In the long way that I must tread alone,*
> *Will lead my steps aright,—*

gave to him the comfort that it has given to many others, and he went on bravely.

Dana soon brought it about that Bryant should be invited to read the annual poem before the Phi Beta Kappa Society at Harvard. The poem which he presented was *The Ages.* This, together with *Thanatopsis, To a Waterfowl,* and four other poems, was published in a slender little volume, in 1821.

Bryant was recognized as the first poet in the land, but even poets must buy bread and butter. Thus far, his poems had brought him a vast amount of praise and about two dollars apiece, and his law business had never given him a sufficient income. In 1825 he decided to accept a literary position that was offered him in

New York. He soon became editor of *The Evening Post,* and this position he held for nearly fifty years. As an editor, he was absolutely independent, but always dignified and calm; and he held his paper to a high literary standard. It was during those years that he wrote *The Fringed Gentian, The Antiquity of Freedom, The Flood of Years,* and other poems that our literature could ill afford to lose. He said that he had little choice among his poems. Irving liked *The Rivulet;* Halleck, *The Apple Tree;* Dana, *The Past.* Bryant also translated the *Iliad* and the *Odyssey.* His life extended long after the lives of Irving and of Cooper had closed. Other poets had arisen in the land. They wrote on many themes; he wrote on few save death and nature. Their verses were often more warm-hearted, more passionate than Bryant's, and often they were easier reading; but Bryant never lost the place of honor and dignity that he had so fairly earned. He is the Father of American Poetry; and it is well for American poetry that it can look back to the calmness and strength and poise of such a founder. Lowell says:—

He is almost the one of your poets that knows
How much grace, strength, and dignity lie in Repose.

22. The Minor Knickerbocker Poets

Among the crowd of minor poets of the Knickerbocker School were Halleck, Drake, and Willis. Fitz-Greene Halleck was a Connecticut boy who went to New York when he was twenty-one years old. He found work in the counting-room of John Jacob Astor. He also found a poet friend in a young man named Joseph Rodman Drake. Together they wrote

The Croakers, satirical poems on the New York of the day. These are rather bright and witty, but it is hard to realize that they won intense admiration. The story has been handed down that when the editor of the paper in which they appeared first met his unknown contributors, he exclaimed with enthusiasm, "I had no idea that we had such talent in America." It was from the friendship between Halleck and Drake that Drake's best known poem arose, *The Culprit Fay.* If we may trust the tradition, the two poets, together with Cooper, were one day talking of America. Halleck and Cooper declared that it was impossible to find the poetry in American rivers that had been found in Scottish streams, but Drake took the contrary side. "I will prove it," he said to himself; and within the next three days he produced his *Culprit Fay*, as dainty a bit of slight, graceful, imaginative verse as can be found. The scene is laid in Fairyland, and Fairyland is somewhere among the Highlands of the Hudson. The fairy hero loves a beautiful mortal, and, as a punishment, is doomed to penances that give room for many poetic fancies and delicate pictures. Drake died only four years later. He left behind him at least one other poem, first published in *The Croakers,* that will hardly be forgotten, *The American Flag,* with its noble beginning:—

When Freedom from her mountain height
Unfurled her standard to the air.

Halleck sorrowed deeply for the death of his friend. He himself lived for nearly half a century longer and wrote many poems, but nothing else as good as his loving tribute to Drake, which begins:—

Green be the turf above thee,
Friend of my better days!
None knew thee but to love thee,
Nor named thee but to praise!

One other poem of Halleck's, *Marco Bozzaris,* has always been a favorite because of its vigor and spirit. Bryant said, "The reading of Marco Bozzaris... stirs up my blood like the sound of martial music or the blast of a trumpet." Parts of it bring to mind the demand of King Olaf for a poem "with a sword in every line." Worn as these verses are by much declaiming, there is still a good old martial ring in such lines as:—

Strike—till the last armed foe expires;
Strike—for your altars and your fires;
Strike—for the green graves of your sires;
God and your native land.

At the end of this rousing war-cry are two lines that are as familiar as anything in the language:—

One of the few, the immortal names
That were not born to die.

Another member of the Knickerbocker School was Nathaniel Parker Willis, a Maine boy who found his way to New York. He had hardly unpacked his trunk before it was decided that if he would go to Europe and send home a weekly letter for publication, it would be greatly to the advantage of the journal with which he was connected. Europe was still so distant as to make letters of travel interesting. These sketches, afterwards published as *Pencillings by the Way,* were light and graceful, and they were copied by scores of papers. When Willis came home, five years later, he edited the

Home Journal, wrote pretty, imaginative sketches and many poems. There was nothing deep or thoughtful in them, rarely anything strong; but they were easily and gracefully written and people liked to read them. A few of the poems, such as *The Belfry Pigeon, Unseen Spirits, Saturday Afternoon,* and *Parrhasius,* are still favorites.

While in college, Willis wrote a number of sacred poems. Lowell wickedly said of them, "Nobody likes inspiration and water." But Lowell was wrong, for they found a large audience, and their author tasted all the sweets of popularity. He was not spoiled, however, and he was, as Halleck said, "one of the kindest of men." His own path to literary success had been smooth, but he was always ready to sympathize with the struggles of others and to aid them by every means in his power. He died in 1867; but many years before his death it was evident that the literary leadership had again fallen into the hands of New England.

SUMMARY

A. The Knickerbocker School

Washington Irving	*Fitz-Greene Halleck*
James Fenimore Cooper	*Joseph Rodman Drake*
William Cullen Bryant	*Nathaniel Parker Willis*

The progress of the country during the early years of the century inspired progress in literature. The literary centre had moved from Massachusetts to Philadelphia, but now New York began to hold the place of honor.

The authors belonging to the Knickerbocker School are Irving, Cooper, and Bryant, with the minor poets, Halleck, Drake, and Willis. *Knickerbocker's History of New York* made Irving somewhat known on both sides of the ocean, but his *Sketch Book* was the first American book to win a European reputation. He afterwards wrote much history and biography. Cooper attempted first an English novel, then wrote *The Spy*, which made him famous in both England and America. He wrote many other tales of the forest and the ocean. He was popular as a novelist, but unpopular as a man. The third great writer of the Knickerbocker School was Bryant. He wrote his masterpiece, *Thanatopsis,* before he was eighteen. His early poems were highly praised, but brought him little money. He was editor of *The Evening Post* for nearly fifty years, wrote many poems, and translated the *Iliad* and the *Odyssey.* He was the Father of American Poetry. Among the minor Knickerbocker Poets were Halleck, Drake, and Willis. Long before the death of Willis, it was evident that the literary centre was again to be found in New England.

CHAPTER IV

THE NATIONAL PERIOD — EARLIER YEARS

1815–1865

B. THE TRANSCENDENTALISTS

23. The Transcendentalists

Before the year 1840 had arrived, a remarkable group of writers of New England ancestry and birth had begun their work. They were fortunate in more than one way. They had the inspiration of knowing that good literature had already been written in America; and they had the stimulus arising from a movement, or manner of thought, known as transcendentalism. This movement began in Germany, was felt first in England and then in America, introduced by the works of Carlyle and Coleridge. Three of its "notes" were: (1) There are ideas in the human mind that were "born there" and were not acquired by experience; (2) Thought is the only reality; (3) Every one must do his own thinking. The Transcendental Club was formed, and the new movement had its literary organ, *The Dial,* whose first editor was the brilliant Margaret Fuller. It had also its representatives in the pulpit, for the persuasive charm of William Ellery Channing and the impassioned eloquence of Theodore Parker were employed to proclaim the new gospel. Another advocate was Amos Bronson Alcott, gentle, visionary, and immovable, who is so well pictured in the opening chapters of his daughter's *Little Women.*

The first thrill of all new movements leads to extremes, and transcendentalism was no exception. Freedom! Reform! was the war-cry; and to those who were inclined to act first and think afterwards, the new impulse was merely an incitement to tear down the fences. There were wild projects and fantastic schemes innumerable. A sense of humor would have guided and controlled much of this unbalanced enthusiasm; but it is only great men like Lincoln who can see any fellowship between humor and earnestness. The very people who were to profit by this movement were the loudest laughers at these dreamers who gazed in rapture upon the planets and sometimes stubbed their toes against the pebbles. Nevertheless, the ripened fruits of transcendentalism were in their degree like those of the Renaissance; it widened the horizon and it inspired men with courage to think for themselves and to live their own lives. This atmosphere of freedom had a noble effect upon literature. Two of the authors of the New England group, the poet-philosopher Emerson and the poet-naturalist Thoreau, were so imbued with its spirit that in literary classifications they are usually ranked as *the* transcendentalists; and Hawthorne is often classed with them, partly by virtue of a few months' connection with a transcendental scheme, and even more because in his romances the thought and the spirit are so much more real than the deeds by which they are manifested and symbolized.

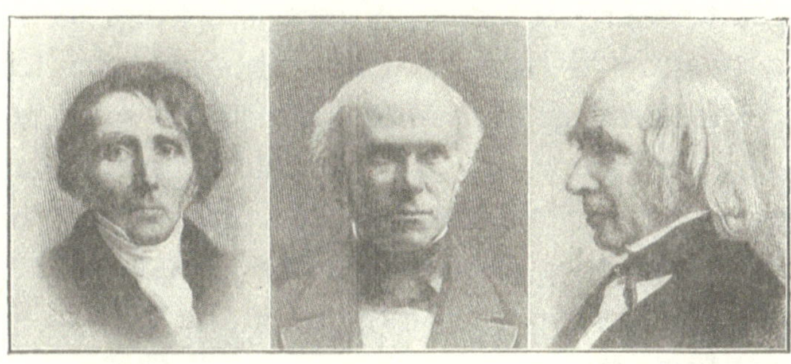

Channing *1780–1842* *Parker* *1810–1860* *Alcott* *1799–1888*

Three Transcendentalists

24. Ralph Waldo Emerson, 1803–1882

The poet-philosopher was one of five boys who lived with their widowed mother in Boston. They were poor, for clergymen do not amass fortunes, and their father had been no exception to the rule. The famous First Church, however, of which he had been in charge, did not forget the family of their beloved minister. Now and then other kind friends gave a bit of help. Once a cow was lent them, and every morning the boys drove her down Beacon Hill to pasture. In spite of their poverty it never entered the mind of any member of the family that the children could grow up without an education. Four of the boys graduated at Harvard. The oldest son, who was then a sedate gentleman of twenty, opened a school for young ladies; and his brother Ralph, two years younger, became his assistant. The evenings were free, and the young man of eighteen was even then jotting down the thoughts that he was to use many years later in his essay, *Compensation.* He was a descendant of eight generations of ministers, and there seems to have been in his mind hardly a thought of entering any other profession than the ministry. A minister he became; but a few years later he told his congregation frankly that his belief differed on one or two points from theirs and it seemed to him best to resign. They urged him to remain with them, but he did not think it wise to do so.

A year later he went to Europe for his health. He wanted to see three or four men rather than places, he said. He met Coleridge and Wordsworth; and then he sought out the lonely little farm of Craigenputtock, the home of Carlyle. His coming was "like the visit of an angel," said the Scotch philosopher to Longfellow. The two men became friends, and the friendship lasted as long as their lives.

When Emerson came back to America, he made his home in Concord, Massachusetts, but for a long while he was almost as much at home on railroad trains and in stages. Those were the times when people were eager to hear from the lecture platform what the best thinkers of the day could tell them. In 1837 Emerson delivered at Harvard his Phi Beta Kappa address entitled *The American Scholar;* and then for the first time the American people were told seriously and with dignity that they must no longer listen to "the courtly muses of Europe." "We will walk on our own feet; we will work with our own hands; we will speak our own minds," said Emerson. These last words were the keynote of his message to the world. Whoever listens may hear the voice of God, he declared; and for that reason each person's individuality was sacred to him. Therefore it was that he met every man with a gently expectant deference that was far above the ordinary courtesy of society. A humble working woman once said that she did not understand his lectures, but she liked to go to them and see him look as if he thought everybody else just as good as he. On the lecture platform Emerson's manner was that of one who was trying to interpret what had been told to him, of one who was striving to put his thoughts into a language which had no words to express them fully.

Some parts of Emerson's writings are simple enough for a little child to understand; other parts perhaps no one but their author has fully comprehended. It is not easy to make an outline of his essays. Every sentence, instead of opening the gate for the next, as in Macaulay's prose, seems to stand alone. Emerson said with truth, "I build my house of boulders." The connection is not in the words, but in a subtle undercurrent of thought. The best way to enjoy his writings is to turn the pages of some one of his simpler essays, *Compensation*, for instance, that he planned when a young man of eighteen, and read whatever strikes the eye. When one has read: " 'What will you have?' quoth God; 'pay for it and take it,' "—"The borrower runs in his own debt,"—"The thief steals from himself,"—"A great man is always willing to be little;"—when one has read a few such sentences, he cannot help wishing to begin at the beginning to see how they come in. Then let him take from each essay that he reads the part that belongs to him, and leave the rest until its day and moment have fully come.

Among Emerson's poems, *Each and All, The Rhodora, The Humblebee, The Snow-Storm, Forbearance, Woodnotes, The Mountain and the Squirrel, Concord Hymn,* and *Boston Hymn* are all easy and all well worth knowing by heart. He who has learned this handful of poems has met their author face to face, and can hardly fail to have gained a friendliness for him that will serve as his best interpreter.

25. Henry David Thoreau, 1817–1862

In that same village of Concord was a young man named Thoreau who was a great puzzle to his neighbors. He had graduated at Harvard, but he took no step to become clergyman, lawyer, physician, or teacher. He wrote and sometimes he lectured; he read many books; and he spent a great deal of time out of doors. His father was a maker of lead pencils, and the son also learned the trade. Before long he made them better than the father; then he made them equal to the best that were imported. "There is a fortune for you in those pencils," declared his friends; but the young man made no more. "Why should I?" he queried. "I would not do again what I have done once."

Thoreau loved his family, little children, and a few good friends; but not a straw did he care about people in the mass. Emerson said of him that his soul was made for the noblest society; but when he was about twenty-eight, he built himself a tiny cottage on the shore of Walden Pond, and there he lived for the greater part of two years and a half. He kept a journal, and in this he noted when the first bluebird appeared, how the little twigs changed in color at the coming of the spring, and many other "common sights." He knew every nook and cranny of the rocks, every bend of the stream, every curve of the shore. The little wild creatures had no fear of him; the red squirrels played about his feet as he wrote; the flowers seemed to hasten their blooming to meet the dates of his last year's diary. He told Emerson that if he waked up from a trance in his favorite swamp, he could tell by the plants what time of year it was within two days. He could find his way through the woods at night by the feeling of the ground to his feet. He saw everything around him. "Where can arrowheads be found?" he was asked. "Here," was his reply, as he stooped and picked one up. It is no wonder that he felt small patience with the blindness of other folk. "I have never yet met a man who was quite awake," he declared. He loved trees, and once, when the woodchoppers had done their worst, he exclaimed devoutly, "Thank God, they cannot cut down the clouds."

Henry David Thoreau
1817-1862

He found so much to enjoy that he could not bear to give his time to any profession. To be free, to read, and to live with nature,—that was happiness. "A man is rich in proportion to the number of things which he can afford to let alone," declared this philosopher of the wilderness. The few things that he could not "let alone," he supplied easily by the work of his hands. Emerson said that he himself could split a shingle four ways with one nail; but Thoreau could make a bookcase or a chest or a table or almost anything else. He knew more about gardening than any of the farmers around him. Six weeks of work as carpenter or surveyor supplied his needs for the rest of the year; then he was free.

In 1839 he made a boat, and in it he and his brother took a voyage on the Concord and Merrimack rivers. He was still in the habit of keeping a journal, and he wrote in it an account of the trip. This is something more than a guide-book, for on one page is a disquisition on the habits of the pickerel; on another a discourse on friendship or Chaucer or the ruins of Egypt, as it may chance. Occasionally there is a poem, sometimes with such a fine bit of description as this, written of the effect of the clear light of sunset:—

Mountains and trees
Stand as they were on air graven.

Of a churlish man whom he met in the mountains he wrote serenely, "I suffered him to pass for what he was,— for why should I quarrel with nature?—and was even pleased at the discovery of such a singular natural phenomenon." Thoreau is always interesting. What he says has ever the charm of the straightforward thought of a wise, honest, widely read, and keenly observant man; but he is most delightful when his knowledge of nature and his tender, sympathetic humor are combined; as, for instance, in his little talk about the shad, that, "armed only with innocence and a just cause," are ever finding a "corporation with its dam" blocking the way to their old haunts. "Keep a stiff fin," he says cheerily, "and stem all the tides thou mayst meet."

These quotations are from his journal of the little voyage *A Week on the Concord and Merrimack Rivers,* as it is called. He prepared it for the press, and offered it to publisher after publisher; but no one was willing to run the financial risk of putting it into print. At last he published one thousand copies at his own expense. Four years later, 706 unsold volumes were returned to him. He wrote in his journal, "I have now a library of nearly 900 volumes, over 700 of which I wrote myself." Then he calmly went to work at surveying to finish paying the printer's bills.

Thoreau's House at Walden

Only one other volume of Thoreau's writings, *Walden,* was published during his life; but critics discovered, one by one, that his wide reading, his minute knowledge of nature, his warm sympathy with every living creature, and his ability to put his knowledge and his thoughts on paper, were a rare combination of gifts. His thirty-nine volumes of manuscript journals were carefully read, and the greater part of them published; but not until Thoreau had been dead for many years.

26. Nathaniel Hawthorne, 1804–1864

The connection of Hawthorne with the transcendentalists came about through his joining what was known as the Brook Farm project. A company of "dreamers" united in buying this farm in the expectation that it could be carried on with profit if they all worked a few hours each day. The rest of the time they were to have for social enjoyment and intellectual pursuits. Hawthorne was engaged to a brilliant, charming woman, and he hoped to be able to make a home for them at Brook Farm. The project failed, but he married and went to live at the Old Manse in Concord, to find perfect happiness in his home, and to work his way toward literary fame.

He had led a singular life. When he was four years old, his father, a sea-captain, died in South America. His mother shut herself away from the outside world and almost from her own family. The little boy was sent to school; but soon a football injury confined him to the silent house for two years. There was little to do but read; and he read from morning till night. Froissart, *Pilgrim's*

Progress, and Spenser carried him away to the realms of the imagination, and made the long days a delight. At last he was well again; and then came one glorious year by Sebago Lake, where he wandered at his will in the grand old forests of Maine. He graduated at Bowdoin College in the famous class of 1825. There were names among those college boys that their bearers were afterwards to make famous: Henry W. Longfellow, J. S. C. Abbott, George B. Cheever, and Horatio Bridge; and in the preceding class was Franklin Pierce. The last two became Hawthorne's warmest friends.

Nathaniel Hawthorne
1804-1864

Graduation separated him from his college companions; indeed, for twelve years he was isolated from almost every one. He had returned to his home in Salem. His older sister had become nearly as much of a recluse as her mother. Interruptions were almost unknown, and the young man wrote and read by day and by night. He published a novel which he was afterwards glad did not sell. He wrote many short stories. Most of them he burned; some he sent to various publishers. At the end of the twelve years, Bridge urged him to publish his stories in a volume, and offered to be responsible for the expense. This book was the *Twice-Told Tales.* Soon after his marriage he published the second series of *Tales,* and a few years later, *Mosses from an Old Manse.* Most people who read these stories were pleased with them, but few recognized in their author the promise of a great romancer. Meanwhile, the romancer needed an income, and he was glad to retain the Custom House position in Boston that George Bancroft had secured for him. After a while he was transferred to the Salem Custom House. Then came a change in political power, and one day he had to tell his wife that he had been thrown out of his position. "I am glad," she said, "for now you can write your book." She produced a sum of money which she had been quietly saving for some such emergency, and her husband took up his pen with all good cheer. Not many months later, "a big man with brown beard and shining eyes, who bubbled over with enthusiasm and fun," knocked at the door. He was James T. Fields, the publisher. He had read the manuscript, and he had come to tell its author what a magnificent piece of work it was. "It is the greatest book of the age," he declared. Even Fields, however, did not know what appreciation it would meet, and he did not stereotype it. The result was that, two weeks after its publication, the type had to be reset, for the whole edition had been sold. This book was *The Scarlet Letter,* that marvellous picture of the stern old Puritan days, softened and illumined by the touch of a genius. One need not fear to say that it is still the greatest American book.

Hawthorne had now come to the atmosphere of appreciation that inspired him to do his best work.

Within three short years he wrote *The House of the Seven Gables,* a book of weird, pathetic humor and flashes of everyday sunshine. Then came *The Wonder-Book,* the little volume that is so dear to the hearts of children. *The Blithedale Romance* followed, whose suggestion arose from the months at Brook Farm. The life of his dear friend, Franklin Pierce, and *Tanglewood Tales* came next,—a glorious record for less than three years.

Franklin Pierce had become President, and he appointed his old friend consul at Liverpool. Four years of the consulship and three years of travel resulted in the *Note-Books* and *The Marble Faun,* the fourth of his great romances. Four years after its publication, Hawthorne died.

It is as difficult to compare Hawthorne's romances with the novels of other writers of fiction as to compare a strain of music with a painting, for their aims are entirely different. Novelists strive to make their characters lifelike, to surround them with difficulties, and to keep the reader in suspense as to the outcome of the struggle. Hawthorne's characters are clearly outlined, but they seem to belong to a different world. We could talk freely with Rip Van Winkle, but we should hardly know what to say to Clifford or Hepzibah, or even to Phebe. Nor are the endings of Hawthorne's books of supreme interest. The fact that four people in *The House of the Seven Gables* finally come to their own is not the most impressive fact of the story.

Hawthorne's power lies primarily in his knowledge of the human heart and in his ability to trace step by step the effect upon it of a single action. His charm comes from a humor so delicate that sometimes we hardly realize its presence; from a style so artistic that it is almost without flaw; from a manner of treating the supernatural that is purely his own. He has no clumsy ventriloquistic trickery like Brown; he gives the suggestive hint that sets our own fancy to work, then with a half smile he quietly offers us the choice of a matter-of-fact explanation,—which, of course, we refuse to accept. But the magic that removes Hawthorne's stories farthest from everyday life is the different atmosphere in which they seem to exist. The characters are real people, but they are seen through the thought of the romancer. In *The House of the Seven Gables,* Hawthorne ponders on how "the wrong-doing of one generation lives into the successive ones;" and everything is seen through the medium of that thought. No other American author has shown such profound knowledge of the human heart or has put that knowledge into words with so accurate and delicate a touch. No one else has treated the supernatural in so fascinating a manner or has mingled so gracefully the prosaic and the ideal. No one else has manifested such perfection of literary style. Longfellow has well said:—

Ah! who shall lift that wand of magic power,
And the lost clew regain?
The unfinished window in Aladdin's tower
Unfinished must remain!

SUMMARY

B. The Transcendentalists

Ralph Waldo Emerson
Henry David Thoreau
Nathaniel Hawthorne

Transcendentalism had a strong effect upon New England literature. Its literary organ was *The Dial*. Among its special advocates were Channing, Parker, and Alcott. It aroused at first much unbalanced enthusiasm; but later it led toward freedom of thought and of life. Emerson and Thoreau are counted as *the* transcendentalists of American literature. Hawthorne is often classed with them.

Emerson became a minister, but resigned because of disagreement with the belief of his church. He delivered many lectures. His Phi Beta Kappa oration in 1837 was an "intellectual Declaration of Independence." Respect for one's own individuality was the keynote of his teaching.

Thoreau cared little for people in the mass, but loved his friends and nature. *His Week on the Concord and Merrimack Rivers* and *Walden* were published during his lifetime. The value of his work as author and naturalist was not fully appreciated until long after his death.

Hawthorne was connected with the transcendentalists through the Brook Farm project and the spirit of his writings. His early life was singularly lonely, though he made warm friends in college. For twelve years after graduation, he was a literary recluse. Losing his position in the Salem Custom House, he produced *The Scarlet Letter*, which made him famous. Other works followed. Seven years abroad as consul resulted in the *Note-Books* and *The Marble Faun*. In American literature he is unequalled for knowledge of the human heart, for fascinating treatment of the supernatural, for graceful mingling of the prosaic and the ideal, and for perfection of literary style.

CHAPTER V

THE NATIONAL PERIOD — EARLIER YEARS

1815–1865

C. The Anti-Slavery Writers

27. The Anti-Slavery Movement

Side by side with the transcendental movement was a second which strongly affected literature, the anti-slavery movement. The second was the logical companion of the first. "Let every man be free to live his own life," proclaimed the transcendentalists. "How can a man be free to live his own life if he is held in bondage?" retorted the anti-slavery advocates. After the struggle concerning the extension of slavery which resulted in the Missouri Compromise of 1820, the subject had been gradually dropped. To be sure, the Quakers were still unmoved in their opposition, but the masses of the people in the free States had come to feel that to attempt to break up slavery was to threaten the very existence of the Union. The revival of the question was due to William Lloyd Garrison, who took this ground. Slavery is wrong; therefore every slave should be freed at once, and God will take care of the consequences. This was a direct challenge to the conscience of every man in the nation. It was complicated by questions of social safety and of business and financial interests as well as by sympathetic and sectional feelings. There was no dearth of material for thought, discussion, and literature.

Among the many New England writers whose names will ever be associated with the emancipation of the slave are the poet Whittier and the novelist Harriet Beecher Stowe.

28. John Greenleaf Whittier, 1807–1892

In a quiet Quaker farmhouse in the town of Haverhill, there lived a boy who longed for books and school, but had to stay at home and work on the farm. The family library consisted of about thirty volumes, chiefly the lives of prominent Quakers. The boy read these over and over and even made a catalogue of them in rhyme. One day the schoolmaster came to the house with a copy of Burns's poems in his pocket. He read aloud poem after poem, and the bright-eyed boy listened as if his mind had been starved. "Shall I lend it to you?" the master asked, and the boy took the book gratefully. After a while he paid a visit to Boston and came home happy but a little conscience-smitten, for he had bought a copy of Shakespeare, and he knew that Quakers did not approve of plays.

One day when the boy and his father were mending a stone wall, a man rode by distributing Garrison's *Free Press* to its subscribers. He tossed a paper to the boy, who glanced from page to page, looking especially, as was his wont, at the corner where the poetry was usually printed. He read there "The Exile's Departure."

"Thee had better put up the paper and go to work," said his father; but still the boy gazed, for the poem was signed "W.," and it was his own! His older sister Mary had quietly sent it to the editor without saying anything to her brother. The next scene was like a fairy story. Not long afterwards a carriage stopped at the door. A young man, well dressed and with the easy manner of one used to society, inquired for his new contributor. "I can't go in," declared the shy poet. "Thee must," said the sister Mary. Mr. Garrison told the family that the son had "true poetic genius," and that he ought to have an education. "Don't thee put such notions into the boy's head," said the father, for he saw no way to afford even a single term at school. A way was arranged, however, by which the young man could pay his board; and he had one year at an academy. This was almost his only schooling, but he was an eager student all the days of his life.

Through Garrison's influence an opportunity to do editorial work was offered him. He became deeply interested in public matters. The very air was tingling with the question: Slavery or no slavery? He threw the whole force of his thought and his pen against slavery. From the peace-loving Quaker came lyrics that were like the clashing of swords.

The years passed swiftly, and Whittier gained reputation as a poet slowly. He published several early volumes of poems, but it was not until 1866 that he really touched the heart of the country, for then he published *Snow-Bound*. There are poems by scores that portray passing moods or tell interesting stories or describe beautiful scenes; but, save for *The Cotter's Saturday Night,* there is hardly another that gives so vivid a picture of home life. We almost feel the chill in the air before the coming storm; we fancy that we are with the group who sit "the clean-winged hearth about:"

The Kitchen of "Snowbound"

we listen to the "tales of witchcraft old," the stories of Indian attacks, of life in the logging camps; we see the schoolmaster, the Dartmouth boy who is teasing "the mitten-blinded cat" and telling of college pranks. The mother turns her wheel, and the days pass till the storm is over and the roads are open. The poem is true, simple, and vivid, and it is full of such phrases as "the sun, a snow-blown traveller;" "the great throat of the chimney laughed;" "between the andirons' straddling feet,"—phrases that outline a picture with the sure and certain touch of a master. The poem is "real," but with the reality given by the brush of an artist. *Snow-Bound* is Whittier's masterpiece; but *The Eternal Goodness* and some of his ballads, *The Barefoot Boy, In School-Days, Among the Hills, Telling the Bees,* and a few other poems, come so close to the heart that they can never be forgotten.

Whittier was always fond of children. The story is told that he came from the pine woods one day with his pet, Phebe, and said merrily, "Phebe is seventy, I am seven, and we both act like sixty." He lived to see his eighty-fifth birthday in the midst of love and honors. One who was near him when the end came tells us that among his last whispered words were "Love to the world."

29. Harriet Beecher Stowe, 1811–1896

When the future novelist was a child in school in Litchfield, Connecticut, her father, Dr. Beecher, one day went to visit the academy. Classes were called up to recite; then compositions were read. One of these was on this subject: "Can the Immortality of the Soul be proved from the Light of Nature?" It was remarkably well written, and Dr. Beecher asked quickly, "Who wrote that?" "Your daughter, sir," was the reply of the teacher. This daughter was then a girl of only twelve; and it is hardly surprising that when she was fourteen she was teaching a class in Butler's *Analogy* in her sister's school in Hartford. She taught and studied until she was twenty-four. She compiled a small geography, but the idea of writing a novel seems not to have entered her mind.

At twenty-four Harriet Beecher became Harriet Beecher Stowe by her marriage to Prof. C. E. Stowe. In their Cincinnati home they heard many stories from runaway slaves who had crossed the Ohio River to escape to a free State. After some years her husband was called to Bowdoin College, but the stories lingered in her mind; and in 1852 her *Uncle Tom's Cabin* was published in book form. It had received no special attention in coming out as a serial, but its sale as a book was astounding,—half a million copies in the United States alone within five years. The sale in other countries was enormous, and the work has been translated into more than twenty languages.

There were several reasons for this remarkable sale. To be sure, the book was carelessly written and is of unequal excellence; its plot is of small interest and is loosely connected. On the other hand, its humor is irresistible; its pathos is really pathetic; and some of its characters are so vividly painted that the names of two or three have become a part of everyday speech. Moreover, it came straight from the author's heart, for she believed every word that she wrote. Another reason, and the strongest reason, for its large immediate sales, was the condition of affairs in the United States at the time when it was issued. It was only nine years before the opening of the Civil War. The South protested, "This book is an utterly false representation of the life of the Southern States." The North retorted, "We believe that it is true." And meanwhile, every one wanted to read it. The feeling on both sides grew more and more intense. When President Lincoln met Mrs. Stowe, he said, "Is this the little woman who made this great war?"

Mrs. Stowe wrote a number of other books. Her best literary success was in her New England stories, *The Minister's Wooing, The Pearl of Orr's Island,* and *Oldtown Folks.* She wrote in the midst of difficulties. One of her friends has given us an amusing account of her dictating a story in the kitchen, with the inkstand on the teakettle, the latest baby in the clothes basket, the table loaded with all the paraphernalia of cooking, and an unskilled servant making constant appeals for direction in her work. More than one of Mrs. Stowe's books were written in surroundings much like these. It is no wonder that she left punctuation to the printer.

30. Oratory

It was in great degree the question of slavery that made the New England of this period so rich in orators. Feeling became more and more intense. The printed page could not express it; the man must come face to face with the people whom he was burning to convince. The power to move an audience is eloquence, and eloquence there was in the land in liberal measure. There was William Lloyd Garrison, with his scathing earnestness of conviction; there was Edward Everett, who used words as a painter uses his colors; there was Wendell Phillips, whose magnetism almost won over those who were scorched by his invective; there was Charles Sumner, brilliant, polished, logical, sometimes reaching the sublime; there was Rufus Choate, with his richness of vocabulary, his enchanting splendor of description, his thrilling appeals to the imagination; and there was Daniel Webster, greatest of them all in the impression that he gave of exhaustless power ever

Charles Sumner *Edward Everett*

Daniel Webster

William Lloyd Garrison *Wendell Phillips*

lying behind his sonorous phrases. Such was the oratory of New England. Eloquence, however, makes its appeal not only by words, but by voice, gesture, manner,—by personality. Its rewards are those of the moment. An hour after the delivery of the most brilliant oration, its glory is but a memory; in a few years it is but a tradition. Literature recognizes no tools but printed words. It often lacks immediate recognition, but whatever there is in it of merit cannot fail to win appreciation sooner or later. Oratory is not necessarily literature; but the orations of Webster lose little of their power when transferred to the printed page; they not only *hear well* but *read well.*

Webster was a New Hampshire boy whose later home was Massachusetts. He won early fame as a lawyer and speaker, but his first great oratorical success was his oration delivered at Plymouth in 1820. He spoke at the laying of the corner-stone of the Bunker Hill monument, and again at its completion. As a man in public life, as a member of Congress, and as Secretary of State, many of his orations were of a political nature, the greatest of these being his reply to Hayne. His law practice was continued, and even some of his legal speeches have become classics. Perhaps the most noted among them is the one on the murder of Captain Joseph White, with its thrilling account of the deed of the assassin, of the horror of the possession of the "fatal secret," on to the famous climax, "It must be confessed; it will be confessed; there is no refuge from confession but in suicide,—and suicide is confession!"

Webster's words, spoken with his sonorous, melodious voice, and strengthened by the impression of power and immeasurable reserved force, might easily sway an audience; but what is it that has made them literature? How is it that while most speeches pale and fade in the reading, and lose the life and glow bestowed by the personality of the orator, Webster's are as mighty in the domain of literature as in that of oratory? It is because his thought is so clear, his argument so irresistible and so logical in arrangement, his style so dignified and vigorous and finished, and above all so perfectly adapted to the subject. When we read his words, we forget speaker, audience, and style, we forget to notice how he has spoken and think only on what he has spoken,—and such writings are literature.

SUMMARY

C. The Anti-Slavery Writers

John Greenleaf Whittier
Harriet Beecher Stowe

Orators

William Lloyd Garrison
Edward Everett
Wendell Phillips
Charles Sumner
Rufus Choate
Daniel Webster

The anti-slavery movement strongly affected literature. It was aroused by Garrison. Among the many names associated with its literature are those of Whittier and Mrs. Stowe. Whittier's first published poem was in Garrison's *Free Press.* By Garrison's influence he was sent to school and later entered upon editorial work. He wrote many ringing anti-slavery poems. In 1866 his *Snow-Bound* touched the heart of the country. Many of his ballads are of rare excellence.

Mrs. Stowe founded *Uncle Tom's Cabin* upon the stories of escaped slaves. Its enormous sale was due to its humor, pathos, and earnestness, and to the time of its publication. Her best literary success was in her New England stories.

During this period New England was also rich in orators. Among them were Garrison, Everett, Phillips, Sumner, Choate, and Webster. Not all oratory is literature, but many of Webster's orations are also literature. He was equally eloquent in occasional addresses and in legal and political speeches.

CHAPTER VI

THE NATIONAL PERIOD — EARLIER YEARS

1815–1865

D. THE CAMBRIDGE POETS

31. The Cambridge Poets

To this period belongs the greater part of the work of the three New England poets, Longfellow, Lowell, and Holmes. In the early lives of these three there was a somewhat remarkable similarity. They were all descendants of New England families of culture and standing. They grew up in homes of plenty, but not of undignified display. They were surrounded by people of education and intellectual ability. They came to feel, as Holmes puts it, as much at ease among books as a stable boy feels among horses. Each held a professorship at Harvard. Here the resemblance ends, for never were three poets more unlike in work and disposition than the three who are known as the Cambridge Poets.

32. Henry Wadsworth Longfellow, 1807–1882

The birthplace of Longfellow was Portland, Maine, which he calls "the beautiful town that is seated by the sea." He had all the advantages of books, college, and home culture; and he made such good use of them that while he was journeying homeward from Bowdoin College with his diploma in his trunk, the trustees were

Cambridge in 1824

meditating upon offering the young man of nineteen the professorship of modern languages in his Alma Mater. He accepted gladly, spent three years in Europe preparing for the position, and returned to Bowdoin, where he remained for six years. Then came a call to become professor at Harvard; and a welcome professor he was, for his fame had gone before him. The boys were proud to be in the classes of a teacher who, with the exception of George Ticknor, a much older man, was the best American scholar of the languages and literature of modern Europe. He was a poet, too; his *Summer Shower* had been in their reading-books. Some of them had read his *Outre Mer,* a graceful and poetical mingling of bits of travel, stories, and translations. Moreover, he was a somewhat new kind of professor to the Harvard students of 1836, for he persisted in treating them as if they were gentlemen; and, whatever they might be with others, they always were gentlemen with him.

Up to 1839, the mass of Longfellow's work was in prose; but in that year he published first *Hyperion* and then *Voices of the Night.* In the latter volume were translations from six or seven languages. There were also *A Psalm of Life* and *The Reaper and the Flowers.* These have had nearly seventy years of hard wear; but read them as if no one had ever read them before, and think what courage and inspiration there is in—

Let us, then, be up and doing,
With a heart for any fate;
Still achieving, still pursuing,
Learn to labor and to wait.

The lovers of poetry were watching the young professor at Harvard. What would be his next work? When his next volume came out, it contained, among other poems, *The Skeleton in Armor.* Thus far, his writings had been thoughtful and beautiful, but in this there was something more; there was a stronger flight of the imagination, there was life, action, a story to tell, and generous promise for the future.

So Longfellow's work went on. He lived in the charming old Craigie House in Cambridge, where, as he wrote,

Once, ah, once, within these walls,
One whom memory oft recalls,
The Father of his Country, dwelt.

His longest narrative poems are *Evangeline, The Courtship of Miles Standish,* and *The Song of Hiawatha,* which have been favorites from the first. He translated Dante's *Divine Comedy* and wrote several dramas. His translations are much more literal than those of most writers; but they are never bald and prosy, for he gives to every phrase the master touch that makes it glow with poetry. Few, if any, poems are more American and more patriotic than his *Building of the Ship*, with its impassioned apostrophe:—

Thou, too, sail on, O Ship of State!
Sail on, O Union, strong and great!

Nevertheless, Longfellow loved the Old World and the literatures of many peoples. In his translations he

Craigie House

brought to his own country the culture of the lands across the sea. In so doing he not only enabled others to share in his enjoyment, but did much to prove to the youthful literature of the New World that there were still heights for it to ascend.

Longfellow knew how to beautify his verse with

exquisite imagery, but this imagery was never used merely for ornament; it invariably flashed a light upon the thought, as in—

Feeling is deep and still; and the word that floats on the surface
Is as the tossing buoy, that betrays where the anchor is hidden.

He had the ability to produce beauty from the simplest materials. Once, for instance, he chose a time-worn subject, he made a time-worn comparison, he used in his fifteen lines of verse but fifty-six different words, all everyday words and five sixths of them monosyllables; and with such materials he composed his *Rainy Day!* His writings are so smooth and graceful that one sometimes overlooks their strength. *Evangeline,* for instance, is "A Tale of Love in Acadie," but it is also a picture of indomitable purpose and unfaltering resolution. *Miles Standish* is more than a charming Puritan idyl, centring in an archly demure, "Why don't you speak for yourself, John?" It is a maiden's fearless obedience to the voice of her heart, and a strong man's noble conquest of himself. The keynote of much of Longfellow's lyric verse is his sympathy. When sorrow came to him, his pity did not centre in himself, but went out into the world to all who suffered. In the midst of his own grief, he wrote:—

There is no fireside, howsoe'er defended,
But has one vacant chair.

"Read me that poem," said a bereaved mother, "for Longfellow understood." That is why Longfellow is great. In his *Hiawatha* he introduced a Finnish metre; in *Evangeline* he first succeeded in using the classic hexameter in English. Thus he gave new tools to the wrights of English verse; but it was a far greater glory to be able to speak directly to the hearts of the people. This gift, together with his pure and blameless life, won for him an affection so peculiarly reverent that, even while he lived, thousands of his readers spoke his name with the tenderness of accent oftenest given to those who are no longer among us. Happy is the man who wins both fame and love!

33. James Russell Lowell, 1819–1891

A big, roomy house, fields, woods, pastures, libraries, a college at hand, older brothers and sisters, a father and mother of education and refinement,—such were the surroundings of Lowell's early life. *The Vision of Sir Launfal* shows how well he learned the out-of-door world; his essays prove on every page how familiar he became with the world of books.

When the time for college had come, there were difficulties. The boy was ready to read every volume not required by the curriculum, and to keep every rule except those invented by the faculty. When graduation time drew near, his parents were in Rome. Some one hastened to tell them that their son had been rusticated to Concord for six weeks and had also been chosen class poet. "Oh, dear!" exclaimed the despairing father, "James promised me that he would quit writing poetry and go to work."

Fortunately for the lovers of good poetry, "James" did not keep his word. He struggled manfully to become a lawyer, but he could not help being a poet. Just ten years after graduating, he brought out in one

Elmwood

short twelvemonth three significant poems. The first was *The Vision of Sir Launfal,* with its loving outburst of sympathy with nature. He knew well how the clod—

> *Groping blindly above it for light,*
> *Climbs to a soul in grass and flowers.*

Sir Launfal, too, climbs to a soul, for the poem is the story of a life. The second poem was *A Fable for Critics.* The fable proper is as dull as the preposterous rhymes and unthinkable puns of Lowell will permit; but its pithy criticisms of various authors have well endured the wear and tear of half a century. The third was *The Biglow Papers.* Here was an entirely new vein. Here the Yankee dialect—which is so often only a survival of the English of Shakespeare's day—became a literary language. Lowell could have easily put his thoughts into the polished sentences of the scholar; but the homely wording which he chose to employ gives them a certain everyday strength and vigor that a smoother phrasing would have weakened. When he writes,—

Ez fer war, I call it murder;
There you hev it plain an' flat;
I don't want to go no furder
Than my Testyment fer that,—

he strikes a blow that has something of the keenness of the sword and the weight of the cudgel.

These three poems indicate the three directions in which Lowell did his best work; for he was poet, critic, and reformer,—sometimes all three in one. In such poems as *The Present Crisis,* that stern and solemn arraignment of his countrymen, there is as much of earnest protest as of poetry. So in *The Dandelion,* his "dear, common flower" reveals to him not only its own beauty, but the thought that every human heart is sacred.

Lowell's lyrics are only a small part of his work; for he took the place of Longfellow at Harvard, he edited the *Atlantic* and the *North American Review;* he wrote many magazine articles on literary and political subjects; he delivered addresses and poems, the noble *Commemoration Ode* ranking highest of all; and he was minister, first to Spain, and then to England. In his prose writings one is almost overwhelmed with the wideness of his knowledge, yet there is never a touch of pedantry. He always writes as if his readers were as much at home in the world of books as himself. The serious thought is ever brightened by gleams of humor, flashes of wit. When we take up one of his writings, it will "perchance turn out a song, perchance turn out a sermon." It may be full of strong and manly thought, and it may be all a-whirl with rollicking merriment; but whatever else it is, it will be sincere and honest and interesting. It is easier to label and classify the man who writes in but one manner, and it may be that he wins a surer fame; but we should be sorry indeed to miss either scholar, critic, wit, or reformer from the work of the poet Lowell.

34. Oliver Wendell Holmes, 1809–1894

On the page for August in a copy of the old *Massachusetts Register* for 1809, the twenty-ninth day is marked, and at the bottom of the page is a foot-note, "Son b." In this laconic fashion was noted the advent of the physician-novelist-poet. He had also a chance of becoming a clergyman and a lawyer; for his father favored the one profession, and he himself gave a year's study to the other. It was while he was poring over Blackstone that the order was given to break up the old battleship *Constitution.* Then it was that he wrote *Old Ironsides.* The poem was printed on handbills. They were showered about the streets of Washington, and the Secretary of the Navy revoked his order. Holmes was twenty-one. The question of a profession was still unsettled. Finally he decided to be a physician; but, as he said, "The man or woman who has tasted type is sure to return to his old indulgence sooner or later." In Holmes's case, it was sooner, for he had hardly taken his degree before the publishers were advertising a volume of his poems. Here were *My Aunt, The September Gale,* and best of all, *The Last Leaf,* the verses that one reads with a smile on the lips and tears in the eyes.

The young physician's practice did not occupy much of his time, chiefly because he wrote poetry and made witty remarks. These were a delight to the well folk, but the sick people were a little afraid of a doctor whose interest and knowledge were not limited to pills and powders. Moreover, the man who lay ill of a fever could not forget that the brilliant young M. D. had said jauntily of his slender practice, "Even the smallest fevers thankfully received." Soon an invitation came to teach anatomy at Dartmouth; and, a few years later, to teach the same subject at Harvard. Holmes was successful in both places; for with all his love of literature, he had a genuine devotion to his profession. He wrote much on medical subjects, and three times his essays gained the famous Boylston prize, offered annually by Harvard College for the best dissertations on questions in medical science.

In 1857, the publishers, Phillips, Sampson and Co., decided to establish a new magazine. "Will you be its editor?" they asked Lowell; and he finally replied "Yes, if Dr. Holmes can be the first contributor to be engaged." Dr. Holmes became not only the first contributor, but he named the magazine *The Atlantic*. Some twenty-five years earlier he had written two papers called *The Autocrat of the Breakfast Table*. He now continued them, beginning, "I was just going to say when I was interrupted." The scene is laid at the table of a boarding-house. The Autocrat carries on a brilliant monologue, broken from time to time by a word from the lady who asks for original poetry for her album, from the theological student, the old gentleman, or the young man John; or by an anxious look on the face of the landlady, to whom some paradoxical speech of the Autocrat's suggests insanity and the loss of a boarder. Howells calls *The Autocrat* a "dramatized essay;" but,

The Autocrat Leaving his Boston Home for a Morning Walk

whatever it is called, it will bear many readings and seem brighter and fresher at each one. Among the paragraphs of *The Autocrat* and *The Professor,* which followed, a number of poems are interspersed. Among them are *The One-Hoss Shay,* with its irrefutable logic; *Contentment,* with its modest—

I only wish a hut of stone
(A very plain brown stone will do),—

and the exquisite lines of *The Chambered Nautilus*, with its superb appeal,—

Build thee more stately mansions, O my soul!

Holmes was also a novelist; for he produced *Elsie Venner* and two other works of fiction, all showing power of characterization, and all finding their chief interest in some study of the mysterious connection between mind and body. "Medicated novels," a friend mischievously called them, somewhat to the wrath of their author.

Nearly half of Holmes's poems were written for some special occasion,—some anniversary, or class reunion, or reception of a famous guest. At such times he was at his best; for the demand for occasional verse, which freezes most wielders of the pen, was to him a breath of inspiration.

Holmes's wit is ever fascinating, his pathos is ever sincere; but the charm that will perhaps be even more powerful to hold his readers is his delightful personality, which is revealed in every sentence. A book of his never stands alone, for the beloved Autocrat is ever peeping through it. His tender heart first feels the pathos that he reveals to us; his kindly spirit is behind every flash of wit, every sword-thrust of satire.

SUMMARY

D. The Cambridge Poets

Henry Wadsworth Longfellow
James Russell Lowell
Oliver Wendell Holmes

The Cambridge Poets were all descendants of cultivated New England families and grew up among intellectual surroundings. All held professorships at Harvard.

Longfellow graduated at Bowdoin, and became professor of modern languages, first at Bowdoin and then at Harvard. Until 1839, when he published *Voices of the Night,* he wrote chiefly prose. *The Skeleton in Armor* established his reputation as a poet. His longest narrative poems are *Evangeline, The Courtship of Miles Standish,* and *The Song of Hiawatha.* His translations are both literal and poetic, and were of great value to the young American literature. He can beautify his work with figures, or he can make a poem with the simplest materials. His sympathy was the keynote of much of his lyric verse. He introduced a Finnish metre, and was the first to succeed in English hexameter.

Lowell's serious work began in 1848, when he brought out *The Vision of Sir Launfal, A Fable for Critics,* and *The Biglow Papers.* He succeeded Longfellow at Harvard, edited *The Atlantic,* wrote many magazine articles and addresses, was foreign minister to Spain and England. His writings show broad scholarship, love of nature, and much humor. He was scholar, wit, critic, reformer, and poet.

Holmes's *Old Ironsides* was his first prominent poem. He studied medicine, became professor of anatomy, first at Dartmouth, then at Harvard. In 1857 he named *The Atlantic*, and wrote *The Autocrat* for it. He wrote three novels, and was especially successful as an occasional poet.

CHAPTER VII

THE NATIONAL PERIOD — EARLIER YEARS

1815–1865

E. THE HISTORIANS

35. Historical Writing

In the midst of this composition of poetry and novels and philosophy, the early New England tendency toward the historical had by no means disappeared. Here, two opposing influences were at work. On the one hand, the Spanish studies of Irving, the *History of Spanish Literature* of Ticknor, and the translations of Longfellow, had turned men's minds toward European countries. On the other hand, the War of 1812 and the rapid development of the United States had stimulated patriotism. Moreover, with the passing of the heroes of the Revolution, Americans began to realize that the childhood of the United States had vanished, that the youthful country had already a history to be recorded. The proper method of historical composition was pointed out to his countrymen by Jared Sparks, first a professor and then president of Harvard College.

Before the days of Sparks, few writers had felt the responsibility of historical writing. It was enough if a history was made interesting and romantic; there was little attempt to make it accurate. Even if original sources were at hand and the author took pains to examine them, he paid little attention to any study of causes or results, he made no careful comparison of conflicting accounts. One manuscript was as good as another, and any so-called fact was welcome if it filled a vacant niche in the story. Sparks followed a different method. To gather his information, he consulted not only the records stored in the dignified archives of the great libraries of Europe and America, but also the family papers stuffed away into the corners of ancient garrets. He examined old newspapers and pamphlets and diaries. He traced legends and traditions back to their origins. It was in this way that his *Life and Writings of George Washington,* his partially completed *History of the American Revolution,* and his other works were produced. Unfortunately, Sparks lacked the good fairy gift of the power to make his work interesting; that was left for other writers; but in thoroughness in collecting materials he was the pioneer. During this period, there were at least four historians whose fame is far greater than his; but to Sparks they owe the gratitude that is ever due to him who has pointed out the way. These four are Bancroft and Parkman, who wrote on American themes; and Prescott and Motley, who chose for their subjects different phases of European history.

36. George Bancroft, 1800–1891

On a hill in the city of Worcester, Massachusetts, stands a tower of massive stone. It was erected in honor of George Bancroft, who as a boy roamed over the hills and valleys of what is now a part of the city.

He graduated at Harvard, and then went to Germany, where he studied with various scholars branches of learning which ranged from French literature to Scriptural interpretation. At twenty he had chosen his lifework,—to become a historian. Fourteen years later the first volume of his *History of the United States* came out, a scholarly record of the progress of our country from the discovery of America to the adoption of the Constitution in 1789.

Bancroft's historical work extended over nearly fifty years; but during that time he did much other writing, he was minister to England and to Berlin, and he was Secretary of the Navy. While holding this last office he decided that the United States ought to have a naval school. Congress did not agree, but Mr. Bancroft went quietly to work. He found that he had a right to choose a place where midshipmen should remain while waiting for orders, also that he could direct that the lessons given them at sea should be continued on land. He obtained the use of some military buildings at Annapolis, put the boys into them, and set them to work. Then he said to Congress, "We have a naval school in operation; will you not adopt it?" Congress adopted it, and thus the United States Naval Academy was founded.

37. William Hickling Prescott, 1796–1859

A crust of bread thrown in a students' frolic at Harvard made Prescott nearly blind, and prevented him from becoming a lawyer as he had planned. With what little eyesight remained to him, and with an inexhaustible fund of courage and cheerfulness, he set to work to become a historian. He made a generous preparation. For ten years he read by the eyes of others scores of volumes on ancient and modern literature. He had chosen for the title of his first book *The History of the Reign of Ferdinand and Isabella.* He must learn Spanish, of course; and he describes with a gentle humor the weeks spent under the trees of his country residence, listening to the reading of a man who understood not a word of the language. As the different authorities were read aloud, many of them conflicting, Prescott dictated notes. When he had completed his reading for one chapter, he had these notes read to him. Then he thought over all that he meant to say in the chapter,—thought so exactly, and so many times, that when he took up his noctograph, he could write as rapidly as the contrivance would permit.

It was under such discouragements that Prescott wrote; but he said bravely that these difficulties were no excuse for "not doing well what it was not necessary to do at all." His work needs small excuse. He had chosen the Spanish field; he wrote *The Conquest of Mexico,* then *The Conquest of Peru.* Three volumes he completed of *The History of the Reign of Philip the Second;* then came death.

Prescott was most painstaking in collecting facts and comparing statements, but the popularity of his books is due in part to their subject and in even greater part to their style. He wrote of the days of romance and wild adventure, it is true; but yet the most thrilling subject will not make a thrilling writer out of a dull one. Prescott has written in a style that is strong, absolutely clear, and often poetic. He describes a battle or a procession or a banquet or even a wedding costume as if he loved to do it. Few writers have combined as successfully as he the accuracy of the historian and the marvellous picturing of the poet and novelist.

38. John Lothrop Motley, 1814–1877

When Bancroft was a young man, he taught for a year at Northampton. One of his pupils was a handsome, bright-eyed boy named Motley. This boy's especial delight was reading poetry and novels, and a few years after he graduated from Harvard he wrote a novel which was fairly good. He wrote another, which was better; but by this time he had become so deeply interested in the Dutch Republic that he determined to write its history. Ten years later he sent a manuscript to the English publisher, Murray. It was promptly declined, and the author published it at his own expense. Then Murray was a sorry man, for *The Rise of the Dutch Republic* was a decided success.

John Lothrop Motley
1814–1877

The lavish amount of work that had been bestowed upon it ought to have brought success. Motley could not obtain the needed documents in America, therefore he and his family crossed the ocean. When he had exhausted the library in one place, they went to another. He had a hard-working secretary, and in two or three countries he had men engaged to copy rare papers for his use. When his material was well in hand, he had the critical ability to select and arrange his facts, the literary instinct to present them in telling fashion, and the artistic talent to make vivid pictures of famous persons and dramatic scenes.

One of the pleasantest facts about our greater authors is the almost invariable absence of envy among them. This book could hardly fail to trench upon the field of Prescott; yet the blind historian was ready with the warmest commendations, as were Irving and Bancroft. Prescott, indeed, in the first volume of his *Philip the Second*, published a year earlier, had inserted a cordial note in regard to the forthcoming *Dutch Republic.*

Motley's next book was *The United Netherlands.* One more work would have completed the history of the whole struggle of the Dutch for liberty. He postponed preparing this until he should have written *The Life and Death of John of Barneveld.* Then came the long illness which ended his life, and the story of the epoch was never completed.

39. Francis Parkman, 1823–1893

Some years before Longfellow wrote, "The thoughts of youth are long, long thoughts," Francis Parkman was proving the truth of the line; for he, a young man of eighteen, had already planned his lifework. He would be an historian, and he would write on the subject that appealed to him most strongly,—the contest between France and England for the possession of a continent. The preparation for such a work required more than the reading of papers—though an enormous quantity of these demanded careful attention. The Indians must be known. Their way of living and thinking must be as familiar to the historian as his own. The only way to gain this knowledge was to share their life; and this Parkman did for several months. His health failed, his eyesight was impaired, but he did not give up the work that he had planned. Before beginning it, however, he tried his hand by writing *The Oregon Trail*, an account of his western journeyings and his life among the red men.

Francis Parkman
1823–1893

His health was so completely broken down that for some time he could not listen to his secretary's reading for more than half an hour a day; but he had no thought of yielding. He visited the places that he intended to describe; he wrote when he could; when writing was impossible, he cultivated roses and lilies; but whatever he did, and even when he could do nothing, he was always cheerful and courageous.

So it was that Parkman's work was done; but he writes so easily, so gracefully, and with such apparent pleasure that the mere style of his composition would make it of value. He seldom stops to consider motives and determine remote causes, but he gives us a clear narrative, with dramatic and picturesque descriptions of such verisimilitude that we should hardly be surprised to see a foot-note saying, "I was present. F. P." He lived to carry out his plan, comprising twelve volumes which cover the ground from *Pioneers of France in the New World* to *The Conspiracy of Pontiac.* Higginson's summary of the characteristics of the four historians is as follows: "George Bancroft, with a style in that day thought eloquent, but now felt to be overstrained and inflated; William H. Prescott, with attractive but colorless style and rather superficial interpretation. . . . John Lothrop Motley, laborious, but delightful; and Francis Parkman, more original in his work and probably more permanent in his fame than any of these."

40. Minor Authors

These last four chapters have been devoted to the authors of highest rank during the early part of New England's second period of literary leadership; but there are many others whose names it is not easy to omit from even so brief a sketch. In history, there are not only John Gorham Palfrey, whose *History of New England,* and Jeremy Belknap, whose *History of*

New Hampshire are still standards; but there is Richard Hildreth, whose *History of the United States*, written from a political point of view opposed to Bancroft's, lacks only an interesting style to win the popularity which its research and scholarship deserve. In criticism, there is Edwin Percy Whipple, who reviewed literary work with sympathetic good sense and expressed his opinions in so vigorous and interesting a style that his own writings became literature. He and Richard Henry Dana ought to have worked hand in hand: Whipple, to criticise completed writings; Dana, to cultivate the public taste to demand the best. Dana wrote poetry also, but it lacked the warmth of feeling that makes a poem live. *The Little Beach-Bird* is now his best-known poem. Whipple calls it "delicious, but slightly morbid;" and it certainly has neither the tenderness of Henry Vaughan's *The Bird* nor the joyous comradeship of Mrs. Thaxter's *The Sandpiper*. Among essayists, there are two whose names first became well known during this period, Donald Grant Mitchell and George William Curtis. The story is told of Mitchell that to make sure of a winding, picturesque pathway from the road to his house, he had a heavy load of stone brought to the gate and bade the driver make his way up the hill by the easiest grades. It is "by the easiest grades" that his *Dream Life* and *Reveries of a Bachelor*, his earliest books, roam on gently and smoothly. They are full of sentiment; but it is a good, clean sentiment that should be not without honor, even in a book. His latest work, *English Lands, Letters, and Kings*, has not quite the winsome charm of his earlier writings, but it is vigorous and picturesque.

Here is his description of William the Conqueror: "It was as if a new, sharp, eager man of business had on a sudden come to the handling of some old sleepily conducted counting-room: he cuts off the useless heads; he squares the books: he stops waste; pity or tenderness have no hearing in his shop." He says of Elizabeth: "She would have been great if she had been a shoemaker's daughter, . . . she would have bound more shoes, and bound them better, and looked sharper after the affairs of her household than any cobbler's wife of the land."

George William Curtis spent some of his schooldays at Brook Farm among the transcendentalists. Graceful sketches of travel were in vogue, and he wrote *Nile Notes of a Howadji;* dreamy sentiment was in fashion, and he wrote his ever-charming *Prue and I.* Then he became an editor, a lecturer, a political speaker. Meanwhile he had entered upon a long and honored career in the *Easy Chair* department of *Harper's Magazine.* For nearly forty years the readers of *Harper's* cut open the *Easy Chair* pages expectantly, for there they were sure to find some pleasant chat on topics of the day,—on The American Girl, or The Game of Newport, or Honor, or The New England Sabbath, or on some man who was in the public eye. Grave or satirical, they were always marked by a liquid, graceful style, a gentle, kindly humor, and sound thought. Then there were two books, a big one and a little one, written by Noah Webster. They were not literature, and they did not have any special "inspiring influence" toward the making of literature; but they were exceedingly useful tools. The big book was Webster's *Dictionary,* and the little one was the thin, blue-covered Webster's *Spelling-book*. Long ago it went far beyond copyrights and publishers' reports; but it is estimated that sufficient copies have been printed to put one into the hand of every child in the nation.

Taking this literature of New England, or almost of Massachusetts, as a whole, we cannot fail to note its atmosphere of conscientious work. It is not enough for the poet that an inspiring thought has flashed into his mind; he feels a responsibility to interpret it to the best of his power. In Longfellow's work, for instance, there is no poem that we would strike out as unworthy of his pen. Hawthorne's slightest sketch is as carefully finished as his *Scarlet Letter*. Nothing is done heedlessly. The Puritan conscience had been enriched with two centuries of culture; but it was as much of a power in the literature of New England as in the lonely little settlements that clung to her inhospitable coast.

SUMMARY

E. The Historians

Jared Sparks
George Bancroft
William Hickling Prescott
John Lothrop Motley
Francis Parkman

The Spanish studies of Irving and Ticknor and the translations of Longfellow drew men's minds toward the Old World; the War of 1812 and the rapid development of the United States stimulated patriotism. Sparks first pointed out the thorough and accurate method of historical writing. The four leading historians of the period were: (1) Bancroft, who wrote the *History of the United States;* (2) Prescott, who wrote clearly and attractively on Spanish themes, and whose last book, the *History of the Reign of Philip the Second,* was left incomplete; (3) Motley, who wrote "laboriously but picturesquely" of the Dutch Republic, but died without completing its history; (4) Parkman, who chose for his subject the contest between France and England for the possession of North America, and lived to carry out his plan so excellently as to win permanent fame.

Among the many minor authors of this period were the historians, Palfrey, Belknap, and Hildreth; the critic, Whipple; the critic and poet, Dana; the essayists, Mitchell, and Curtis of the *Easy Chair;* while Noah Webster of the *Dictionary* and *Spelling-book* must not be forgotten.

CHAPTER VIII

THE NATIONAL PERIOD — EARLIER YEARS

1815–1865

F. THE SOUTHERN WRITERS

41. Why there was little writing in the South

Thus it was that literature centred about the great cities of the North. There were several reasons why it could hardly be expected to flourish in the South. In the first place, there were no large towns where publishing houses had been established and where men of talent might gain inspiration from one another. Again, there was small home market for the wares of the author. There were libraries in many of the stately homes of the South, but their shelves were filled with the English classics of the eighteenth century. There was no lack of intellectual power; but plantation life called for executive ability and led naturally to statesmanship and oratory rather than to the printed page. There were orators, such men as Henry Clay, "the great leader;" the ardent, brilliant Patrick Henry of earlier times; Robert Young Hayne, equally eloquent in address and in debate; and John Caldwell Calhoun, whom Webster called "a senator of Rome." There was almost from the beginning a poem written in one place and a history or a biography in another. The most famous of these scattered writings were produced by William Wirt, a

William Wirt
1772–1834

Maryland lawyer. Early in the century he wrote his *Letters of a British Spy,* which contains his touching description of *The Blind Preacher.* In 1817 his eminence as a lawyer was proved by his being chosen Attorney-General of the United States, and his ability as an author by the publication of his *Life of Patrick Henry.* This book is rather doubtful as to some of its facts, and rather flowery as to its rhetoric, but so vivid that the picture which it draws of the great orator has held its own for nearly a century. Charleston was the nearest approach to a literary centre, for it was the home of Simms, Hayne, and Timrod.

42. William Gilmore Simms, 1806–1870

In 1827, when the Knickerbocker writers had already brought forth some of their most valuable productions, Simms published a little volume of poems. He published a second, a third, and many others; but his best work was in prose. He wrote novel after novel, as hastily and carelessly as Cooper, but with a certain dash and vigor. *The Yemassee* is ranked as his best work. It has no adequate plot, but contains many thrilling adventures and narrow escapes. Simms is often called the "Cooper of the South;" and in one important detail he is Cooper's superior, namely, his women are real women. They are not introduced merely as pretty dummies whose rescue will exhibit the prowess of the hero: they are thoughtful and intelligent, and, in time of need, they can take a hand in their own rescue. In *The Yemassee,* for instance, "Grayson's wife" has a terrible struggle with an Indian at her window. She faints, but—like a real woman—not until she has won the victory. In one respect Simms did work that is of increasing value; he laid his scenes in the country about his own home, he studied the best historical records, he learned the traditions of the South. The result is that in his novels there is a wealth of information about Southern colonial life that can hardly be found elsewhere.

William Gilmore Simms
1806–1870

43. Paul Hamilton Hayne, 1830–1886

Simms was of value to the world of literature in another way than by wielding his own pen. He was a kind and helpful friend to the younger authors who gathered around him. The chief of these was Hayne, who is often called "the poet-laureate of the South." Hayne had a comfortable fortune and a troop of friends, and there was only one reason why his life should not have flowed on easily and pleasantly. That reason was the Civil War. He enlisted in the Confederate Army, and, even after he was sent home too ill for service, his pen was ever busied with ringing lyrics of warfare. When peace came, he found himself almost penniless. Many a man has taken up such a struggle with life bravely; Hayne did more, for he took it up cheerfully. He built himself a tiny cottage and "persisted in being happy." Before the war, he had published three volumes of verse, and now from that little home came forth many graceful, beautiful lyrics. This is part of his description of the song of the mocking-bird at night:—

It rose in dazzling spirals overhead,
Whence to wild sweetness wed,
Poured marvellous melodies, silvery trill on trill;
The very leaves grew still
On the charmed trees to hearken; while for me,
Heart-trilled to ecstasy,
I followed—followed the bright shape that flew,
Still circling up the blue,
Till as a fountain that has reached its height,
Falls back in sprays of light
Slowly dissolved, so that enrapturing lay
Divinely melts away
Through tremulous spaces to a music-mist,
Soon by the fitful breeze
    How gently kissed
Into remote and tender silences.

He wrote narrative verse, but was especially successful in the sonnet, with its harassing restrictions and limitations. Hayne's writings have one charm that those of greater poets often lack; his personality gleams through them. He trusts us with his sorrows and his joys. He writes of the father whom he never saw, of the dear son "Will," of whom he says:—

We roam the hills together,
In the golden summer weather,
Will and I.

He writes of his wife's "bonny brown hand,"—

The hand that holds an honest heart, and rules a happy hearth.

He writes of the majestic pine against which his poet friend laid his weary head. In whatever he writes, he shows himself not only a poet, but also a sincere and lovable man.

44. Henry Timrod, 1829–1867

The friend who leaned against the pine was Henry Timrod. Their friendship began in the days when "Harry" passed under his desk a slate full of his own verses. Life was hard for the young poet. Lack of funds broke off his college course, and for many years he acted as tutor in various families. In 1860 a little volume of his poems was brought out in Boston by Ticknor and Fields. It was spoken of kindly—and that was all. Then came the war, and such poverty that he wrote of his verse, "I would consign every line of it to eternal oblivion, for—one hundred dollars in hand!"

Timrod writes in many tones. He is sometimes strong, as in *The Cotton Boll;* sometimes light and graceful, as in *Baby's Age,* wherein the age is counted by flowers, a different flower for each week. This ends:—

But soon—so grave, and deep, and wise
The meaning grows in Baby's eyes,
So VERY *deep for Baby's age—*
We think to date a week with sage.

Sometimes he rises to noble heights, as in his description of the poet, at least one stanza of which is not unworthy of Tennyson:—

And he must be as armèd warrior strong,
And he must be as gentle as a girl,
And he must front, and sometimes suffer wrong,
With brow unbent, and lip untaught to curl;
For wrath, and scorn, and pride, however just,
Fill the clear spirit's eyes with earthly dust.

In whatever tone he writes, there is sincerity, true love of nature, and a frequent flash of poetic expression, that make us dream pleasant dreams of what a little money and a little leisure might have brought from his pen.

45. Edgar Allan Poe, 1809–1849

Another Southern writer, in some respects the greatest of all, was Edgar Allan Poe. He was left an orphan, and was taken into the family of a wealthy merchant of Baltimore named Allan. He was somewhat wild in college, and was brought home and put to work in Mr. Allan's office. He ran away, joined the army under an assumed name, was received at West Point through Mr. Allan's influence, but later discharged for neglect of his duties. Mr. Allan refused any further assistance, and Poe set to work to support himself by his pen. In the midst of poverty he married a beautiful young cousin whom he loved devotedly. He wrote a few poems and much prose. He held various editorial positions; he filled them most acceptably, but usually lost them through either his extreme sensitiveness or his use of stimulants. His child-wife died, and two years later Poe himself died.

These are the facts in the life of Poe; but his various biographers have put widely varying interpretations upon them. One pictures him, for instance, as a worthless drunkard; another, probably more truly, as of a sensitive, poetic organization that was thrown into confusion by a single glass of liquor.

As a literary man, Poe was first known by his prose, and especially by his reviews. He had a keen sense of literary excellence, and recognized it at a glance. He was utterly fearless—and fearlessness was a new and badly needed quality in American criticism. On the other hand, he had not the foundation of wide reading and study necessary for criticism that is to abide; and, worse than that, he was not great enough to be fair to the man whom he disliked or of whom he was jealous. His most valuable prose is his tales, for here he is a master. They are well constructed and the plot is well developed; every sentence, every word, counts toward the climax. That is the more mechanical part of the work; but Poe's power goes much further. He has a marvellous ability to make a story "real." He brings this about sometimes in Defoe's fashion, by throwing himself into the place of the character in hand and thinking what *he* would do in such a position; sometimes by noting and emphasizing some significant detail, as, for instance, in *The Cask of*

Amontillado. Here he mentions three times the webwork of nitre on the walls that proves their fearful depth below the river bed, and the victim's consequent hopelessness of rescue. Sometimes the opening sentence puts us into the mood of the story, so that, before it is fairly begun, an atmosphere has been provided that lends its own coloring to every detail. For instance, the first sentence of *The Fall of the House of Usher* is:—

"During the whole of a dull, dark, and soundless day in the autumn of the year, when the clouds hung oppressively low in the heavens, I had been passing alone, on horseback, through a singularly dreary tract of country, and at length found myself, as the shades of evening drew on, within view of the melancholy House of Usher."

Here is the keynote of the story, and we are prepared for sadness and gloom. The unusual expressions, "soundless day" and "singularly dreary," hint at some mystery. The second sentence increases these feelings; and with each additional phrase the gloom and sadness become more dense.

No one knows better than Poe how to work up to a climax of horror, and then to intensify its awfulness by dropping in some contrasting detail. In *The Cask of Amontillado,* for instance, the false friend, in his carnival dress of motley with cap and bells, is chained and then walled up in the masonry that is to become his living tomb. A single aperture remains. Through this the avenger thrusts his torch and lets it fall. Poe says, "There came forth in return only a jingling of bells."

The awful death that lies before the false friend grows doubly horrible at this suggestion of the merriment of the carnival.

Poe's poetry is on the fascinating borderland where poetry and music meet. His poems are not fifty in number, and many of them are but a few lines in length. The two that are best known are *The Bells,* a wonderfully beautiful expression of feeling through the mere sound of words, and *The Raven.* Poe has left a cold-blooded account of the "manufacture" of this latter poem. He declares that he chose beauty for the atmosphere, and that beauty excites the sensitive to tears; therefore he decided to write of melancholy. The most beautiful thing is a beautiful woman, the most melancholy is death; therefore he writes of the death of a beautiful woman. So with the refrain. *O* is the most sonorous vowel, and when joined with *r* is capable of "protracted emphasis;" therefore he fixes upon "Nevermore." He may be believed or disbelieved; but in *The Raven,* as in whatever else he writes, there is a weird and marvellous music. To him, everything poetical could be interpreted by sound; he said he "could distinctly hear the sound of the darkness as it stole over the horizon." He has a way of repeating a phrase with some slight change, as if he could not bear to leave it. Thus in *Annabel Lee* he writes:—

But our love it was stronger by far than the love
Of those who were older than we—
Of many far wiser than we—
And neither the angels in heaven above,

Nor the demons down under the sea,
Can ever dissever my soul from the soul
Of the beautiful Annabel Lee.

This repetition is even more marked in *Ulalume:—*

The leaves they were crispéd and sere—
The leaves they were withering and sere.

These phrases cling to the memory of the reader as if they were strains of music. We find ourselves saying them over and over. It is not easy to analyze the fascination of such verse, but it has fascination. Many years ago, when Poe was a young man, Higginson heard him read his mystic *Al Aaraaf.* He says, "In walking back to Cambridge my comrades and I felt that we had been under the spell of some wizard." When we look in the poems of Poe for the "high seriousness" that Matthew Arnold names as one of the marks of the best poetry, it cannot be found; but in the power to express a mood, a feeling, by the mere sound of words, Poe has no rival.

46. Sidney Lanier, 1842–1881

A few years after the death of Poe, a Southern college boy was earnestly demanding of himself, "What am I fit for?" He had musical genius, not merely the facility that can tinkle out tunes on various instruments, but deep, strong love of music and rare ability to produce music. His father, a lawyer of Macon, Georgia, felt that to be a musician was rather small business; and his son had yielded to this belief so far as the genius within him would permit. Another talent had this rarely gifted boy,—for poetry.

The Civil War was a harsh master for such a spirit, but in its first days he enlisted in the Confederate army, and saw some terrible fighting. More than three years later he was taken prisoner—he and his flute. After five months they were released. For sixteen years he taught, he read, he wrote, he lectured at Johns Hopkins University and elsewhere, and for several winters he played first flute in the Peabody Symphony Orchestra in Baltimore. All those years he was in a constant struggle with consumption and poverty. Sometimes for many months he could do nothing but suffer. Between the attacks of illness he did a large amount of literary work. It was not always the kind of writing that he was longing to do,—some of it would in other hands have been nothing but hack work; but with a spirit like Lanier's there could be no such thing as hack work, for he threw such talent into it, such pleasure in using the pen, that at his touch it became literature. He edited Froissart and other chronicles of long ago, and he wrote a novel. He wrote also on the development of the novel, on the science of English verse, on the relations of poetry and music, and on Shakespeare and his forerunners. He was always a student, and always original.

Lanier had the lofty conscientiousness of a great poet. Some truth underlies each of his poems, whether it is the simple—and profound—*Ballad of the Trees and the Master,—*

Into the woods my Master went,
Clean forspent, forspent.
Into the woods my Master came,
Forspent with love and shame.

But the olives they were not blind to Him;
The little gray leaves were kind to Him:
The thorn tree had a mind to Him
When into the woods He came.

Out of the woods my Master went,
And He was well content.
Out of the woods my Master came,
Content with death and shame.
When Death and Shame would woo Him last,
From under the trees they drew Him last:
'T was on a tree they slew Him—last
When out of the woods He came,—

the nobly rhythmical *Marshes of Glynn*, or *The Song of the Chattahoochee,—*

All down the hills of Habersham,
All through the valleys of Hall,
The rushes cried ABIDE, ABIDE,
The willful water weeds held me thrall,
The laving laurel turned my tide,
The ferns and the fondling grass said STAY,
The dewberry dipped for to work delay,
And the little weeds sighed ABIDE, ABIDE,
HERE IN THE HILLS OF HABERSHAM,
HERE IN THE VALLEYS OF HALL.

Poe had a melody of unearthly sweetness, but little basis of thought; Lanier had a richer, if less bewitching melody, *and* thought. He had the balance, the self-control, in which Poe was lacking. It is almost a sure test of any kind of greatness if its achievements carry with them an overtone that murmurs, "The man is greater than his deed. He could do more than he has ever done." We do not feel this in Poe; we do feel it in Lanier. In his rare combination of Southern richness with Northern restraint, he will ever be an inspiration to the poetry that must arise from the luxuriant land of the South. He is not only the greatest Southern poet; he is one of the greatest poets that our country has produced. "How I long to sing a thousand various songs that oppress me unsung!" he wrote; and no lover of poetry can turn the last leaf of his single volume of verse without an earnest wish that a longer life had permitted his desire to be gratified.

SUMMARY

THE SOUTHERN WRITERS

William Wirt	*Henry Timrod*
William Gilmore Simms	*Edgar Allan Poe*
Paul Hamilton Hayne	*Sidney Lanier*

There was little writing in the South, because of the lack of large cities, the small home market for modern books, and the tendencies of plantation life toward statesmanship and oratory rather than literary composition. The best of this scattered writing was done by Wirt. Later, Simms, the "Cooper of the South," published many volumes of poems and many novels. *The Yemassee* is regarded as his best novel. He is Cooper's superior in the delineation of women. His novels give much information about colonial life in the South. Hayne, the "poet-laureate of the South," lost his property by the war. He wrote many beautiful poems, and was especially successful in the sonnet. His personality gleams through his writings. Henry Timrod had a hard struggle with poverty. He writes in many tones with sincerity, love of nature, and frequent flashes of poetic expression. The facts in Poe's life have been variously interpreted. He first became known through his reviews. His tales are his most valuable prose. They are well constructed and remarkably realistic. His poetry is on the borderland of poetry and music. He wrote fewer than fifty poems. He has left a doubtfully true account of his manufacture of *The Raven.* There is a fascinating music in whatever he writes. He has not the "high seriousness" of the great poet, but in the power to express feeling by the mere sound of the words he has no rival. Lanier had musical and poetical genius. He enlisted in the Confederate army. At the close of the war, he taught, lectured, read, wrote, played first flute in the Baltimore Symphony Orchestra. He struggled with ill health and narrow means. He did much editing, wrote on the development of the novel, on the science of English verse, on the relations of poetry and music, and on Shakespeare and his forerunners. His poems are rarely without a rich melody, and never without underlying truth. It proves his genius that he ever seemed greater than his writings. He is one of our greatest poets.

CHAPTER IX

THE NATIONAL PERIOD — LATER YEARS

1865—

47. Present Literary Activity

Since the war an enormous amount of printed matter has been produced. We can hardly be said to have a literary centre, for no sooner has one place begun to manifest its right to the title than, behold, some remarkably good work appears in quite another quarter. The whole country seems to have taken its pen in hand. Statesman, financier, farmer, general, lawyer, minister, actor, city girl, country girl, college boy,—everybody is writing. The result of this literary activity is entirely too near us for a final decision as to its merits, and any criticism pronounced upon it ought to have the foot-note, "At least, so it seems at present."

48. Fiction

The lion's share of this printed matter, in bulk, at any rate, falls under the heading of fiction. Its distinguishing trait is realism, and the apostles of realism are William Dean Howells (1837–1920) and Henry James (1843–1916). What they write is not thrilling, but the way they write it has charmed thousands of readers. Wit, humor, and grace of style are the qualities of their productions that are seldom lacking. They write of commonplace people; but there is a certain restful charm in reading of the behavior of ordinary mortals under ordinary circumstances. Howells lays the scenes of most of his novels on this side of the ocean; James generally lays his scenes abroad. Francis Marion Crawford (1854–1909) sometimes brings his characters into America, but the scenes of his best novels are laid elsewhere. Edward Everett Hale (1822–1909) is such a master of realism that his *Man without a Country* persuaded thousands that it was the chronicle of an actual and unjustifiable proceeding. And there is Frank Richard Stockton (1834–1902), whose realism-with-a-screw-loose has given us most inimitable absurdities. Our country is so large and manners of life vary so widely in its different regions that an American novel may have all the advantages of realism and yet be as truly romantic to three-fourths of its readers as the wildest dreams of the romanticists. George Washington Cable (1844–1925) has painted in *The Grandissimes* and other works a fascinating picture of Creole life in New Orleans. Richard Malcolm Johnston (1822–1898) tells us of the "Crackers" of Georgia; John Esten Cooke (1830–1866), most of whose work belongs to a somewhat earlier period, has written of the days when chivalry was in flower in the Old Dominion; Thomas Nelson Page (1853–1922) brings before us the negro slave of Virginia, with his picturesque dialect, his devotion to "the fambly," and his notions of things visible and invisible; Joel Chandler Harris (1848–1908) has the honor of contributing a new character, *Uncle Remus*, to the world of literature; Mary

Noailles Murfree (1850–1922), whose very publishers long believed her to be "Mr. Charles Egbert Craddock," has almost the literary monopoly of the mountainous regions of Tennessee. In this the regions are fortunate, for no gleam of beauty, no trait of character, escapes her keen eye. James Lane Allen (1850–1925) has taken as his field his own state of Kentucky. He is as realistic as Henry James, but his realism is softened and beautified by a delicate and poetic grace. Edward Eggleston's (1837–1902) *Hoosier Schoolmaster* revealed the literary possibilities of southern Indiana in pioneer days. Several writers have pictured life in New England. Among them is John Townsend Trowbridge (1827–1916) with his *Neighbor Jackwood* and other stories. Mary E. Wilkins Freeman (1862–1930) writes interesting stories, but almost invariably of the exceptional characters. Sarah Orne Jewett, (1849–1909), with rare grace and humor and finer delicacy of touch, has gone far beyond surface peculiarities, and has found in the most everyday people some gleam of poetry, some shadow of pathos. Alice Brown (1857–1948) writes frequently and charmingly of the unusual; but with her the unusual is the natural manifestation of some typical quality. Elizabeth Stuart Phelps Ward (1844–1911) in 1866 ventured to treat our notions of heaven in somewhat realistic fashion in *Gates Ajar.* She has proved in many volumes her knowledge of the New England woman. Some of her best later work has been in the line of the short story, as, for instance, her *Jonathan and David.* Rose Terry Cooke (1827–1892) has found the humor which is thinly veiled by the New England austerity. The stories of Kate Douglas Wiggin

Louisa M. Alcott	*Helen Hunt Jackson*	*Mary Noailles Murfree*
Sarah Orne Jewett	*Harriet Beecher Stowe*	*Elizabeth Stuart Phelps Ward*
Alice Brown	*Kate Douglas Wiggin Riggs*	*Agnes Repplier*

Riggs (1857–1923) are marked by a keen sense of humor and sparkle with vivid bits of description. The early days of California have been pictured by Helen Hunt Jackson (1831–1885) in *Ramona,* a novel which voiced the author's righteous indignation at the harshness and injustice shown to the Indians by the United States government. Her earlier work was poetry; and in this, too, she has taken no humble place. Mary Hallock Foote (1847–1938) has sympathetically interpreted with both brush and pen the life of the mining camp of what used to be the "far West." Frances Hodgson Burnett (1849–1924) won her first popularity by *That Lass o' Lowrie's,* which pictures life in the Lancashire districts of England. During the last few years the popular favor has swung between the historical novel and the one-character tale; but the fiction, whether of the one class or the other, that has had the largest sale has laid its scenes in America and has been written by American authors.

American fiction has become especially strong in the short story; not merely the story which is short, but the story which differs from the tale in somewhat the same way as the farce differs from the play, namely, that its interest centres in the situation rather than in a series of incidents which usually develop a plot. *Cranford,* for instance, is a tale. It pictures the life of a whole village, and is full of incidents. Stockton's *The Lady or the Tiger* is a short story; it gives no incidents, and no more detail than is necessary to explain the peculiar situation of the princess. It is a single series of links picked out of a broad network. A tale is a field; a short story is a narrow path running through the field. The short story, with its single aim, its determination to make every word count toward that aim, its rigid economy of materials, its sure and rapid progress, has proved most acceptable to our time-saving and swiftly-moving nation.

49. Poetry

The writers of the last fifty years have had an immense advantage in the existence of the four monthlies, *The Atlantic, Harper's, Scribner's,* and *The Century,* for these magazines have provided what was so needed in earlier days,—a generous opportunity to find one's audience. They have been of special value to the poets, and the last half-century has given us much poetry. Not all of it is of the kind that makes its author's name immortal; but it would not be difficult to count at least a score of Americans who in these latter days have written poems that are of real merit. So far as a poetic centre now exists, New York, with its many publishing houses and its favorable geographical position, holds the honor.

50. Bayard Taylor, 1825–1878

Eight years after Bryant published *Thanatopsis,* two of these later poets, Taylor and Stoddard, were born. Bayard Taylor began life as a country boy who wanted to travel. He wandered over Europe, paying his way sometimes by a letter to some New York paper, sometimes by a morning in the hayfield. His account of these wanderings, *Views Afoot,* was so boyish, so honest, enthusiastic, and appreciative, that it was a delight to look at the world through his eyes; and the young man of twenty-one found that he had secured his audience. He continued to wander and to write about his wanderings. He wrote novels also; but, save for the money that this work brought him, he put little value upon it. Poetic fame was his ambition, and he won it in generous measure. His *Poems of the Orient* is wonderfully fervid and intense. Some of these poems contain lines that are as haunting as Poe's. Such is the refrain to his *Bedouin Song:*—

From the desert I come to thee
On a stallion shod with fire;
And the winds are left behind
In the speed of my desire.
Under thy window I stand,
And the midnight hears my cry:
I love thee, I love but thee,
With a love that shall not die
Till the sun grows cold,
And the stars are old,
And the leaves of the Judgment
Book unfold!

Another favorite is his Song of the Camp, with its famous lines,—

Each heart recalled a different name,
But all sang "ANNIE LAURIE."

He wrote *Home Pastorals* (1875), ballads of home life in Pennsylvania; several dramatic poems; and a most valuable translation of Faust (1870–1871). Bayard Taylor seems likely to attain his dearest wish,—to be remembered by his poetry rather than his prose.

51. Richard Henry Stoddard, 1826–1903

One of Taylor's oldest and best beloved friends was Richard Henry Stoddard, a young ironworker. He had hard labor and long hours; but he managed to do a vast amount of reading and thinking, and he had much to contribute to this friendship. He held no college degree, but he knew the best English poetry and was an excellent critic. He, too, was a poet. In a few years he published a volume of poems; but poetry brought little gold, and by Hawthorne's aid he secured a position in the Custom House. He did much reviewing and editing; but poetry was nearest to his heart. There is a certain simplicity and finish about his poems that is most winning. The following is a special favorite:—

The sky is a drinking cup,
That was overturned of old;
And it pours in the eyes of men
Its wine of airy gold.

We drink that wine all day,
Till the last drop is drained up,
And are lighted off to bed
By the jewels in the cup!

52. Edmund Clarence Stedman, 1833–1908

Another poet and critic is Edmund Clarence Stedman. He reversed the usual order, and, instead of going from business to poetry, he went from poetry to business, and became a broker. When he had won success in Wall Street, he returned to poetry with an easy mind. He has a wide knowledge of literature, and is a keen and appreciative critic. Moreover, he can criticise his own work as well as that of other people. He has written many New England idylls, many war lyrics, and many occasional poems. Everything is well proportioned and exquisitely finished, but sometimes we miss warmth and fire. It is like being struck by a cool wind to come from Taylor's *Bedouin Song* to Stedman's *Song from a Drama:—*

Thou art mine, thou hast given thy word;
Close, close in my arms thou art clinging;
Alone for my ear thou art singing
A song which no stranger has heard:
But afar from me yet, like a bird,
Thy soul, in some region unstirred,
On its mystical circuit is winging.

One of his poems that no one who has read it can forget is *The Discoverer;* graceful, tender, with somewhat of Matthew Arnold's Greek restraint, and so carefully polished that it seems simple and natural. This begins:—

I have a little kinsman
Whose earthly summers are but three,
And yet a voyager is he
Greater than Drake or Frobisher,
Than all their peers together!
He is a brave discoverer,
And, far beyond the tether
Of them who seek the frozen Pole,
Has sailed where the noiseless surges roll.
Ay, he has travelled whither
A winged pilot steered his bark
Through the portals of the dark,
Past hoary Mimir's well and tree,
Across the unknown sea.

53. Thomas Bailey Aldrich, 1836–1907

Thomas Bailey Aldrich is counted with the New York group of poets by virtue of his fifteen years' residence in the metropolis. His tender little poem on the death of a child, *Baby Bell,* beginning,—

Have you not heard the poets tell
How came the dainty Baby Bell
Into this world of ours?

touched the sympathetic American heart and won him the name of poet. If he had been a sculptor, he would have engraved cameos, so exquisitely finished is everything that he touches. The thought that some writers would expand into a volume of philosophy or a romance of mysticism, he is satisfied to condense into a lyric, as in his *Identity:*—

Somewhere—in desolate wind-swept space—
In Twilight-land—in No-man's-land—
Two hurrying Shapes met face to face,
And bade each other stand.

"And who are you?" cried one a-gape,
Shuddering in the gloaming light.
"I know not," said the second Shape,
"I only died last night!"

In 1870 Aldrich returned to Boston. He then edited *Every Saturday,* and later *The Atlantic Monthly.* He published several volumes of poems and some charming stories. The most original of the latter is the delicious *Marjorie Daw,* which won such popularity as to verify the favorite dictum of Barnum, "People like to be humbugged." This story is marked by the same artistic workmanship and nicety of finish that beautifies whatever Aldrich touches. One cannot imagine him allowing a line to go into print that is in any degree less perfect than he can make it.

54. Francis Bret Harte, 1839–1902

In 1868 a new voice came from the Pacific coast. *The Overland Monthly* had been founded, and Francis Bret Harte had become its editor. He had gone from Albany to California, had tried teaching and mining, had written a few poems, and also *Condensed Novels,* an irreverent and wisely critical parody on the works of various authors whom he had been taught to admire. In his second month of office he published *The Luck of Roaring Camp.* This was followed by other stories and poems, and in a twinkling he was a famous man. The flush of novelty has passed, and he is no longer hailed as the American laureate; but no one can help seeing that within his own limits he is a master. When he takes his pen, the life of the mining camp stands before us in bold outline. He is a very missionary of light to those who think there is no goodness beyond their own little circle. In *How Santa Claus Came to Simpson's Bar,* for instance, the dirty little boy with "fevier. And childblains. And roomatiz," gets out of bed to show to the rough men who are his visitors a hospitality which is genuine if somewhat soiled; and the roughest of them all gallops away on a dare-devil ride over ragged mountains and through swollen rivers to find a city and a toy-shop, because he has overheard the sick child asking his father what "Chrismiss" is, and the question has touched some childhood memories of his own. Harte's one text in both prose and poetry is that in every child there is some bit of simple faith, and that in the wildest, roughest, most desperate of men there is some good. Several of his poems are exceedingly beautiful lyrics; those that are called "characteristic," because written in the line wherein he made his first fame, are vivid pictures of the mining camp,—coarse, but hardly vulgar, and with a never-failing touch of human sympathy and warm confidence in human nature.

55. Walt Whitman, 1819–1892

A few years ago, an old man with long white hair and beard, gray vest, gray coat, and a broad white collar well opened in front, walked slowly and with some difficulty to an armchair that stood on a lecture platform in Camden, New Jersey. He spoke of Lincoln, and at the end of the address he said half shyly: "My hour is nearly gone, but I frequently close such remarks by reading a little piece I have written—a little piece, it takes only two or three minutes—it is a little poem, 'O Captain! My Captain!' " This is what he read:—

O Captain! my Captain! our fearful trip is done,
The ship has weathered every rack, the prize we sought is won,
The port is near, the bells I hear, the people all exulting,
While follow eyes the steady keel, the vessel grim and daring;
But O heart! heart! heart!
But O the bleeding drops of red,
Where on the deck my Captain lies,
Fallen cold and dead.

O Captain! my Captain! rise up and hear the bells;
Rise up—for you the flag is flung—for you the bugle trills,
For you bouquets and ribboned wreaths—for you the shores acrowding,

For you they call, the swaying mass, their eager faces turning;
Here Captain! dear father!
This arm beneath your head!
It is some dream that on the deck
You've fallen cold and dead.

My Captain does not answer, his lips are pale and still,
My father does not feel my arm, he has no pulse nor will,
The ship is anchored safe and sound, its voyage closed and done,
From fearful trip the victor ship comes in with object won;
Exult, O shores, and ring, O bells!
But I, with mournful tread,
Walk the deck my Captain lies,
Fallen cold and dead.

This speaker was Walt Whitman. In 1855 he brought out his first volume of poems, *Leaves of Grass.* Seven years later he became the good angel of the army hospitals, writing a letter for one sufferer, cheering another by a hearty greeting, leaving an orange or a piece of bright new scrip or a package of candy at bed after bed. Northerner or Southerner, it was the same to him as he went around, carrying out the little wishes that are so great in a sick man's eyes. A few years later he suffered from a partial paralysis. His last days were spent in a simple home near the Delaware, in Camden.

The place of Walt Whitman as a poet is in dispute. Some look upon him as a "literary freak;" others as the mightiest poetical genius of America. He is capable of writing such a gem as *O Captain! my Captain!* and also of foisting upon us such stuff as the following and calling it poetry:—

The latest dates, discoveries, inventions, societies,
authors old and new,
My dinner, dress, associates, looks, compliments, dues.

Whitman believed that a poet might write on all subjects, and that poetic form and rhythm should be avoided. Unfortunately for his theories, when he has most of real poetic passion, he is most inclined to use poetic rhythm. He writes some lists of details that are no more poetic than the catalogue of an auctioneer; but he is capable of painting a vivid picture with the same despised tools, as in his *Cavalry Crossing a Ford:—*

A line in long array where they wind betwixt green islands,
They take a serpentine course, their arms flash in the sun,—hark
to the musical clank,
Behold the silvery river, in it the splashing horses loitering stop
to drink,
Behold the brown-faced men, each group, each person, a picture,
the negligent rest on the saddles,
Some emerge on the opposite bank, others are just entering the
ford—while
Scarlet and blue and snowy white,
The guidon flags flutter gayly in the wind.

This is hardly more than an enumeration of details; but hc has chosen and arranged them so well that he brings the moving picture before us better than even paint and canvas could do. When he persists in telling us uninteresting facts that we do not care to be told, he is a writer of prose printed somewhat like poetry; but when he allows a poetic thought to sweep him onward to a glory of poetic expression, he is a poet, and a poet of lofty rank.

56. Minor Poets

It is especially difficult to select a few names from the long list of our minor poets, for the work of almost every one of them is marked by some appealing excellence of subject or of treatment. Celia Thaxter (1835–1894) is ever associated with the Isles of Shoals, and, as Stedman says, "Her sprayey stanzas give us the dip of the sea-bird's wing, the foam and tangle of ocean." Lucy Larcom (1826–1893), too, was one of those who love the sea. The one of her poems that has perhaps touched the greatest number of hearts is *Hannah Binding Shoes,* that glimpse into the life of the lonely woman of Marblehead with her pathetic question:—

Is there from the fishers any news?

John Hay (1838–1905) forsook literature for the triumphs of a noble diplomacy, but not until he had shown his ability as biographer and as poet. The first readers of his *Pike County Ballads* were not quite certain that he was not a bit irreverent; but they soon recognized the manliness of his sentiment, however audacious its expression might appear. Jones Very (1813–1880) is still winning an increasing number of friends by his graceful, delicate thought and crystalline clearness of expression. Edward Rowland Sill (1841–1887), though with few years of life and scanty leisure, made himself such an one as the king's son of his own *Opportunity,* who with the broken sword

Saved a great cause that heroic day.

His poems are marked by the insight which sees the difficulties of life and also the simple faith which bestows the courage to meet them and to look beyond them. Richard Watson Gilder (1844–1909), greatest of the New York group, ever charms us by the delicate music of his verse. His finish is so artistic, so flawless, that sometimes the first reading of one of his poems does not reveal to us the strength of feeling half hidden by the bewitching gleams of its beauty. Although we can boast of no poet of the first rank among these later writers, yet poetic ability is so widely distributed among American authors and so much of its product is of excellence that we certainly have reason to expect a rapid progress to some worthy manifestation before many years of the twentieth century shall have passed.

57. Humorous Writings

There is no lack of humor in the writings of Americans. Indeed, we are a little inclined to look askance at an author who manifests no sense of the humorous, and to feel that something is lacking in his mental make-up. The works of Irving, Holmes, Lowell, the charming essays of Warner, Mitchell, and Curtis, and the stories of Frank Stockton and others, are lighted up by humor on every page, sometimes keen and swift, sometimes graceful and poetic. These are humorists that make us smile. There are lesser humorists who make us laugh. Such was Charles Farrar Browne (1834–1867), "Artemus Ward," who wrote over his show, "You cannot expect to go in without paying your money, but you can pay your money without going in." Such was Benjamin Penhallow Shillaber (1814–1890), "Mrs. Partington," who "could desecrate a turkey better" if she "understood its anathema," and who thought "Men ought not to go to war, but admit their disputes to agitation." His fun depended almost entirely upon the misuse of words, Sheridan's old device in "Mrs. Malaprop" of *The Rivals.* Such was David Ross Locke (1833–1888), "Petroleum Vesuvius Nasby," who was a political power in the years immediately following the Civil War. Henry Wheeler Shaw (1818–1885), "Josh Billings," gave plenty of good, substantial advice. "Blessed is he who kan pocket abuse, and feel that it iz no disgrace tew be bit bi a dog."—"Most everyone seems tew be willing to be a phool himself, but he cant bear to have enny boddy else one."—"It is better to kno less, than to kno so mutch that ain't so." These are bits of the philosopher's wisdom. He, as well as Browne and Locke, depended in part upon absurdities of spelling to attract attention, a questionable resort save where, as in the *Biglow Papers,* it helps to bring a character before us. American humor is accused, and sometimes with justice, of depending upon exaggeration and irreverence. This humor has, nevertheless, a solid basis of shrewdness and good sense; and, however crooked its spelling may be, it always goes straight to the point. Another characteristic quality is that in the "good stories" that are copied from one end of the land to the other, the hero does not get the better of the "other man" because the other man is a fool, but because he himself is bright.

Our best living humorist is Samuel Langhorne Clemens, or "Mark Twain." He was born in Missouri, and became printer, pilot, miner, reporter, editor, lecturer, and author. His *Innocents Abroad,* the record of his first European trip, set the whole country laughing.

The "Innocents" wander through Europe. They distress guides and cicerones by refusing to make the ecstatic responses to which these tyrants are accustomed. When they are led to the bust of Columbus, they inquire with mock eagerness, "Is this the first time this gentleman was ever on a bust?" The one place where they deign to show "tumultuous emotion" is at the tomb of Adam, whom they call tearfully a "blood relation," "a distant one, but still a relation." The book is a witty satire on sham enthusiasm; but it is more than a satire, for Mark Twain is not only a wit but a literary man. He can describe a scene like a poet if he chooses; he can paint a picture and he can make a character live. Among his many books are two that show close historical study, *The Personal Memoirs of Joan of Arc,* and his ever delightful *The Prince and the Pauper.* The latter is a tale for children, wherein the prince exchanges clothes with the pauper, is put out of the palace grounds, and has many troubles before he comes to his own again. Mark Twain abominates shams of all sorts and looks upon them as proper targets for his artillery. His reputation as a humorist does not depend upon vagaries in spelling, or amusing deportment on the lecture platform. He is a clear-sighted, original, honest man, and his fun has a solid foundation of good sense.

58. History and Biography

Our later historians have found their field in American chronicles. John Fiske (1842–1901) has made scholarly interpretations of our colonial records. Henry Adams (1838–1918), James Schouler (1839–1920), Thomas Wentworth Higginson (1823–1911), Justin

Winsor (1831–1897), Edward Eggleston, and others have written of various periods in the history of our country. John Bach McMaster's (1852–1932) work is so full of vivid details that any stray paragraph is interesting reading. Hubert Howe Bancroft's (1832–1918) *History of the Pacific Coast* is a monumental work. Besides histories, we have many volumes of reminiscences, and biographies without number. Surely, the future student of American life and manners will not be without plentiful material. Among the biographers, James Parton (1822–1891) and Horace Elisha Scudder (1838–1902) are of specially high rank. Scudder and Higginson deserve lasting gratitude, not only for the quality of their own work, but for their resolute opposition to all that is not of the best. The biography of the beasts and birds has not been forgotten. Many writers on nature are following in the footsteps of John Burroughs (1837–1921), a worthy

John Burroughs

disciple of Thoreau, who sees nature like a camera and describes her like a poet. Among these writers is Olive Thorne Miller (1831–1918), whose tender friendliness for animals is shown even in the titles of her books, *Little Brothers of the Air* and *Little Folks in Feathers and Fur.*

59. The Magazine Article

In American prose there has been of late a somewhat remarkable development of the magazine article, which is in many respects the successor of the lecture platform of some years ago. Its aim is to present information. The subject may be an invention, a discovery, literary criticism, reminiscence, biography, a study of nature, an account of a war,—what you will; but it must give information. It must be brief and readable. Technicalities must be translated into common terms, and necessarily it must be the work of an expert. Written with care and signed with the name of the author, these articles become a progressive encyclopædia of the advancement and thought of the age.

Another type of magazine article is that written by Agnes Repplier, Samuel McChord Crothers, and others, which does not apparently aim at giving information but seems rather to be the familiar, half-confidential talk of a widely read person with a gift for delightful monologue.

The scope of our magazine articles suggests the breadth and diversity of pure scholarship in America. Among our best-known scholars are Charles Eliot Norton (1827–1908), biographer and translator of

Dante as well as critic of art; Francis James Child (1825–1896), editor of *English and Scottish Ballads;* Francis Andrew March (1825–1911), our greatest Anglo-Saxon scholar; Felix Emanuel Schelling (1858–1945), our best authority on the literature of the Elizabethan Age; Horace Howard Furness (1833–1912), the Shakespeare scholar; and Cornelius Felton (1807–1862), president of Harvard College, with his profound knowledge of Greek and the Greeks.

60. Juvenile Literature

Books for children have been published in enormous numbers. Even in the thirties they came out by scores in half a dozen cities of New England, in Cooperstown, Baltimore, New York, and elsewhere. In 1833 there was a "Juvenile Book-Store" in New York City. Many authors, Hawthorne, Mrs. Ward, Mark Twain, Trowbridge, and others have written books for children, but few have written for children alone. Among these latter, the principal ones are Jacob Abbott and Louisa May Alcott. More than two hundred books came from Abbott's pen,—the *Rollo Books,* the *Lucy Books,* and scores of simple histories and biographies. He is always interesting, for he always makes us want to know what is coming next. When, for instance, Rollo and Jennie and the kitten in the cage are left by mistake to cross the ocean by themselves, even a grown-up will turn the page with considerable interest to see how they manage matters. Abbott never "writes down" to children. Even when he is giving them substantial moral advice, he writes as if he were talking with equals; and few childish readers of his books ever skip the little lectures.

Louisa May Alcott was a Philadelphia girl who grew up in Concord. She wrote for twenty years without any special success. Then she published *Little Women,* and this proved to be exactly what the young folk wanted. It is a clean, fresh, "homey" book about young people who are not too good or too bright to be possible. They are not so angelic as Mrs. Burnett's Little Lord Fauntleroy; but they are lovable and thoroughly human. A number of other books followed *Little Women,* all about sensible, healthy-minded boys and girls. Within the last fifty years or more many papers and magazines have been published for young people; such as *Merry's Museum, Our Young Folks, Wide Awake,* and *St. Nicholas.* The patriarch of them all is *The Youth's Companion,* whose rather priggish name suggests its antiquity. It was founded in 1827 by the father of N. P. Willis. In its fourscore years of life it has kept so perfectly in touch with the spirit of the age that to read its files is an interesting literary study. It seems a long way back from its realistic stories of to-day to the times when, for instance, a beggar—in a book—petitioned some children, "Please to bestow your charity on a poor blind man, who has no other means of subsistence but from your beneficence." *The Youth's Companion* has followed literary fashions; but throughout its long career its aim to be clean, wholesome, and interesting has never varied.

61. Literary Progress

Counting from the very beginning, our literature is not yet three hundred years old. The American colonists landed on the shores of a new country. They had famine and sickness to endure, the savages and the wilderness to subdue. It is little wonder that for many decades the pen was rarely taken in hand save for what was regarded as necessity. What literary progress has been made may be seen by comparing Anne Bradstreet with Longfellow and Lanier, Cotton Mather with Parkman and Fiske, the *New England Primer* with the best of the scores of books for children that flood the market every autumn. We have little drama, but in fiction, poetry, humorous writings, essays, biography, history, and juvenile books, we produce an immense amount of composition. The pessimist wails that the motto of this composition is the old cry, "Bread and the games!"—that we demand only what will give us a working knowledge of a subject, or something that will amuse us. The optimist points to the high average of this writing, and to the fact that everybody reads. Many influences are at work; who shall say what their resultant will be? One thing, however, is certain,—he who reads second-rate books is helping to lower the literary standard of his country, while he who lays down a poor book to read a good one is not only doing a thing that is for his own advantage, but is increasing the demand for good literature that almost invariably results in its production.

SUMMARY

THE NATIONAL PERIOD

II. LATER YEARS

Writers of Fiction

William Dean Howells
Henry James
Francis Marion Crawford
Edward Everett Hale
Frank Richard Stockton
George Washington Cable
Richard Malcolm Johnston
John Esten Cooke
Thomas Nelson Page
Joel Chandler Harris
Mary Noailles Murfree
Edward Eggleston
John Townsend Trowbridge
Mary E. Wilkins Freeman
Sarah Orne Jewett
Alice Brown
Elizabeth Stuart Phelps Ward
Rose Terry Cooke
Kate Douglas Wiggin Riggs
Helen Hunt Jackson
Frances Hodgson Burnett
Mary Hallock Foote
James Lane Allen

Poets

Bayard Taylor
Richard Henry Stoddard
Edmund Clarence Stedman
Thomas Bailey Aldrich
Francis Bret Harte
Walt Whitman
Celia Thaxter
Lucy Larcom
John Hay
Jones Very
Edward Rowland Sill
Richard Watson Gilder

Humorists

Washington Irving
Oliver Wendell Holmes
James Russell Lowell
Charles Dudley Warner
Donald Grant Mitchell
George William Curtis
Frank Richard Stockton
Charles Farrar Browne
Benjamin Penhallow Shillaber
David Ross Locke
Henry Wheeler Shaw
Samuel Langhorne Clemens

Historians and Biographers

John Fiske
Henry Adams
James Schouler
Thomas Wentworth Higginson
John Bach McMaster
Hubert Howe Bancroft
James Parton
Horace Elisha Scudder
Justin Winsor

Naturalists

John Burroughs.
Olive Thorne Miller.

Writers for Children

Jacob Abbott
Louisa May Alcott

Much literature has been produced since the war. The greater part of it is fiction. This is marked by realism, whose apostles are Howells and James. Many authors have revealed the literary possibilities of different parts of our country. The short story has been successfully developed. Historical novels and also the one-character novel are in favor. To the poets especially, the monthly magazines have been of much advantage. New York stands at present as our poetic centre. Taylor, Stoddard, Stedman, and Aldrich are counted as part of the New

York group. In 1868 Bret Harte was made famous by his stories and poems of the mining camp. Walt Whitman is a poet of no humble rank. He believed in writing on all subjects and in avoiding poetic form and rhythm, but is at his best when he forgets his theories. There is much humor in American writings. Of the lesser humorists, Browne, Locke, and Shaw depended in part upon incorrect spelling, and Shillaber upon a comical misuse of words. Our best humorist is Clemens. He is not only a wit, but also a man of much literary talent. His fun is always founded upon common sense. Most of our historians have chosen American history as their theme. Many volumes of biographies and reminiscences have been published. The magazine article has taken the place of the lecture platform and the magazines form a progressive encyclopædia of the advancement of the world. Great numbers of children's books have appeared. Among those authors that have written for children alone are Abbott and Miss Alcott. Many juvenile magazines and papers have been founded. *The Youth's Companion* is the oldest of all. Many literary influences are at work. What the resultant will be is still unknown.

WRITERS WHO ARE REMEMBERED BY A SINGLE WORK:

Ethelinda Beers,
All quiet along the Potomac
David Everett,
You'd scarce expect one of my age
Albert G. Greene,
Old Grimes

James Fenno Hoffman,
Sparkling and Bright
Francis Hopkinson,
The Battle of the Kegs
Joseph Hopkinson,
Hail Columbia
Julia Ward Howe,
The Battle-Hymn of the Republic
Francis Scott Key,
The Star-Spangled Banner
Guy Humphrey McMaster,
Carmen Bellicosum
Clement C. Moore,
'T was the night before Christmas
George Perkins Morris,
Woodman, spare that tree
William Augustus Muhlenberg,
I would not live alway
Theodore O'Hara,
The Bivouac of the Dead
John Howard Payne,
Home, Sweet Home
Albert Pike,
Dixie
James Rider Randall,
Maryland, My Maryland
Thomas Buchanan Read,
Sheridan's Ride
Abraham Joseph Ryan,
The Conquered Banner

Epes Sargent,
A Life on the Ocean Wave
Samuel Francis Smith,
My Country, 'tis of thee
Frank O. Ticknor,
Virginians of the Valley
Samuel Woodworth,
The Old Oaken Bucket

REFERENCES

ENGLAND'S LITERATURE

THE following lists of books are of course not expected to be in any degree exhaustive. Their main object is, first, to suggest some few of the great number of criticisms and histories of literature that may be helpful to the student; second, to tell where good editions of complete works or selections from some of the less accessible authors may be found.

For general consultation throughout the course the following authorities are recommended:—

For history, manners, and customs; Green's *Short History of the English People,* Gardiner's *Student's History of England,* Traill's *Social England.* For history of literature, Jusserand's *Literary History of the English People from the Origins to the Renaissance.* For history of the language, Lounsbury's *History of the English Language.* For biography, the *Dictionary of National Biography* is the standard work. See also the *English Men of Letters Series.* Three works, Craik's *English Prose Selections* (5 vols.), Ward's *English Poets* (4 vols.), and Morley's *English Writers* (11 vols.), contain well-chosen selections from the works of nearly all the authors named, and are almost a necessity to students who are not able to consult a large library. For separate texts the volumes of the *Riverside Literature Series* are of special value because of their careful editing, good binding, and reasonable price. Cassell's *National Library* is also inexpensive and convenient.

CENTURIES V-XIII

Freeman's *Old English History.*

Sharon Turner's *History of the Anglo-Saxons.*

Brooke's *English Literature from the Beginning to the Norman Conquest.*

Brother Azarias's *Development of English Literature.*

Beowulf has been translated by C. G. Child *(Riverside Literature Series),* Garnett, Hall, Morris and Wyatt, and others. Much of the poem is given in Brooke's *History of Early English Literature* and Morley's *English Writers.* Morley, vol. I, contains *Widsith,* passages from Cædmon and Cynewulf, and also specimens of the old Celtic literature.

The Exeter Book has been translated by Gollancz (Early English Text Society); also by Benjamin Thorpe.

Bede's *Ecclesiastical History* and the *Anglo-Saxon Chronicle* are contained in one volume of Bohn's *Antiquarian Library.*

Alfred's *Orosius* and *Pauli's Life of Alfred* are in one volume of Bohn's *Antiquarian Library.* Asser's *Life of Alfred* has been edited by A. S. Cook (Ginn).

Extracts from the *Ormulum,* the *Ancren Riwle,* the *History* of Geoffrey of Monmouth, Layamon's *Brut,* and *King Horn* (with glossary) are contained in Morris and Skeat's *Specimens of Early English,* vol. I.

Robin Hood Ballads are contained in Child's *English and Scottish Popular Ballads.*

Geoffrey of Monmouth's *History* is contained in Giles's *Six Old English Chronicles* (Bohn's *Antiquarian Library.)*

CENTURY XIV

Jusserand's *Wayfaring Life in the Fourteenth Century.*

Wright's *History of Domestic Manners and Sentiments in England during the Middle Ages.*

E. L. Cutts's *Scenes and Characters of the Middle Ages.*

Tudor Jenks's *In the Days of Chaucer.*

Mandeville's *Voyages and Travels,* Cassell's *National Library.* Morris and Skeat's *Specimens of Early English,* vol. ii, contains selections from Mandeville, Langland, Wyclif, and Chaucer.

Chaucer's *Prologue, Knight's Tale, and Nun's Priest's Tale* (with glossary) are published in one volume of the *Riverside Literature Series.* Lowell's *Literary Essays,* vol. III, contains a delight ful appreciation of Chaucer.

CENTURY XV

Green's *Town Life in the Fifteenth Century.*

Denton's *England in the Fifteenth Century.*

Jusserand's *Romance of a King's Life* (James I).

The King's Quair, edited by Skeat.

Malory's *Morte d'Arthur,* edited by Sommer and also by Gollancz. Morris and Skeat's *Specimens of Early English,* vol. III, contains selections from the *King's Quair, the Morte d'Arthur,* and Caxton's *Recuyell of the Historyes of Troye.*

Ballads. Child's *English and Scottish Popular Ballads* is the great authority. Percy's *Reliques.* Gummere's *Old English Ballads* contains a well-chosen group and also a valuable introduction.

Mystery plays and Moralities. *The York Plays,* edited by Lucy Toulmin Smith; *The English Religious Drama,* by K. L. Bates. *English Miracle Plays, Moralities, and Interludes,* by A. W. Pollard, contains *Everyman.* Morley's *Specimens of the Pre-Shakespearian Drama* contains *The Foure P's, Ralph Roister Doister, Gorboduc, Campaspe, etc.*

CENTURY XVI

Ward's *History of English Dramatic Literature* (3 vols.).

Lowell's *Old English Dramatists.*

Lamb's *Specimens of English Dramatic Poets* (Bohn's *Antiquarian Library*).

Saintsbury's *History of Elizabethan Literature.*

E. P. Whipple's *Literature of the Age of Elizabeth.*

Lowell's *Literary Essays,* vol. IV, contains his essay on Spenser; in vol. III is his essay on Shakespeare.

Schelling's *The English Chronicle Play.*

Schelling's *The Queen's Progress.*

Jusserand's *The English Novel in the Time of Shakespeare.*

Goadby's *The England of Shakespeare.*

Ordish's *Shakespeare's London.*

Warner's *The People for whom Shakespeare wrote.*

Tudor Jenks's *In the Days of Shakespeare.*

Sidney *Lee's A Life of William Shakespeare* and *Shakespeare's Life and Work.*

Rolfe's *Shakespeare the Boy.*

Dowden's *Shakespeare Primer.*

Abbott's *Shakespearian Grammar.*

Lamb's *Specimens of English Dramatic Poets who lived about the Time of Shakespeare* contains *Gorboduc, Tamburlaine, Edward II, The Rich Jew of Malta, Dr. Faustus,* etc. *The Mermaid Series* contains the best plays of Beaumont and Fletcher, Marlowe, and others. Morris and Skeat's *Specimens of Early English,* vol. III, contains selections from Skelton, Tyndale, Surrey, Wyatt, also *Ralph Roister Doister, Euphues,* and *The Shepherd's Calendar.*

The Mermaid Series contains a most valuable selection of the plays of this age.

Utopia. Cassell's *National Library,* Morley's *Universal Library, Camelot Series, Temple Classics,* etc.

Wyatt and Surrey. *Tottel's Miscellany* in Arber's *English Reprints.*

The Foure P's. Full extracts in Morley's *English Plays.*

Ralph Roister Doister, and *Gorboduc.* Morley's *English Plays* and Manly's *Specimens of the Pre-Shakespearian Drama.*

Lyly. *Euphues* in Arber's *Reprints. Endymion,* edited by G. P. Baker (Holt). *Campaspe* is in Manly's *Specimens of the Pre-Shakespearian Drama.*

Spenser. The Riverside edition (3 vols.), edited by F. J. Child, is authoritative. The Globe edition is in one volume. Minor poems in the *Temple Classics* (Macmillan); *The Shepherd's Calendar* in Cassell's *National Library. The Faerie Queene,* Bk. I, in *Riverside Literature Series.*

Sidney. *Arcadia,* edited by H. Friswell. Prose selections, edited by G. Macdonald in the *Elizabethan Library. Defence of Poesie,* in Cassell's *National Library. Astrophel and Stella,* edited by A. Pollard (Scott).

Lyrics. *A Book of Elizabethan Lyrics,* edited by F. E. Schelling. *Lyrics from the Dramatists of the Elizabethan Age,* edited by A. H. Bullen.

Marlowe. Chief plays in the *Mermaid Series. Dr. Faustus* in the *Temple Dramatists,* in Morley's *English Plays,* and in Morley's *Universal Library.*

Hooker. *Ecclesiastical Polity,* Books I—IV, in Morley's *Universal Library.*

Shakespeare. Good editions are numerous. Furness's *Variorum* is best for advanced work. For the beginner, *Julius Cæsar, The Merchant of Venice, Macbeth, The Tempest,* and selections from the sonnets are recommended. *The Winter's Tale* is published in one volume of Cassell's *National Library* together with Greene's *Pandosto.*

CENTURY XVII

Saintsbury's *Elizabethan Literature* (to 1660).

Lowell's *Literary Essays,* vol. IV, contains his essay on Milton; vol. III that on Dryden.

Gosse's *Jacobean Poets.*

Gosse's *Seventeenth Century Studies.*

Lowell's *Old English Dramatists.*

Macaulay's *Essays on Milton and Bunyan.*

Schelling's *Seventeenth Century Lyrics.*

Lamb's *On the Artificial Comedy of the Last Century.*

The chief plays of this age are found in the *Mermaid Series.*

Bacon. *Essays* are published in Morley's *Universal Library,* also in Macmillan's *English Classics* and in Cassell's *National Library. Learning,* Book I, has been edited by A. S. Cook (Ginn).

Jonson. Several of his masques are in H. A. Evans's *English Masques. Timber,* edited by F. E. Schelling (Ginn); three of his best plays and *The Sad Shepherd* are in Morley's *Universal Library.*

Beaumont and Fletcher. Best plays are in the *Mermaid Series.*

Donne's poems are in the *Muses' Library*, edited by E. K. Chambers.

Milton. Masson's *Poetical Works of John Milton* (3 vols.) is the standard edition. *Paradise Lost,* Books I—III, and earlier poems with notes and biographical sketch in *Riverside Literature Series;* also in Cassell's *National Library* (2 vols.). Milton's *Minor Poems* (Allyn and Bacon).

Herbert. *The Temple* is in Morley's *Universal Library,* also in Cassell's *National Library.*

Crashaw. Poems, edited by Turnbull, are in *Library of Old Authors;* edited by Grosart, in *Fuller's Worthies' Library.*

Vaughan. Poems, edited by E. K. Chambers, in *Muses' Library.*

Taylor. *Holy Living and Holy Dying,* in Bohn's *Standard Library.* Selections, edited by E. E. Wentworth (Ginn).

Carew, Lovelace, Suckling. Selections are in *Cavalier and Courtier Lyrists, Canterbury Poets Series* (Scott).

Herrick. *Hesperides* and *Noble Numbers,* edited by A. Pollard. Selections in *Athenæum Press Series* (Ginn). Lyrics, selected from *Hesperides* and *Noble Numbers,* by T. B. Aldrich (Century Co.).

Walton. *Combleat Angler,* in Cassell's *National Library.*

Lives of Donne and Herbert in Morley's *Universal Library.*

Butler. Selections from *Hudibras* in Morley's *Universal Library.*

Bunyan. *The Pilgrim's Progress* in *Riverside Literature Series.*

Dryden. *Religio Laici,* etc. in Cassell's *National Library;* also selections from his poems. *Poetical Works,* edited by W. P. Christie; select poems edited by Christie (Clarendon Press). *Palamon and Arcite,* edited by Arthur Gilman, *Riverside Literature Series.*

CENTURY XVIII

Gosse's *History of English Literature in the Eighteenth Century.*

Ashton's *Social Life in the Reign of Queen Anne.*

Susan Hale's *Men and Manners of the Eighteenth Century.*

Thackeray's *English Humorists.*

Johnson's *Lives of the Poets* (see Johnson's works).

Leslie Stephen's *Hours in a Library.*

Macaulay's *Essay on Addison,* edited by W. P. Trent, *Riverside Literature Series.*

De Quincey's *Essay on Pope.*

Lowell's *Among my Books.*

Eighteenth Century Letters, edited by R. B. Johnson.

Lanier's *The English Novel.*

Carlyle's *Essay on Burns,* edited by George R. Noyes, *Riverside Literature Series.*

Carlyle on Burns and Scott, Cassell's *National Library.*

Pope. *Essay on Man,* edited by Mark Pattison (Clarendon Press); *Essay on Man, Rape of the Lock,* etc. edited by Henry W. Boynton, *Riverside Literature Series.*

Addison and Steele. *The Sir Roger de Coverley Papers,* edited by Eustace Budgell, *Riverside Literature Series;* also edited by Samuel Thurber, Allyn and Bacon. Selections, *Athenæum Press, Golden Treasury Series,* etc. *Selections from the Spectator,* edited by J. Habberton (Putnam): from the *Tatler* and the *Guardian,* together with Macaulay's *Essays on Steele and Addison* (Bangs). Steele's plays are in the *Mermaid Series.*

Swift. *Gulliver's Voyage to Brobdingnag* and *Voyage to Lilliput, Riverside Literature Series.* Selections, Ginn, Clarendon Press, etc. *Selected Letters* in R. B. Johnson's *Eighteenth Century Letters and Letter-Writers. Battle of the Books* in Cassell's *National Library.*

Defoe. *Robinson Crusoe, Riverside Literature Series; Journal of the Plague Year,* numerous school editions. Essay on Projects, Cassell's *National Library.*

Johnson. *Lives of the Poets,* Cassell's *National Library. Six Chief Lives* from Johnson's *Lives of the Poets* together with Macaulay's *Life of Johnson,* edited by M. Arnold (Macmillan). *Rasselas* in Morley's *Universal Library;* and also in Cassell's *National Library.*

Goldsmith. *Vicar of Wakefield, Poems, and Plays,* in Morley's *Universal Library; The Vicar of Wakefield,* edited by Mrs. H. A. Davidson, in *Riverside Literature Series* (with introduction, notes, aids to study, etc.).

Burke. *On Conciliation,* edited by Robert Andersen, *Riverside Literature Series. American Speeches* with *Essay on the Sublime and Beautiful* (Macmillan).

Percy. *Reliques of Ancient English Poetry.* Bohn and other editions.

Gray. *Elegy and Other Poems;* Cowper's *John Gilpin and Other Poems* (1 vol.), *Riverside Literature Series.* Selections from Cowper in *Athenæum Press Series, Canterbury Poets,* etc.

Burns. Selected poems in *Riverside Literature Series;* also in *Athenæum Press Series.*

CENTURY XIX

Leslie Stephen's *Hours in a Library.*

Saintsbury's *A History of Nineteenth Century Literature.*

Stedman's *Victorian Poets.*

Bagehot's *Literary Studies* (Thackeray, Dickens, Macaulay, Tennyson, Browning).

McCarthy's *History of Our Own Times.*

Dowden's *Studies in Literature* (1789-1877).

Wordsworth. *Selected Poems, Riverside Literature Series;* also in *Golden Treasury Series;* Cassell's *National Library.*

Coleridge. *Selections from Coleridge,* in *Athenæum Press Series. Selections from Prose Writings,* edited by H. A. Beers (Holt); *Selections from Coleridge and Campbell, Riverside Literature Series.*

Southey. *Life of Nelson, Curse of Kehama, Cassell's National Library.* Selections in *Canterbury Poets Series; Life of Nelson* in Morley's *Universal Library,* also in Longmans' *English Classics.*

Scott. *The Lady of the Lake,* Cassell's National Library; *The Lay of the Last Minstrel,* edited by W. J. Rolfe, *Riverside Literature Series; Ivanhoe, Riverside Literature Series.*

Byron. *Selected Poems, Riverside Literature Series,* edited by F. I. Carpenter (Holt).

Shelley. Selections in *Riverside Literature Series;* also in *Golden Treasury Series.*

Keats. *Ode on a Grecian Urn and Other Poems, Riverside Literature Series. Endymion,* etc., Cassell's *National Library. Selected Poems in Athenæum Press Series* and *Golden Treasury Series.*

Lamb. *Tales from Shakespeare, Riverside Literature Series. Essays of Elia,* in *Camelot Classics,* and elsewhere. *Specimens of English Dramatic Poets,* Bohn. *Selected Essays of Elia, Riverside Literature Series.*

De Quincey. *The Flight of a Tartar Tribe, Riverside Literature Series. Confessions of an English Opium-Eater,* Morley's *Universal Library, Temple Classics.* Selections, edited by Bliss Perry (Doubleday, Page and Co.).

Macaulay. *Essays on Johnson and Goldsmith* (1 vol.), *Essays on Milton and Addison* (1 vol.), *Riverside Literature Series and* Cassell's *National Library. Lays of Ancient Rome, Riverside Literature Series.*

Carlyle. *Heroes, Hero-Worship and the Heroic in History,* in *Athenæum Press Series.*

Ruskin. *Sesame and Lilies, Riverside Literature Series. Selected Essays and Letters* (Ginn). *Selections,* edited by V. D. Scudder (Heath).

Arnold. *Sohrab and Rustum and Other Poems, Riverside Literature Series,* edited by Louise Imogen Guiney. *Poems* (1 vol.) (Macmillan). Introduction to Ward's *English Poets,* vol. i.

Browning. *The Pied Piper of Hamelin and Other Poems, Riverside Literature Series.*

Tennyson. *Enoch Arden and Other Poems, Riverside Literature Series. The Princess,* edited by W. J. Rolfe, *Riverside Literature Series. Idylls of the King,* edited by W. J. Rolfe (Houghton Mifflin and Co.); edited by H. W. Boynton (Allyn and Bacon).

REFERENCES

AMERICA'S LITERATURE

THE following works are of value for general reference:—

Stedman and Hutchinson's *Library of American Literature* (11 vols.) (W. E. Benjamin), containing selections from nearly all the authors named in this book.

Hart's *American History told by Contemporaries* (4 vols.) (Macmillan).

Richardson's *History of American Literature* (2 vols.) (Putnam).

Whipple's *History of American Literature,* Harper's Magazine, 1876.

Stedman's *An American Anthology* (Houghton, Mifflin and Co.).

Stedman's *Poets of America* (Houghton, Mifflin and Co.).

COLONIAL AND REVOLUTIONARY TIMES

Tyler's *History of American Literature during the Colonial Times* (Putnam).

R. C. Winthrop's *Life and Letters of John Winthrop* (Little, Brown and Co.)

Helen Campbell's *Anne Bradstreet and her Time* (Lothrop).

Bradford's *History of Plymouth*, published by the Commonwealth of Massachusetts.

Winthrop's *History of New England* (2 vols.) (Little, Brown and Co.).

Bay Psalm Book (reprint) (Dodd, Mead and Co.)

Wigglesworth's *Day of Doom*, edited by J. W. Dean.

The New England Primer, edited by Paul Leicester Ford (Dodd, Mead and Co.).

Trent and Wells's *Colonial Prose and Poetry* (3 vols.) (Crowell).

Tyler's *History of the Literature of the American Revolution* (2 vols.) (Putnam).

Wendell's *Life of Cotton Mather* (Dodd, Mead and Co.).

Kate M. Cone's *Cotton Mather's Daughter* (The Outlook, vol. LXXXI, nos. 6, 7).

Allen's *Life of Jonathan Edwards* (Houghton, Mifflin and Co.).

McMaster's *Life of Benjamin Franklin* (Houghton, Mifflin and Co.).

Ford's *The Many-Sided Franklin* (The Century Co.).

Tyler's *Three Men of Letters* (Berkeley, Dwight, Barlow) (Putnam).

Todd's Barlow's *Life and Letters* (Putnam).

Austin's *Philip Freneau, A History of his Life and Times* (A. Wessels Co.).

Dunlap's *Life of Charles Brockden Brown* (2 vols.) (James P. Parke).

Smyth's *The Philadelphia Magazines and their Contributors* (Lindsay).

Mather's *Magnalia Christi,* reprinted 1853 (Silas Andrews and Son).

Edwards's *Works* (2 vols.) (Bohn).

Franklin's *Works,* edited by John Bigelow (10 vols.) (Putnam).

Franklin's *Autobiography* (3 vols.), edited by John Bigelow (Putnam).

Franklin's *Autobiography,* Riverside Literature Series.

Franklin's *Poor Richard's Almanac,* Riverside Literature Series.

The Federalist, edited by Paul Leicester Ford (Holt).

Trumbull's *M'Fingal* (Samuel G. Goodrich).

Freneau's *Poems* (3 vols.), edited by Pattee (Princeton University Library).

Songs and Ballads of the American Revolution, edited by Frank Moore (Appleton).

THE NATIONAL PERIOD

For biography, consult the *American Men of Letters Series* (Houghton, Mifflin and Co.). This contains lives of Irving, Thoreau, Cooper, Emerson, Poe, Willis, Franklin, Bryant, Simms, Taylor, Hawthorne, Longfellow, Whittier, Prescott, Parkman, Bret Harte, Holmes, Motley, Whitman, Curtis, Margaret Fuller, and Noah Webster.

Irving's *Life and Letters* (4 vols.), edited by P. M. Irving (Putnam).

J. G. Wilson's *Bryant and his Friends* (Fords).

Halleck's *Life and Letters,* edited by J. G. Wilson (Appleton).

The Poetical Writings of Halleck, edited by J. G. Wilson (Appleton).

Samuel Longfellow's *Life and Letters of Longfellow* (3 vols.) (Houghton, Mifflin and Co.).

Higginson's *Contemporaries* (Houghton, Mifflin and Co.).

F. H. Underwood's *Henry Wadsworth Longfellow* (Houghton, Mifflin and Co.).

S. T. Pickard's *Life and Letters of John Greenleaf Whittier* (2 vols.) (Houghton, Mifflin and Co.).

E. E. Hale's *James Russell Lowell and his Friends* (Houghton, Mifflin and Co.).

H. E. Scudder's *James Russell Lowell: A Biography* (2 vols.) (Houghton, Mifflin and Co.).

J. T. Morse's *Life and Letters of Oliver Wendell Holmes* (2 vols.) (Houghton, Mifflin and Co.)

J. E. Cabot's *Ralph Waldo Emerson, a Memoir* (2 vols.) (Houghton, Mifflin and Co.).

The Correspondence of Emerson and Carlyle (2 vols.) (Houghton, Mifflin and Co.)

Houghton, Mifflin and Co. are the only authorized publishers of the works of the following writers: Longfellow in 11 vols.; Whittier in 7; Lowell in 11; Holmes in 14; Emerson in 12; Thoreau in 11; Hawthorne in 13; Mrs. Stowe in 16. The same publishers have also brought out one-volume editions of the above New England poets. Many selections are published in various numbers of the *Riverside Literature Series* and in *American Poems* and *American Prose,* edited by H. E. Scudder. The *Riverside Literature Series* contains a large number of selections from their writings.

Julian Hawthorne's *Nathaniel Hawthorne and His Wife* (2 vols.) (Houghton, Mifflin and Co.).

Henry James's *Life of Hawthorne* (Harper).

Mrs. James T. Fields's *Life and Letters of Harriet Beecher Stowe* (Houghton, Mifflin and Co.)

Bancroft's *History of the United States* (6 vols.) (Little, Brown and Co.).

Prescott's *Works* (12 vols.) (Lippincott).

Motley's *Works* (17 vols.) (Harper).

Parkman's *Works* (12 vols.) (Little, Brown and Co.).

Ticknor's *Life of Prescott* (Ticknor and Fields).

Motley's *Letters,* edited by G. W. Curtis (2 vols.) (Harper).

Holmes's *A Memoir of Motley* (Houghton, Mifflin and Co.).

C. H. Farnham's *Life of Francis Parkman* (Little, Brown and Co.).

Manly's *Southern Literature* (Johnson).

Baskervill's *Southern Writers* (Barbee).

S. A. Link's *Pioneers of Southern Literature*, including Hayne, Timrod, Simms, Cooke, Poe, and others (2 vols.) (Barbee and Smith).

Simms's *Novels* (10 vols.) (Armstrong).

Simms's *Poems* (2 vols.) (Redfield).

Hayne's *Poems* (Lothrop).

Timrod's *Poems* (Houghton, Mifflin and Co.).

Poe's *Works* (11 vols.) (Stone and Kimball), (17 vols.) (Crowell).

The works of the later authors are so generally accessible as to make special reference unnecessary. For biographical data, consult *Who's Who in America,* and for both criticism and biography, consult the magazine articles which may be found through *Poole's Index* and the *Cumulative Index.*

An exceedingly valuable list of references to poems and magazine articles as well as books relating to Bryant, Poe, Emerson, Longfellow, Whittier, Holmes, Lowell, Whitman, and Lanier may be found in *The Chief American Poets,* by Curtis Hidden Page (Houghton, Mifflin and Co.).

www.ingramcontent.com/pod-product-compliance
Lightning Source LLC
LaVergne TN
LVHW050913080826
845145LV00001B/73

* 9 7 8 1 6 3 3 3 4 1 4 8 7 *